# MANAGING PEOPLE

*Across Cultures*

*For Frits Haselhoff*
*Thank you for teaching us the basics of strategy and*
*leadership as dilemmas and hanging out in Philadelphia's*
*divine bars*

FONS TROMPENAARS
CHARLES HAMPDEN-TURNER

# MANAGING PEOPLE

*Across Cultures*

CAPSTONE

Copyright © 2004 by Fons Trompenaars and Charles Hampden-Turner

The right of Fons Trompenaars and Charles Hampden-Turner to be identified as the authors of this work has been asserted in accordance with the Copyright, Designs and Patents Act 1988

First published 2004 by
**Capstone Publishing Ltd** (a Wiley Company)
The Atrium
Southern Gate
Chichester
West Sussex PO19 8SQ
England
www.wileyeurope.com

CIP catalogue records for this book are available from the British Library and the US Library of Congress

ISBN 1-84112-472-9

Typeset by Forewords, 109 Oxford Road, Cowley, Oxford

Printed and bound by T.J. International Ltd, Padstow, Cornwall

This book is printed on acid-free paper responsibly manufactured from sustainable forestry in which at least two trees are planted for each one used for paper production.

Substantial discounts on bulk quantities of Capstone Books are available to corporations, professional associations and other organizations. For details contact John Wiley & Sons: tel. (+44) 1243 770441, fax (+44) 1243 770517, email corporatedevelopment@wiley.co.uk

# Contents

INTRODUCTION

# Human resource management: a leading force or a palliative?

This book challenges Human Resource Management (HRM) to assume its rightful place at the leading edge of knowledge management and innovation. But in order to do so Human Resources (HR) must first come to terms with its origins and the role it has played in the past and still plays in many companies. Only then are those of us in HR in a position to take our companies into a future of perpetual renewal.

In this introduction we will be asking the following questions:

- Is HRM a genuine specialty or part of a wider human endowment?
- Who were the first human resources?
- How did HRM come to be?
- What are HRM's dilemmas?
- What should HRM's future direction be?

## IS HRM A GENUINE SPECIALTY OR PART OF A WIDER HUMAN ENDOWMENT?

The problem with HRM is that it has been with us from the beginning of time but no one bothered to notice it until recently. The hunter-gatherer tribes that once peopled the earth had no need of it and the herders who replaced them were too busy with their animals and their crops. Even the early industrialists were most excited about the new machines that increased productivity severalfold. We are all human; we all "relate" and "behave," so what is new? Does HRM have a genuine specialty, or is this something we all do and we all have?

There is a dilemma that exists when a group of professionals claim special expertise in something most people take for granted. It is hard to imagine a more disastrous tactic than informing someone with whom you have a relationship that you are the expert on that relationship because of your profession. Let's hope that the bloody nose you'll receive when you do so will only be metaphorical!

This is really a matter of credibility. Why should other functions listen to HRM? Are we simply attempting to "colonize common sense" and claiming that this is our area of expertise? In this book we hope to show that HRM is a genuine profession and, because it pervades the entire corporation, an essential discipline for leaders and leadership. But we must first answer another question.

## WHO WERE THE FIRST HUMAN RESOURCES?

The prime human resource of early capitalism, a resource that predated machinery, was the entrepreneur. The word is from the French, meaning "to take a stand between." The entrepreneur stood between the factors of production, land, labor, and capital and recombined these in ways that generated new wealth and value. Schumpeter has described this as a "gale of creative destruction." Note the dilemma or paradox implied by these words. There are non-human resources, land and capital, and human resources, labor and the entrepreneur. If HRM is to be taken seriously, we must include entrepreneurship and innovation in our definition of "human." We must pay attention to those forces of vitality that created the corporation in the first place.

So long as the great nineteenth-century entrepreneurs still lived, a vital human resource remained at the helm of big companies. No one spoke of human resources in those days, but they did speak of genius, innovation, creativity, and the mobilization of the greatest mass of resources the world had ever seen. It is these pre-bureaucratic manifestations of human enterprise that we need to revive.

Yet as the nineteenth century ended, the great American and European entrepreneurs began to die off and by the 1930s very few were left. This produced a crisis of legitimacy. By what right did the cronies of these great men rule over million-dollar empires? What, if any, were their qualifications? Everyone agreed that the founders were worthy, but what of their acolytes? Andrew Carnegie had left Henry C. Frick in charge of the Homestead works and Frick had allowed scores of trade unionists and their families to be massacred by Pinkerton agents. Carnegie, then retired in Scotland, found he could not even attend the theater, so great was the rage of the audience. He had to leave his box so that those shouting curses at him would stop and the play could start.

The managers left behind by the deaths of founders felt an urgent need to become professionals, but in what profession? In 1926 the Harvard Business School was founded as a professional school for graduate students. It immediately began to specialize in such sub-divisions as Finance, Production, Control, Business Policy, and a strangely titled subject, "Administrative Practices," later to become Human Behavior in Organizations and Human Resource Management. The school and its successors taught the "mastery" of business administration, assuming a set of principles capable of being generalized across a vast canvas. HRM had moved from entrepreneurial genius to "relating" to fellow employees, from heading the corporation to trying to make its pieces fit together.

All growing corporations face a "span of control" problem as their numbers increase beyond their founder's capacity to know employees personally. At this point rules, procedures, and processes need to be invented and HRM steps into the picture. But what kind of substitutes are these for the founder's actual presence? How much of the original genius is lost?

## HOW DID HRM COME TO BE?

Let us now look at the birth pangs of HRM as we know it today. One pattern is very clear. HRM persistently reacts to the problems caused by advancing technology and burgeoning bureaucracy. Such a reaction was responsible for its initial birth.

The push for professionalism had actually started some years before the Harvard Business School was founded. Its chief proponent was Frederick Winslow Taylor, engineer–inventor of carbon-tipped machine tools. He proposed nothing less than that management should be regarded as a science. Not surprisingly, perhaps, he regarded Scientific Management as an extension of the engineering principles necessary to organizing a factory. A "one best way" of subdividing and organizing work could be calculated in advance and could be proven by demonstration. All conflict would cease as science showed the way.

These procedures were also known as "Fordism," after Henry Ford, as they were practiced in the mass production of the Model T. Yet the human costs turned out to be very high, leading to extreme job simplification and chronic deskilling of the workforce. With tens of thousands of immigrants desperate for work and not yet proficient in English, it proved possible to keep wages very low, train new workers in a hour or so, and fire them even more quickly if they gave the least trouble. Work was seen as entirely made up of the physical energy necessary for keeping up with the ever-moving assembly line. Almost no intelligence was necessary.

Henry Ford famously doubled the pay of his workers so that they could afford to buy the cars they were producing and saw off vigorous complaints by shareholders, but as he aged he began to see anti-Fordist conspiracies everywhere. The workforce was seeded with spies and workers spoke in a "Ford whisper" in case their disloyal sentiments were overheard. In the end Ford became a violent opponent of the United Automobile Workers and a fervent supporter of Hitler and Nazi Germany, where strikes were suppressed.

The first real blow for an independent, non-engineering vision of HRM occurred in 1927 at the Hawthorne Plant of Western Electric. From this series of experiments arose ideas and practices that constitute much of HRM today. Some of these ideas were latent and bore fruit many years later, but it's fair to say that this one series of studies was the inspiration for much that followed.

Elton Mayo was a philosopher with a strong aversion to Taylorism and Fordism, and he believed that if business schools like Harvard were to flourish, they must stake out independent, critical positions. When his student Fritz Roethlisberger, together with William Dickson, the company's representative, wrote *Management and the Worker* in 1939 Mayo's HR thesis about the discontents of industrial society was nailed firmly to the mast.

The book took direct aim at the flaws of Scientific Management. This constituted the Formal System in most factories, wherein workers received piecework incentives for producing above set standards and could be dismissed for failing to reach standard output. Ranged against this Formal System was the workers' Informal System, sometimes called Emergent System. The latter deliberately restricted output. By tacit consent among workers daily production was limited. Those working "too hard," known as rate busters, were sanctioned by fellow workers and punished socially or even physically. The workers believed, often rightly, that increased productivity would lead to an increase in the minimum standard required and that they would have to work harder for the same low wages. Instead they organized to beat the system. If they discovered more effective ways of working, they would hide these from their foremen and use the time they had won to relax.

Among the experiments carried out at Hawthorne was the Relay Test Room Experiment and it was this, more than any other, that made the researchers famous. Six immigrant women, of Irish and Polish descent, were removed from the factory floor and put in a small group where they assembled telephone relays. This was a classic psychological experiment with "independent variables" which, it was hoped, might "cause" productivity to rise. These variables included lighting, seating, height of workbenches, better food, rest periods, medicals, and shorter or longer hours. It was found that whichever variables were added or subtracted production steadily rose. The women had found ways of improving their relationships and of eliciting from each other more of their "human resources." They had also engaged with the researchers.

From that single event arose most of the ideas that characterize HRM today. For example, it gave rise to a counseling program and to private coaching, which is increasingly practiced to this day – albeit with managers, not workers. It spawned studies of job enrichment: Did the women work better because they had something challenging to work on? It gave rise to the creation of superordinate goals: Was it better to take part in an important experiment than simply assemble relays?

Douglas McGregor drew from this the conclusion that the belief in the potential of workers to manage themselves responsibly was self-fulfilling. He called this "Theory Y." Others pointed out that the experimenters, not wishing to bias the results by intruding, had instead engaged in facilitation, non-directive leadership, and what Carl Rogers was to call client-centered counseling. As production climbed and climbed the women participated more in the direction the research was taking, and productivity increased further.

Other HRM experts emphasized the small group or team-based nature of this phenomenon. This led to the Sensitivity Group, or T-group movement, to the Managerial Grid seminars of Robert Blake and Jane S. Mouton, wherein Taylor's Concern with Task was reconciled with Mayo's Concern with People. These groups evolved into Quality Circles, Quality of Work Life Groups, the Creativity Groups used in the Scanlon Plan, and the problem-solving teams widely in use today. W. Edwards Deming used groups to sustain Continuous Improvement, which was to revolutionize Japanese productivity in the 60s, 70s and 80s.

As early as the 50s, Peter Drucker had interpreted the Hawthorne Experiment as a way of systematically negotiating and reconciling personal with organizational goals. He called this Management by Objectives. Productivity was monitored daily in the Test Room, while the women discussed those features of the experiment they liked and disliked. Thus there arose an implicit bargain: "Do this for us and you will get more productivity."

Abraham Maslow saw in Hawthorne that the satisfaction of "lower needs," for survival, safety and belonging, could allow for the emergence of "higher needs," the status of helping Harvard researchers with an important project and the self-actualization of creating new awareness.

The sociologist Alvin Goulder described this as the norm of reciprocity. If managers initiated something that the employees appreciated, the latter felt an obligation to reciprocate, whereupon management would do more, and workers more. Even casual examinations of most of the hypotheses being tested reveal these as attempts to benefit workers directly and management indirectly via enhanced output. Workers responded to this kindliness.

Other HR experts argued that increased output was the result (albeit accidental) of system dynamics, fed by daily feedback. The Test Room team was a self-organizing system developing spontaneously through autopoeisis. Here was an organic model of the organization, which challenged the mechanical model of Taylor and Ford. Extrinsic motivation through the receipt of external piecework incentives had been replaced or qualified by intrinsic motivation: pleasure in the company of other people, a challenging problem to solve together, a journey of self-discovery.

Meanwhile, in Britain, Trist and Emery at the Tavistock Institute for Human Relations were arguing that the Technical System must be harmonized with the Social System to create a Socio-Technical System. What the Hawthorne researchers had done was reorganize the social system around the technical system.

Those who later became interested in corporate culture saw in the Hawthorne studies a radical change in corporate culture from the alienated factory with its predefined roles and procedures, to the face-to-face encounters of the small, intimate group. There was something in these studies for everyone, and we shall be taking the culture approach very seriously in Chapter 1.

From Adam Smith to F. W. Taylor, the stress had always been on the division of labor, but here at last were clues to the integration of labor. As Paul Lawrence and Jay Lorsch revealed, creative organizations reconciled these contrasting values.

All these discoveries and many more were either explicit or latent within the Hawthorne findings. No single event has done more to shape the field as it later developed.

## WHAT ARE HRM'S DILEMMAS?

Our approach thus far can be expressed as a series of paradoxes or *dilemmas*, which comes from the Greek *"di-lemma"* meaning "two propositions." We have asked whether HRM can really be a special function since everyone does it. We have argued that innovation, entrepreneurship, and the genius of founders are expressions of human resources very different from the style of most HRM functions today. Entrepreneurs actually resolve dilemmas by standing between the factors of production, between human and non-human resources, between destruction and creativity. We have characterized HRM as in part a philosophy of protest against dehumanizing technology and bureaucracy. Dilemmas and paradoxes are often thought of as failures of reason. We believe that the logic of values and of culture is inherently paradoxical. But we also believe that these dilemmas can be *reconciled*. Indeed the Hawthorne experiment we just described did this beautifully, albeit accidentally.

Let's briefly summarize our own view of Hawthorne:

- The *formal* system learned from the *informal* system of the workers.
- *"Independent"* variables became *system* variables, which developed together.
- *Simplified* jobs were *enriched* by the wider research context.
- *Piecework incentives* gave way to shared *superordinate goals*.
- *Directive leadership* became *nondirective* as the women became informants.
- *Authorities*, puzzled by rising output, began to act as *facilitators*.
- *Top-down goals* were transformed by *bottom-up participation*.
- *Individuals* were joined into *teams* to become more productive.
- *Task* orientations were qualified by *people* orientations and their insights.

- *Initiatives* were monitored by *feedback* to help teams learn.
- *Explicit* objectives were implicitly negotiated with the researchers.
- Management's well-intended *initiatives* were promptly *reciprocated.*
- The *experimental* laboratory became a *self-organizing system.*
- A *mechanistic* model of rewards/punishments was transformed into an *organic* one.
- *Extrinsic* inducements were qualified by *intrinsic* group satisfactions.
- The *technical* system was supported and reorganized by the *social* system.
- The *division* of labor became better *integrated* and aligned.

We could go on indefinitely, but there is enough here to recognize a consistent pattern. The values on the left are not wrong, but nor are they the only values that drive enterprise. The values of HRM are on the right and are needed to qualify the usually dominant technological values. The aim is not to defeat the left-hand values, from which the bulk of innovation probably still derives, but to integrate them with those on the right. The need is to be more differentiated and more integrated, more non-directive so as to discover a clearer direction, more individualist because a strong group supports each member, more task-oriented because people are developing around these tasks.

There is one more feature of the Hawthorne Experiment, highly relevant to the subject of this book. This was, for its time, a milestone in the study of diversity. To bother to talk to female immigrant workers and solicit their views was very unusual in 1927. They were semi-skilled and not long off the boat; job notices at that time read,

"No Irish need apply." So another of the key dilemmas in this experiment had to do with Diversity versus New Unity.

Out of what seemed unpromising human resources, "the poor, the huddled masses, yearning to breathe free," came an extraordinary discovery that gave HRM much of the unity it enjoys today. It is when we explore new vistas that answers to old problems come to us. It is when we cross social distance that we discover new reasons for relating. It is only when we try to understand the cultures of other lands and other disciplines that we begin to understand our own culture and our own disciplines.

Yet there is a final feature of the Hawthorne Experiment, which reveals the problem HRM faces today. It was and it remains a reaction to the imperatives of technology. We have to decide if we will wait for new technologies to disturb people and then rush in with supportive services, or whether we will foster the initial process of humane innovations.

## WHAT SHOULD HRM'S FUTURE DIRECTION BE?

We are now in a position to spell out our mission for HRM, our vision of what HRM can and must do in the twenty-first century. HRM must return to the values of entrepreneurship, which first created major industries out of native genius. It must do this because size, scale, and vast physical and capital resources are no longer enough. We have entered the age of non-stop human innovation, where the race goes to the agile and the inventive, and those with huge physical resources and capital are vulnerable as never before. Every big company needs to renew and reinvent itself or value will migrate elsewhere, to those talking to customers rather than to each other. The future of HRM is nothing less than to confront the dilemmas of creativity and destruction, human resources and physical resources, change and continuity, along with similar dilemmas.

Even functions, once regarded as monolithic silos, standing proudly on their own, are in need of reconciliation. Time was when the workplace simply manufactured things that the sales force then tried to sell to customers. But the modern corporation cannot be like that. Increasingly we have customized workplaces, customized not just to what customers are asking for, but to what growing, learning, ever-more-complex employees seek to learn, to discover, and to express. The boundaries between functions are dissolving into integrated capabilities.

This book redefines wealth creation in several important respects. We do not "add value" because only in the simplest cases can one value be simply stacked on top of another. Most values come to us in vivid contrasts, defying us to make a good connection. Hence a high performance automobile confronts us with the dilemma of making it as safe as possible. We need to leave drivers in control, so that they can drive intelligently, but we must also snatch back that control if they get into trouble. Brakes must not lock, tires must not skid, and airbags must open before the driver's body is crushed on impact. Then the doors must unlock to facilitate rescue.

These kinds of resolutions are no mean feats of engineering. Values must be aligned, integrated, synergized, and must mutually transform each other to higher levels of complexity. This book will help to show how this is possible.

But let there be no doubt of what happens when we fail to show leadership. Technological-type change will once again seize the helm as it did in the disastrous dot-com boom and bust. Taylorism simply goes underground to reappear as reengineering or some similar stampede of new instruments.

The proper place for HRM is at the fountainhead, the place where ideas are first generated and mobilized for action. If human con-cerns are not embedded there from the beginning, it can be a long, grim struggle to slow the juggernaut as it runs over people. We can explain what has for so long proved mysterious, "good judgment," "intuition," "flare," "genius." We can map these out and codify them so others can build upon earlier achievements. These are not magical, but forms of values' reconciliation, which can be described and progressed in balanced formats.

We are now in a position to sketch out the sequence and structure of our argument in Chapters 1 to 10; you will find case studies of prob-lems faced by international HRM in each chapter.

In Chapter 1, *Human Resources Management and Corporate Culture*, we show that the culture of an organization is a living system, with pur-pose, direction, and properties of self-conservation, so that cultures often defeat all attempts to change them. Four recognizable cultures are described, each suited to different organizational purposes, each with convictions of its own. It is crucial to grasp the role of corporate cultures, since these do the actual work of the corporation. Leaders lead their cultures, change agents must change cultures, because it is cultures that motivate, inspire, reward, and inform their members, successfully or otherwise.

In Chapter 2, *Recruitment, Selection, and Assessment*, we consider the war for talent. In a world rapidly becoming more complex, it is vital to recruit, select, assess, and develop talents that are becoming increasingly scarce. To accomplish this HRM uses a vast array of instruments. Many of these tools have been in use for years and we admire and describe some of these, yet nearly all suffer a crucial flaw. They measure one side of a dilemma only and, in many cases, force us to choose between values which could – and should – be integrated. We show how extant measures can be qualified by complementary measures to create broader syntheses.

In Chapter 3, *Training Managers to Attain Strategic Goals,* we urge HRM to participate in creating strategy. This is essential to placing the corporation's core competence at the center of its strategic thrust. Unless this is done, HRM's function may shrink to the implementation of cost-cutting agendas and the delivery of redundancy notices. The function may become despised. An obvious role for HRM is to develop the strengths necessary to deliver the corporation's strategy. But there is a snag. Few strategies survive a downturn or upturn in the economic cycle. In addition, most strategies end in paradox. The advice of every strategy guru has been contradicted by at least one other. There is no consensus. What can we do about this?

We need to balance these dilemmas against each other, and the Balanced Scorecard is a good start. But it is only a start because persuading a corporation to weigh contrasting values equally is exceedingly difficult. Try telling most banks that their future learning goals are as important as their past financial results; you won't get far. What we need is an Integrated Scorecard, because learning goals will not be taken seriously until they contribute to financial results.

In Chapter 4, *How HRM can Facilitate the Problem-Solving Power of Teams,* we see that teamwork is crucial to HRM. One of our four corporate cultures, the Guided Missile, consists almost entirely of team activity acting as a lynchpin for the matrix organization. All team members have a dual allegiance. They must be true to their function and true to their team's project. These combined objectives are vital to the cohesion of the larger corporation. Most change in organizations would not be possible without teams to test, champion, and model those changes.

We will argue that teams need to be diverse in order to excel. Once again, the research results are paradoxical. Diverse teams are both more likely to fail and to succeed. Yet superlative and innovative solutions require diversity and do not occur without this.

In Chapter 5, *Building a Learning Organization: A Challenge to HR,* we show that nearly everything an organization does can be framed as a question posed to its environment. When an answer is discovered, knowledge has been created. Top managers can engage in a vital dialogue with those closer to customers than they are. The company must become an Inquiring System.

But what kinds of learning are these? Here too, dilemmas abound. Is learning tacit or explicit? Should we make errors and correct these or go for error-free perfectibility? Do we come up to the standards and benchmarks of our industry or create new standards? Real learning and competitive advantage occurs when such dilemmas are reconciled.

In Chapter 6, *Leadership Development Across Cultures,* we conclude that listing the characteristics of a "good" leader can never be complete. With the permanent white water of the global economy, new challenges are constantly thrown up. It becomes very difficult for HRM to specify the capabilities required.

But one generalization does hold. Leaders must increasingly reconcile an ever-widening spectrum of diversities. Different stages of economic cycles, different national cultures, different corporate cultures, different team roles, functions, status levels, learning styles, disciplines, and personalities all contribute to the distances a leader must somehow bridge. We have designed a questionnaire which taps this capacity to reconcile contrasting values. The top leaders we wrote about in *21 Leaders for the 21st Century* outscored the senior managers in our samples by 20 percent or more.

In Chapter 7, *From Personal Diagnoses to Web-Based Assessments*, we reveal how we diagnose the presence of dilemmas even among those who deny their existence. At Trompenaars Hampden-Turner (THT) we locate dilemmas by interviewing, by examining corporate stories, myths, symbols, and metaphors. When the informants proclaim virtues, we look for the shadow side, the contrasting values that may have been sacrificed. Yet we never negate a client's own convictions, although we may qualify these. Our clients approve of all the dilemmas we find before we proceed further. Web-based instruments are good at picking up ongoing discourse within the corporation but do not surface latent ideas.

In Chapter 8, *Steps Towards Resolving Dilemmas*, we do some "conceptual blockbusting" on the way people habitually think. We cannot guarantee that inspiration will follow, but we can demolish the barriers that stand in the way.

In Chapter 9, *Creating an Assessment Center*, we examine what kind of culture an "assessment center" presupposes. We show that candidates from different corporate cultures will behave differently and need to be assessed according to four different environments. Even visions of "career" depend upon which of our four cultures the manager inhabits. Career patterns also differ markedly, as between Japan, Germany, France, and North America.

Finally in Chapter 10, *Varieties of Culture Shock*, we consider the visceral and emotional toll of crossing cultures and meeting strangers. We introduce a simulation, which exercises "emotional muscles." IQ needs to be supplemented by EQ, emotional capabilities to manage stress.

# CHAPTER 1

# Human resource management and corporate culture

**P**erhaps the prime reality with which HRM must deal is corporate culture. Culture is often powerful and it persists when you try to disturb it. The key point to remember is that corporate cultures are alive. Like superhuman organisms they have their own energy, purpose, direction, values, and ways of processing information. Those who believe cultures can be shaped like clay are in for a surprise. If you mess with cultures in a way that violates their sense of order, they will lash back at you. It is a bit like punching that inflatable children's toy which returns to its equilibrium point following any disturbance – and may well punch you back.

Ed Schein of MIT has given us what is probably the best definition of corporate culture, in his book *Organization, Culture, and Leadership*:

> A pattern of assumptions, invented, discovered, or developed by a given group, as it learns to cope with the problem of external adaptation and internal integration, that has worked well enough to be considered valid, and be taught to new members, as the correct way to perceive, think, and feel in relation to these problems.

Note that Schein also perceives a dilemma, that between external adaptation and internal integration. Can these be reconciled?

But it was Ruth Benedict in *Patterns of Culture* who provided what is, for us, a momentous insight. She had been asked to explain why three Native American tribes were close to cultural breakdown – alcoholic, despairing, apathetic, crime-ridden, etc., and why two were relatively well-adjusted and benign. She discovered, to her dismay, that no single variable could be distinguished consistently between the two groups. Had her whole academic life been wasted?

She then saw that she had been looking for answers in the wrong place. It was not the presence or absence of key values that made the difference. All the tribes emphatically condemned selfish behavior, for example. It was the pattern by which selfishness and unselfishness were joined. In the benign culture, unselfish behavior was swiftly rewarded and reciprocated, so that it was also self-serving. In other words, selfishness versus unselfishness was transcended as a polarity. In contrast, unselfishness was ferociously exploited by selfish conduct in the miserable tribes, while those injured condemned selfish conduct in no uncertain terms.

Benedict called this transcendence of value dichotomies "synergy," a word that comes from *syn-ergo*, "to work with or together." She was the first social scientist to use this term, which was eagerly picked up by Abraham Maslow. Cultures are therefore more or less synergistic depending on the extent to which contrasting values work with each other.

We saw in the Introduction, for example, that creativity works with destruction in successful entrepreneurship, just as human resources work with physical ones. In the Hawthorne Experiment, the Formal System worked with the Informal System; tasks were united with people. The Social System supported the Technical System, instead of trying to subvert it. There was synergy among all our pairs. It is this that distinguishes creative and productive cultures from stagnant and ineffective ones. If Benedict had not looked between values rather than at them, she would have failed to understand the subtlety and power of culture.

We are now in a position to present our own definition of culture:

Culture is the pattern by which a group habitually mediates between value differences, such as rules and exceptions, technology and people, conflict and consensus, etc. Cultures can learn to reconcile such values at ever-higher levels of attainment, so that better rules are created from the study of numerous exceptions. From such reconciliation come health, wealth, and wisdom. But cultures in which one value polarity dominates and militates against another will be stressful and stagnate.

Given this definition, the Four Corporate Cultures appearing in Figure 1.1 may seem to break our own rules, for they are not only very different, they are polarized. Quite so, but Polarity versus Reconciliation must itself be synergized. Without any initial difference or diversity between people or cultures, there would be nothing to reconcile. Polarities are an essential part of processing information. We need to make distinctions and we need to combine them, so let us live with these polarities for a while.

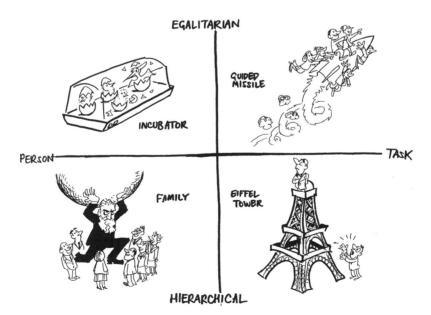

**Figure 1.1** Four corporate cultures

These cultures vary along two dimensions. They are more or less egalitarian or hierarchical and more or less oriented to person or to task. But this does not mean that cultures with an elite hierarchy set no store by equality. There may have been exams in which all entrants had an equal chance. Nor are task-oriented cultures completely dismissive of the people who do these tasks. In a very real sense these four boxes are stereotypes, or archetypes to give them a less opprobrious label. Yet we cannot avoid such labels. They are woven into the mythology and symbolism of all cultures and loom large in the minds of members. Cultures, whether corporate or national, stereotype themselves. The Eiffel Tower, the Sydney Opera House, the Empire State Building. These are flashed on screens to enable audiences to locate the action. When did we ever watch a cowboy hero in an American film whose judgment was overruled by a group? We are still waiting; there the individual is always right.

We all form first impressions quickly. We could not function effectively without doing so. The point is not to avoid stereotypes; these are everywhere. The point is to go beyond superficial impressions to see what lies deeper and half-submerged. This is what we will be doing with the four quadrants in Figure 1.1.

But let us first examine the quadrants, surface manifestations although they are. The *Incubator* at top left, typical of Silicon Valley, is a culture both person-oriented and egalitarian. It is highly creative, incubating new ideas. Here we are not referring to business incubators per se, but using incubation as a metaphor for hatching creative ideas. Such organizations are egalitarian because anyone, at any moment, regardless of their status, may come up with a winning idea. They are person-oriented because the tasks necessary to making and distributing these new products are not yet defined.

The *Guided Missile* is an egalitarian, task-oriented culture in which project groups steer towards the accomplishment of team tasks. They are typically multidisciplinary, taking from the various functions of the organization only those people essential for completing their set task. They are egalitarian because whose expertise is relevant to their shared problems is an ever-open question. NASA was probably the most famous culture of this kind. It took over one hundred disciplines in science and engineering to land on the moon. The relative contributions of each one had to be negotiated among equals. The only boss was the task or mission itself.

The *Eiffel Tower* culture is that described by Max Weber in *The Protestant Ethic and the Spirit of Capitalism* and assumed by Frederick Winslow Taylor and Henry Ford. This is highly structured in the case of a factory processing physical materials and, in the case of a large bureaucracy, it does precise, detailed, and routine tasks without error. Everyone has a precise job description, be it only fixing a mirror to a succession of automobiles on an assembly line, and strict orders come from the top. The culture is stable, predictable, safe, routine, and reliable.

The *Family* culture is perhaps the oldest, since a large number of companies originate from family enterprises even if they eventually go public. On a global scale there are more family-owned companies than any other kind. But we are speaking of the family *culture*, not legal ownership. A family may own an Eiffel Tower or a publicly owned company may have a Family atmosphere.

The Family culture is hierarchical because the gap between "parents" as owners and "children" as employees is very wide. The "old man" may be revered or feared. He – and it is often a "he" – may regard his employees as members of his family, whose burdens he carries. Japanese corporations, even those that are publicly owned, may pride themselves on "elder brother–younger brother" bonding.

Mentoring and coaching are borrowed from the family ideal. MITI, the formidable Japanese government bureaucracy, is even nicknamed "Worried Auntie."

The Family culture is personal rather than task-oriented, because who you are is more important than what you do. Family members may not be fully professional. Those most accomplished at tasks may be passed over in favor of the well connected. Insiders have advantages over outsiders. Such cultures are often warm, intimate, and friendly, but their internal integration may be achieved at the price of poor external adaptation and they can hug and kiss each other into bankruptcy. Creative genius rarely passes down a dynasty, so that the vision of the founder may not be renewed in the generations that follow.

We are now in a position to return to the Hawthorne Experiment, described in the Introduction as the historic fountainhead of HRM. Do our four quadrants help us to make sense of what happened in that case? It should be obvious that Scientific Management was conceived in the image of the Eiffel Tower. Every worker had their task, precisely defined and even calibrated through time and motion study. A hierarchy dominated by a precalculated logic told the worker what to do, when, and at what pace. The worker was considered to be "a pair of hands" (hence "manual worker") obeying a strict sequence of orders from superior intelligences, Taylor and Taylorists. In reality, workers were extensions of big machines that were far more expensive than they.

Notice how cultures confined in one quadrant of our chart become, over time, half-crazed with the potentials of their vision. Taylor himself was neurotic from overcontrol. At night a machine pressed a cool, wet towel upon his brow. He slept tied by a harness to a tilting bed, lest he roll over and suffer the nightmares that tormented him.

Hotels had to be supplied in advance with his paraphernalia for "scientific" sleep. We shall see that to be trapped in any one corner of our chart has potentially catastrophic consequences.

In Figure 1.2 we have depicted the reality of Talyorism and Fordism. It was preponderantly shaped by the culture of the Eiffel Tower represented by the darker square.

Note that even in its extreme form, the Eiffel Tower does not include everyone, but contains influences from the three other cultures. The designers of this system presumably worked as a group in a Guided Missile culture, perhaps one with features of the Family. Almost certainly they believed they were incubating a new science. Mass manufacturing, as we know it, is a testament to their efforts, despite its human costs. The constraints were largely imposed on workers rather than managers.

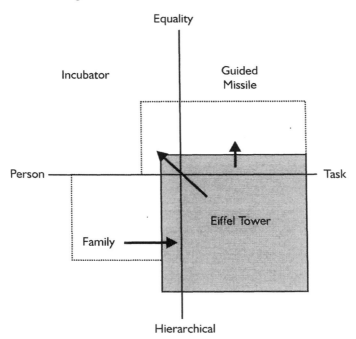

**Figure 1.2**   The reality of Taylorism and Fordism

The arrows pointing to the other quadrants show what the Hawthorne Experiment accomplished, not all of it purposefully. Perhaps the most outstanding changes were triggered accidentally. The Eiffel Tower became a Guided Missile when the women were taken off the factory floor and put in a small group with a shared task, that of becoming more productive. Feedback on their productivity was issued daily, and what today is called a team dashboard monitored their progress, allowing them to nudge it steadily upwards.

The string of hypotheses being tested were like the zigzagging of a missile zeroing in on its target. The group developed over time as the women found out more about each other and became friends. This is not individual development, so much as an overall rise in the social intelligence of the team, who felt in control of their destiny. As their productivity climbed and climbed, the number of visitors increased. The women's combined efforts won them curiosity, respect, and approval from authorities. Like modern problem-solving teams, they were bringing enlightenment to those who sponsored them.

The Eiffel Tower was also strongly qualified by a Family culture. The women became firm friends, baked cakes for each other, and became deeply interested in each other's lives. In fact, it was the family atmosphere that the researchers decided was most responsible for improved performance. The researchers had behaved like permissive parents, not wishing to spoil the experiment by telling their "children" what to do, so that the women behaved autonomously under their fond gaze. They probably thought they were treating the women normally. But what is normal among Harvard co-researchers is not normal among foremen and blue-collar workers. After the first two weeks their regular foreman from the factory floor was forbidden access to them. He was, said the researchers, "upsetting the girls." Hence their treatment was far more benign than usual.

The only permanent institutional change following Hawthorne was a Counseling Program. Motherly women were hired, in whom workers could confide if they wished. This was a form of coaching or monitoring, but one designed to discharge grievances not remedy them, and it was quietly abandoned in the early 60s.

The final direction in which the Eiffel Tower moved was towards the Incubator culture at top left. What was incubated, as we discussed in the Introduction, was nothing less than the contemporary values and beliefs of HRM. It is often forgotten that most of what the researchers "discovered" was told to them by the six subjects of the experiment. Credit for this breakthrough belongs as much to the women as to the researchers. They were no longer assembling tele-phone relays. They were part of an experiment that has opened the eyes of thousands. Experimenting and inquiring is what Incubator cultures do. They frame hypotheses and look for answers. The fact that the hypotheses in the Hawthorne studies were mostly wrong and were subsequently discarded does not distract from the inquir-ing mode. Indeed, it was because the hypotheses were failing while productivity continued to rise that the researchers consulted the six women and gave them power of veto over any feature of the experi-ments they did not like. The researchers became very open to other explanations as their own proved fruitless. The six women *were* researchers. They were no longer just assembling telephone relays, an activity of mind-numbing boredom; they were inquiring into how relays might be better assembled. They were incubating new ways for human beings to work together and learn together.

It is important to grasp that Eiffel Tower cultures do not just disap-pear from the landscape. They are no more dead than volume manufacturing and large bureaucracies. There are still routine, repetitive jobs that need doing and cost pressures and commoditization mean that it is simply too expensive to run these through groups of experts or spend scarce resources in creating a family atmosphere. All four cultures are necessary to effective organizations. What spells trouble is concentrating exclusively on one quadrant.

We have dealt at some length with the cultural vices of the Eiffel Tower culture, but all quadrants if not qualified by other quadrants will produce ill effects. Consider Figure 1.3.

Few of us like the formality, bureaucracy, mechanization, and rigidity of the Eiffel Tower, but are the informality, paternalism, organic relations, and loose procedures of the Family any better? The very warmth and affection of some of these cultures can lure us into complacency and they are not necessarily affectionate either. They can be

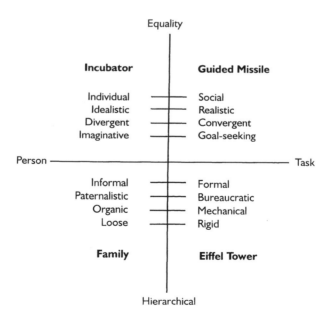

**Figure 1.3** Value polarities corresponding with Person–Task dichotomy

fiefdoms of personal power and arbitrary decisions. Families have their feuds and poor relations.

Similarly, many of us feel drawn to the individualism, idealism, imagination, and divergent thinking typical of new, incubating companies (top left). Yet their failure rate is extremely high and their profitability most precarious. Most new start-ups fail. But is the opposite quadrant any better? Are not over-socialization and group-think also dangerous? If we converge relentlessly on realistic goals (top right) are we not boxed in, unable to reframe issues or revision tasks?

## CULTURES ARE PATTERNS OF DIFFERENCES

The eight pairs of values in Figure 1.3 are all differences, as are the two axes of the model. This is such an important point that we need readers to concentrate and, if necessary, reread this paragraph. What defines "individual" is that to which it has been contrasted, in this case "social." The meanings of both values lie not in themselves but in differences between them. They make no sense without this difference. Thus formality is contrasted with informality, loose with rigid, idealism with realism, and so on.

The implication of all this insight is important. All four quadrants are really differences too. We will go as mad as Taylor if we try to maximize one end of these continua while avoiding the other. The art of creating a viable corporate culture is to reconcile these contrasts or dilemmas, to formalize those informal events that are advantageous, to realize ideals, to diverge in search of new information, and then converge on a new solution, to be loose and tight by turns.

Because values are really differences we get a new set of contrasts by

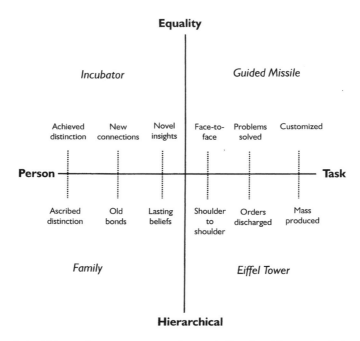

**Figure 1.4**  Value polarities corresponding with Equality–Hierarchy dichotomy

reading from top to bottom on the Equality–Hierarchical axis (Figure 1.4).

The four quadrants are recognizable in many ways by anyone familiar with HR. Let's consider:

1.    Management style.

2.    Power orientation.

3.    Source of cohesion.

4.    Principle of control.

5.    Guiding star or watchword.

6.    Definition of excellence.

What is the best management style (1)? It depends upon the culture

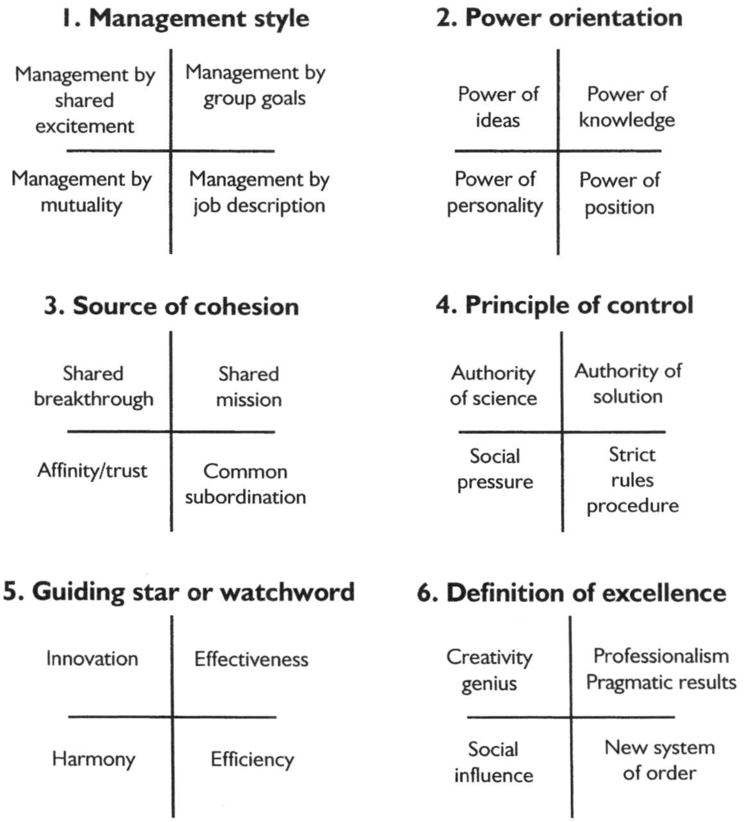

## 1. Management style

| Management by shared excitement | Management by group goals |
|---|---|
| Management by mutuality | Management by job description |

## 2. Power orientation

| Power of ideas | Power of knowledge |
|---|---|
| Power of personality | Power of position |

## 3. Source of cohesion

| Shared breakthrough | Shared mission |
|---|---|
| Affinity/trust | Common subordination |

## 4. Principle of control

| Authority of science | Authority of solution |
|---|---|
| Social pressure | Strict rules procedure |

## 5. Guiding star or watchword

| Innovation | Effectiveness |
|---|---|
| Harmony | Efficiency |

## 6. Definition of excellence

| Creativity genius | Professionalism Pragmatic results |
|---|---|
| Social influence | New system of order |

**Figure 1.5** Typologies suggestive of the four cultures

you inhabit. In the Eiffel Tower (bottom right) it is fulfilling your job description as specified in advance. In the Family culture it is the depth of mutuality, fulfilling your obligations to colleagues (bottom left). In the Incubator culture it is sharing excitement with fellow innovators (top left) and it is meeting team objectives and group goals in the Guided Missile (top right).

How is power oriented (2) in our four cultures? In the Eiffel Tower (bottom right) power is an attribute of your formal position. In the Family culture (bottom left) you have powerful personalities who get their way in family discussions. Power also lies in your historic role as founder or in your relationship to the founder. In the Incubator culture (top left) we deal with ideas whose time has come. In the Guided Missile culture (top right) teams help to constitute and define the knowledge that will guide the company: "Knowledge is power."

What is the source of cohesion (3) for different cultures? What is the glue which holds them together? In the Eiffel Tower we are held together by common subordination to a boss or expert (bottom right). In case of arguments, the duly constituted authority decides and we obey. In the Family culture we are held together by trust and long affinity and empathy (bottom left). In the Incubator culture (top left) we share a momentous breakthrough; we were there when the discovery was made! In the Guided Missile culture (top right) the team shares a mission which it brings to fruition.

By what principle do we accept authority and control (4)? In the Eiffel Tower strict rules and procedures exist and legitimate authority enforces these (bottom right). Actions are either "out of order" or orderly. In the Family culture social pressures are brought to bear by deeply respected persons (bottom left). You are persuaded, often privately. In Incubator cultures the authority belongs to the science or discipline you are using to innovate (top left). If Nature says "yes," you are authorized. In Guided Missile cultures you are justified by the integrity of your own solution (top right). If the problem is solved, then that is your controlling principle. The spacecraft reached Saturn. You were right in your calculations. Late deliveries were halved. Such solutions are your authority.

Each culture has its own Guiding Star or Watchword (5). For Eiffel Towers the supreme virtue is efficiency and accompanying cost reductions (bottom right). Family cultures set great store by harmony, deep insights into each others' needs (bottom left). For

Incubator cultures innovation is the ongoing purpose of the company (top left), while for the Guided Missile effectiveness is most important (top right). Innovation and other qualities must be made to count.

The four cultures also vary in their definitions of excellence (6). For Eiffel Tower cultures excellence is a new system of order by which that culture is structured and disciplined (bottom right). For Family cultures excellence lies in high levels of social influence exercised for the benefit of the company and its employees (bottom left). For Incubator cultures excellence lies in personal creativity and genius (top left), while for Guided Missile cultures being professional and producing the desired results matters most of all (top right).

We can also consider what role HR plays in each quadrant so as to:

1.    Attract, retain, and motivate talent.

2.    Reward staff.

3.    Assess improvement.

4.    Develop staff and leaders.

5.    Effect change.

6.    Use money.

If you want to attract, retain, and motivate talent (1) then different cultures will desire different inducements. In an Eiffel Tower culture job descriptions and precisely qualified job holders are the key (bottom right). In the Family culture (bottom left), loyalty, sociability, diplomacy, and being a trusted "insider" are vital. Incubator cultures need people in search of personal creativity and self-actualization (top left). They yearn to innovate and dedicate themselves totally to this end. Guided Missile cultures want to forge effective

## 1. Attract, retain and motivate talent

| Opportunity for personal creativity and self-actualization | Opportunity to forge team solutions to vital issues |
|---|---|
| Foster loyalty, sociability, diplomacy, trust | Hire those precisely qualified for job as described |

## 2. Reward Staff

| Joy of creating Celebrating discovery | High esteem among close peers |
|---|---|
| Personal recognition Special attention | External incentives for exceeding standards |

## 3. Assess improvement

| People render their own jobs more challenging and creative | Teams set more ambitious targets and go on to realize these |
|---|---|
| The confidence of influential people is won and rapport achieved | Persons come up to standards or fall below these |

## 4. Develop staff and leaders

| Ability to turn creative ideas into genuine innovations | Ability to lead, sponsor and/or debrief teams |
|---|---|
| Read vibes and form fiduciary relationships | Ensure that qualifications match job descriptions |

## 5. Effect change

| Nurture the creative process Champion innovation | Allow teams to self-organize around company's major issues |
|---|---|
| Winning the allegiance of key power brokers | Reengineering the workplace to alter its parameters |

## 6. Use of money

| A resource to be moved to where the innovation is | A symbol of group and personal achievement Group bonus |
|---|---|
| A token of mutua respect, a way of caringl | Compensation for otherwise exacting work |

**Figure 1.6**   Typologies of roles played by HRM

team solutions and enjoy these social crucibles of group effectiveness (top right).

Rewards (2) for staff are very different in the four cultures. In the Eiffel Tower you typically get external (cash) incentives for exceeding set standards (bottom right), plus the security of a stable environment. The Family culture can give you deep respect, personal recognition and very special attention from people you admire, like the best of relationships between master and apprentice (bottom left). In Incubator cultures, the joy of creating and the celebration of discovering new phenomena are foremost (top left). In the Guided Missile culture you can raise the esteem of fellow team members (top right), whose infectious enthusiasm for your ideals and contributions constitute an extended high. Being loved and admired by close colleagues may be the strongest reward on earth.

HR policy needs to deal with the values in all of the forty-eight quadrants. If, for example, you wish to attract, retain, and motivate talent then you must hire qualified people, win their trust and loyalty, organize them into teams, and get them to fulfill themselves through personal creativity. Depending on the culture, one or more of these quadrants will be more crucial than others, but all are involved in overall HR strategies.

Or consider the most appropriate management style. You start by describing the jobs you wish to fill, but you qualify this with the subjective preferences of the job holders. You then manage by objectives, which are in effect a synthesis of what the organization wants and what employees are professionally committed to achieve. As these achievements become more and more innovative, management by shared excitement becomes possible.

It is also arguable that many companies pass through phases in which each quadrant becomes the more influential one. Suppose you start with a Family culture at bottom left, as most companies in the world have done, using combined savings as capital. Family members have a brilliantly creative idea that they Incubate (top left). But there is little profit in just generating ideas. These must be turned into products customized to suit what the markets are demanding. This is where the Guided Missile culture is so appropriate, "guiding" products/services towards customer satisfaction via teams, in a way that makes the customer more effective. It takes a whole team to place products in a rich context of information and service.

Yet markets do inevitably mature. More suppliers are attracted into the industry, margins shrink, profits fall, and commoditization sets in. Companies are forced to cut costs and increase volume through-put, which is where the Eiffel Tower comes back to haunt us. Guided Missile cultures are too expensive for commodity-type output.

The best way to assess improvement (3) also varies between corpo-rate cultures. In the Eiffel Tower (bottom right), you come up to benchmarks and standards or fail to do so. In the Family culture (bottom left), it is who you know, the extent of rapport achieved and the circles of intimacy you have penetrated which count. In the Incu-bator culture you do not so much fulfill your job as transform its significance and challenge (top left). In the Guided Missile culture (top right) you are asked how ambitious the whole team has been and whether it has attained its own stretch goals.

Developing staff and their leadership (4) means different things in our four cultures. In an Eiffel Tower system persons "Improve" by living up to their job descriptions and having the right qualifications (bottom right). In the Family culture it is a question of reading vibes emanating from eminent people and forming fiduciary relationships with them (bottom left). In Incubator cultures creative ideas must become innovative products as the ideal becomes the real (top right). In Guided Missile cultures it is team leadership and sponsor-ship that is most needed (top right).

Effective change (5) takes place in very different ways. Eiffel Towers are often reengineered in a process that is often painful and drastic (bottom right). The whole structure is reconceived. In Family cultures the key power brokers must be on side and their allegiance won (bottom left). Change comes to the Incubator culture through its own innovation, the logic of which prevails (top left). In the Guided Missile culture there is often spontaneous self-organization of teams around issues blocking progress (top right).

Money (6) has meanings dependent on culture. It is literally compensation for work you would not otherwise want to do in the Eiffel Tower culture (bottom right). It is partly symbolic in the Family culture, a token of respect, a way of caring (bottom left). It is used to facilitate innovative activities in the Incubator culture (top left). Indeed the ability of money to follow closely in the wake of innovation is one of the secrets of capitalism. It moves resources to where the breakthrough is. Finally, money is a symbol of team success and the achievement of its members in a Guided Missile culture. It gives them more resources to follow up their gains (top right).

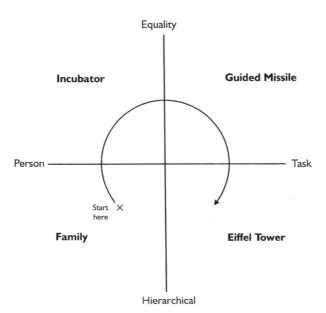

**Figure 1.7**   Coming full circle

But even if a company comes full circle, the Eiffel Tower should be supported by the other quadrants. Quality Circles are ways of punctuating routine production work with Guided Missile deliberations. Routine work can take on an important new meaning provided employees are testing new ideas and reorganizations of their own workplaces. It is even possible to incubate new ideas in Quality Circles and discover their validity by trying these out in the factory or the office in the days following. Having an Eiffel Tower organization does not stop employees thinking, discovering, and learning, as W. Edwards Deming and his cycles of Continuous Improvement demonstrate. He prescribed the sequence of act–plan–implement–check, which is now a standard part of Total Quality Management that fits fairly well into our four quadrants.

An organization learns by using all four quadrants, even where one culture looms larger than the others. If incubation is not connected to the efficient manufacture and marketing of finished products and

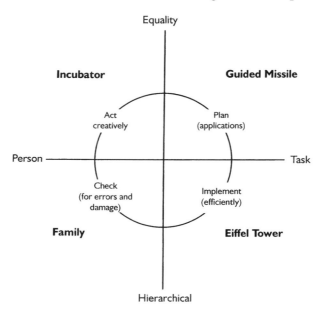

**Figure 1.8** The Deming cycle applied to the four quadrants

services, where are the profits to sustain its creativity going to come from? Every quadrant needs the others to sustain it. Do not trap yourself in the alchemist's dream of creating gold from base metals, nor in Taylor's tilting bed.

## INTERNATIONAL VARIATION IN PREFERRED CORPORATE CULTURES

One serious mistake is to assume that the culture preferred in the domestic HQ of an international company will work throughout the world and that HR can globalize its various tools without serious problems. As Figure 1.9 illustrates, national cultures vary substantially on their relative preferences for the four cultures.

One reason why the Incubator culture is so thinly populated is that creative people are a small minority in all cultures so that using national aggregates tends to hide this preference. In *The Rise of the*

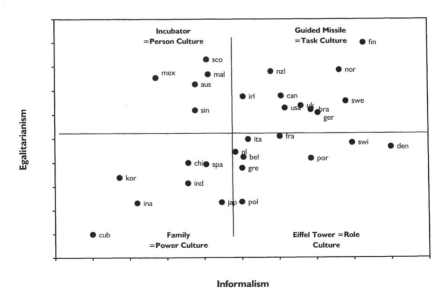

**Figure 1.9** Variation of corporate culture across the world

*Creative Class*, Richard Florida reveals that America's astonishing burst of creativity in the last decade of the twentieth century derives from less than 15 percent of its working population and is confined to a dozen or so urban centers across the USA. This 15 percent produces 85 percent of successful innovations and has transformed America's fortunes and restored the nation to industrial leadership.

## CAPSULE CASE
### The sad history of pay for performance

Pay for performance is one of these incentive systems that "should" work because it seems so logical and fair, but in practice runs foul of corporate culture. So let us consider the (few) circumstances in which it succeeds and the many in which it fails.

It is, of course, an Eiffel Tower concept. Top management is assumed to know how difficult jobs are and therefore how much the successful completion of each task is worth and what reward the employee deserves. Where the job-holder excels, top management even assumes that this excellence will take predictable and measurable forms, increasing in quantities achieved without the quality of the tasks being changed. One consequence of this is that you cannot change a production system to which rewards have been attached without also changing the reward system, which typically leads to strong resistance to change from employees and the need to recalculate pay-for-performance tariffs every time technologies change.

Pay for performance undermines the order and predictability

of Eiffel Tower cultures. It does this by withholding a portion of the employee's pay until after the task has been performed. If the task is held to be unsatisfactory, pay for that period will be less. There is a strong shift of power towards those judging performance and away from those actually performing.

Pay for performance runs into immediate difficulties in any Family culture where motivations and rewards are intrinsic, not extrinsic. You are not paid to be a good parent; you are not rewarded as an individual for what your family group has nurtured in you. Children given monetary incentives for fastening their seat belts in automobiles stopped doing so when the incentives stopped. From a family point of view their lives are precious in themselves and incentives trivialized this. What should a nurse get for holding the hand of a dying teenage joyrider whose auto has crashed and then breaking the news to his parents? Should she get $50, or a T-shirt with a heart on it? Are not many jobs their own reward? Are we all just waiting staff wanting tips?

Pay for performance fails utterly in an Incubator culture. Indeed, it is anti-creative in its influence. When certain tasks are incentivized research shows that employees choose the easiest and avoid the more difficult ones. It is the hard jobs that most need innovation. If and when innovation does occur, it may not be rewarded. It may even be punished, because top management does not know what value to attribute to a task completed in a creative manner. In any case the deep significance of creativity is often insulted by the pin-money used to reward it. What if the innovation is worth millions and you pay

$100? The innovator is likely to feel more aggrieved than if paid nothing.

Finally, the Guided Missile culture quarrels with pay for performance because you have singled out the individual and ignored the team. Why should not those who give help to others be rewarded? Why not give money to whole teams? Indeed, if the group becomes jealous of the high performing individual they will drag that person down to their level. Retail clerks who "sell too much" will have their receipt books stolen by co-workers or be otherwise punished. What is the point of making leaders out of high performers who are disliked by their peers because they received money that others helped them earn?

This capsule case is summarized from Alfie Kohn's book, *Published by Rewards*.

If a single concept like pay for performance is undermined by three out of four corporate cultures just imagine what a mess different national cultures could make of it. No wonder the Italian Employee of the Month calls in sick rather than show her face to the people who made her reward possible. How does an innovative person fill in a time sheet? Perhaps something like, "Tried out several ideas and abandoned them all"!

Although the road is strewn with traps for the unwary, HR still has to recruit, assess, select, and reward employees and do this better than other companies or lose talent. It still has to win the "war for talent" which is the theme of the next chapter.

In conclusion, cultures are living systems that resist being changed save by those who know their underlying logics. We have distinguished four cultures that are, at one and the same time, polar contrasts and interrelated patterns. The traditional business culture is the Eiffel Tower, but as work becomes increasingly complex and the need to learn and innovate increases, the Family culture, the Incubator, and the Guided Missile become more prominent. Any one of these needs help from the others to be effective.

Management styles, sources of cohesion, definitions of excellence, and so on will all vary, depending on which of the four cultures features most prominently. If HR wishes to attract, retain, and motivate talent to reward staff or develop leaders, etc. it needs to be the master of all four cultures, arising to prominence over time, in sequence.

The cultures of different nations may also prefer one corporate culture to another, even within the same multinational company. A tool, often believed to be neutral, like pay for performance, will prove disastrous in certain cultures yet the need to locate and develop talent remains desperately urgent.

But the methods used to reward employees in task-oriented cultures like the USA may fail dismally in person-oriented cultures. Why should I be paid for my performance when I owe all my success to the support of my Family, especially my warm, inspiring teacher and boss? Is it not insulting to him and all my wonderful colleagues to pretend I did everything by myself? How embarrassing to be elected Employee of the Month when my team has done so much to help and sustain me: "I think I will call in sick!"

The effectiveness or otherwise of HR tools depends very much on the corporate culture of that nation and locality. There are no universal measures that can retain exactly the same meanings across cultures.

There is no mistaking what most of the employees we talk to prefer as a culture. Right across the globe they have their eyes on that almost empty top-left quadrant, the Incubator. They vary considerably on what is real for them, the corporate culture they now inhabit, but they vary less in what is ideal. Nearly every senior manager we talk to and test seeks to be more creative and innovative, wants the corporation to renew itself.

An HR department that can create the opportunities to reach this idealized goal, especially among the restless migrants of Generation X, is going to win the war for talent, recruiting, assessing, retaining, and fulfilling the best employees. To this issue we now turn.

CHAPTER 2

# Recruitment, selection, and assessment

Corporations must first go out and recruit talented people. Once they have created a talent pool, they must select from among them the people most valuable to the corporation. Finally their various capabilities need to be assessed. Those assessed highly are given some kind of label, often "high potential," which usually means they will be watched carefully for evidence that this potential is flowering.

In this chapter we show that HR departments face a struggle to attract scarce talent to their own corporations. Knowing how to select and assess the highest quality people is vital in this contest, yet the majority of instruments used for selection and assessment are of doubtful validity in predicting future leadership capacity or high levels of performance.

Here we examine some of the most famous of these instruments:

- the Myers-Briggs Type Indicator (MB TI),
- 360° Feedback,
- Shell's Helicopter, Analysis, Imagination, Realism, and Leadership (HAIRL) system, and
- Hay Job Evaluation.

Each, although full of valuable insights, does not come to terms with the urgent challenge of selecting and assessing the best recruits, which we will demonstrate; we then suggest quite minor modifications to these instruments that would make all the difference.

It is hard to spot talent unless you have some mental image of that talent in mind. Ericcson identifies "Innovators," "Relationship Builders," "Business Managers," and "Competence Developers." Shell looks for Realism, Imagination, Analysis, Helicopter quality, and Leadership. Shell's Amsterdam Laboratories distinguished

Applicators, Integrators, and Creators. The more of these labels you have, the greater the diversity of talents – yet the more difficult it becomes to prioritize different types.

There is not enough talent to go around, especially when the economy turns up and the reputation of the company as an attractive place to work becomes important. There is now a rush of books published in America on "the best companies to work for." These are increasingly broken down into groupings, so that there are "best companies" for women and for minorities, such as gays, African Americans or Hispanics. This trend is very likely to spread. What it promises to become, especially when the economy turns up again, is, in Peter Drucker's words, a "war for talent." It makes good sense to focus on minorities who may have been discriminated against, because their achievements have been wrought despite prejudice against them. For example, for many years Motorola was able to recruit and select some outstanding Japanese women.

## A WAR FOR TALENT

Young people everywhere, especially the most talented and the best educated, want a chance to express themselves through the work they do, to create, innovate, or at least share the excitement of innovative projects. Where once security was sought through long tenure with one company, the recession of the early 90s and cutbacks since have driven jobseekers to increase their own employability. This means that they want a high-profile job with the best chance of learning quickly and being identified with major projects. They will then seek another adventurous job and bid up their salaries in the process.

HR departments have a role of crucial importance to play in this process. Can they identify, hire, assess, monitor, promote, and otherwise reward future leaders and high performers? Can they spot, among the huge variety of candidates, those key traits that other employers have missed?

Two different forms of assessment need to be distinguished. There are instruments whose chief function is to provide self-assessment for the individual. This helps recruits to know themselves. Quite often management does not keep these scores. They are for individuals only, administered by external consultants who then leave. The selection and promotion of preferred candidates uses other kinds of assessment. Here a judgment must be made as to which kinds of talent the organization needs. These two methods are not exclusive of each other. HR would be wise to feedback the results of all assessments for individuals to comment upon and mull over. In that way the value of the instruments used can be assessed, as can the values of individuals. Neither of the two methods is perfect.

By the end of this chapter we hope to have supplied a new lens which can focus upon a key competence missing from existing instruments. We don't advise that these instruments be abolished or replaced, however. Far too much effort has already been expended on them for us to abandon them now. Far too many people know their profiles and set store by these for us to waste this cumulative knowledge. Instead we suggest conserving existing metrics, but extracting new meaning from them and looking at them in new ways. Few assessment instruments are "wrong" *per se*, but most are seriously incomplete.

There are so many assessment instruments offered by rival consultancies that a comprehensive survey would quickly exhaust readers. So, as we previously described, we are going to examine just four well-known instruments, better and longer-lived than others: the Myers-Briggs Type Indicator (MBTI), Shell's famous HAIRL (Helicopter, Analysis, Imagination, Realism, and Leadership) system, 360° Feedback, and Hay Job Evaluation. Our part commendation and part criticism of these four instruments applies to assessment instruments across the board. Almost without exception they answer some questions but miss the most crucial ones of all. The posing of a very few additional questions will permit HR professionals to persevere with existing instruments, yet discover whole new patterns of capability among employees.

## THE MBTI

This was created by a two-woman partnership in the late 30s from the psychology of the Swiss psychiatrist C. J. Jung, with an emphasis on his four functions.

- Introvert–Extrovert
- Sensing–Intuiting
- Thinking–Feeling
- Judgment–Perception

It came into its own when used by the American armed forces following Pearl Harbor to assess millions of volunteers and draftees into military service. One consequence was that a vast number of Americans discovered their MBTI profile. It was also used extensively by business and government after World War II, so that as many as half America's professional managers now know their profiles. Today it is used largely for greater self-awareness. Which psychological types an organization most needs has not been agreed.

For the benefit of readers not familiar with C. J. Jung's Four Functions, we have summarized them below.

The first function has two contrasting types and inquires as to where

**Figure 2.1**   Introvert–Extrovert

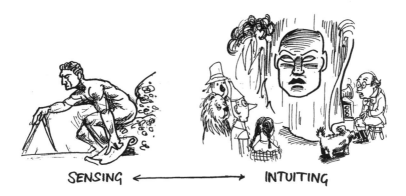

**Figure 2.2**   Sensing–Intuiting

people get their energy from. Introverts spark ideas and convictions within themselves. Extroverts get energy from those they engage with in the social environment.

The second function may seem confusing. Sensing means examining surface and objective facts, those that can be observed and verified. It is close to empiricism and positivism. Intuition, in contrast, looks through the outward appearance of things in search of the larger

**Figure 2.3** Thinking–Feeling

reality. It seeks depth of insight. Hence in *The Wizard of Oz* Dorothy and her friends were able to see through the wizard's imposing façade to reality – a small, balding man pulling levers in an attempt to intimidate them.

The third function contrasts Thinking with Feeling; in Figure 2.3, the dualism of Descartes with the homesickness of ET. Feelings are not without their inner logics. "The heart has its own reasons..." insisted Blaise Pascale.

The final and fourth function is between Judgment and Perception. Judgment at its finest is even said to be blind; it does not look at individuals, only at rules. In contrast, Perception understands all and so forgives all. It waits and waits for the evidence to come in. "There but for the grace of God go I."

The most common American managerial profile is ESTJ, that is Extrovert, Sensing, Thinking, and Judging. The most common British profile is ISTJ, with British Introversion instead of American Extroversion. Latin cultures tend to have an IFNP profile – Introversion, Feeling, Intuiting, Perceiving – the mirror image of America.

JUDGMENT ←—————————→ PERCEPTION

**Figure 2.4** Judgment–Perception

## *Advantages and problems of the MBTI*

The big advantage of MBTI is how readily recognizable it is. We have all encountered extroverts or overwhelming introverts at social gatherings. We have all tried to reason in vain with someone whose feelings are so strong that our efforts were useless, or we have witnessed someone calculating while others visibly suffer. The MBTI is a ready-reckoner of personality types. There are serious problems of superficiality and of proper application, however.

The problem of superficiality stems from either/or classifications of what is manifested at the surface. Is it seriously suggested that we Judge *or* Perceive, Think *or* Feel? Surely judgments are based upon initial perceptions and we feel annoyed at a shoddy argument? Jung himself arranged his "opposite" archetypes in the shape of Tao and wrote of effectance through synthesis. He warned us that ESTJ was the dominant profile of relatively young, brash people in the world of practicality. He regarded these as the dominant Western industrial values.

What he advocated was that we move out of this pattern and mature over time, especially in our later years. He believed that introversion should qualify extraversion, that intuitive faculties should guide sensing, that our feelings could tell us which thoughts were more profound and that good judgment was based on fullness of perception. In short, Jung sought to *reconcile* his four functions, not polarize them. He regarded the less preferred end of any function as lying beneath the persona (the superficial character armor). Where personalities over-emphasized their dominant preferences, the shadow sides of these values – that is, the values repressed and pushed down into unconsciousness – could haunt them. But these values were always there, and were all the more pervasive for being denied.

Jung defined a "complex" as any barrier to moving back and forth between contrasting types. People with complexes came to him for psychotherapy and had these complexes removed.

The problem of applicability is even more troublesome. Suppose a company is predominantly ESTJ. Does that mean that a candidate with this profile should be preferred or not preferred? Clearly he or she would "fit in," but is this necessarily desirable? Have we not missed an opportunity to make the company more diverse? After all, customers come in every shape, size, and function. Might it not be wise to match the preferences of our customer base with our employee base and listen to someone different for a change?

The problem of applicability does not end here. Suppose we decided to achieve a balance. Should this be an aggregate balance, i.e., all employees, a departmental balance, or a peer group balance? And where should this balance take place, within the personality or between personalities? Jung wanted a better balance and a synthesis within the personality but the MBTI is of little use in this respect, because it fails to register our less-preferred types. We are left with the possibility of creating balance within the group, but what do you do when the first INFPs whom you hire feel rejected by the ESTJs?

Is there not some possibility of harm in knowing and accepting your type as fixed? Might you not, like the tragic heroes of world dramas, overplay your winning combination, go on doing what you have habitually done and not change? In our experience, those who administer the MBTI work hard to surface the less preferred type and so make their subjects more whole, but are these efforts enough to compensate for the selective reinforcement of one's customary façade? We think perhaps not.

It is also instructive to consider what the MBTI does not measure. It does not measure the capacity to reach out to another person with the opposite profile and it does not measure how severely the shadow side is repressed within the candidate. Severe repression would, according to Jung, make it very difficult to communicate with someone with the characteristics you so dislike in yourself.

## Can the MBTI be modified?

We have seen that the MBTI brilliantly measures four very impor-tant dimensions, but is unable to assess to what extent these contrasting types have been integrated with each other, as opposed to subordinated to each other. Might it be possible to conserve the best aspects of MBTI while inquiring about the extent to which intro-verted ideas have been extroverted, sense impressions have been intuited, feelings have been thought about, and judgments formed on the basis of strong perceptions?

Given the millions of people who are interested one way or another in MBTI profiles, it is important not to let all this measurement, coaching, mentoring, and insight go to waste. We must, if possible, build on this famous instrument, not try to demolish it or replace it. This is what we have tried to do at THT with our Integrated Type Indicator.

## The Integrated Type Indicator

Let us first look at the MBTI as it is now. A dominant American ESTJ would be: Extrovert not Introvert, Sensing not Intuiting, Thinking not Feeling, and Judging not Perceiving.

The implication is that the second-mentioned attributes are entirely missing although, in fact, all of us have introverted and intuitive feelings and perceptions up to a point. The way of testing for the ESTJ or other preferences is to ask either/or questions and invite the subject to choose one answer in place of another.

The MBTI tests for the relative dominance of, say, Thinking versus Feeling by the following type of question:

*When I make a decision I think it is most important*

a.     *To make sure that I test the opinions of others*

b.     *To reach a decisive conclusion.*

The thinking subject marks "b" and the feeling subject, "a."

But suppose we added two more possibilities:

c.     *To test the opinions of others before deciding*

d.     *To be decisive and thereby elicit others' opinions.*

These four questions tell us much more than the two initial ones. They allow subjects to:

a.      Prefer Feeling to Thinking

b.      Prefer Thinking to Feeling

c.      Feel out opinions before Thinking

d.      Think, and so invite Feelings to be expressed

Our contention is that answers "c" and "d" select more integrated personalities. Answer "c" puts Feelings first and then Thinks about these. Answer "d" puts Thinking first but in a way that elicits Feelings. We believe that employees selecting "c" and "d" are not only more reconciled, but also more able to deal with people of the opposite persuasion.

The four choices can be tabulated as shown in Figure 2.5. Choices "a" and "b" each exclude their opposites, but choice "c" feels in a way inclusive of thinking, while choice "d" thinks in a way inclusive of feeling. Both paths culminate in thoughtful sensibility at the top right. We believe that inclusive or integrated choices reveal leadership potential and predict more effective performances.

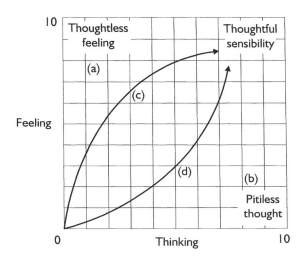

**Figure 2.5**   ITI – Thinking versus Feeling

Let's take a second example, when the MBTI tests for Judgment versus Perception.

*When tackling an issue I would rather work:*

a.     *In a structured and really organized way*

b.     *Flexibly with necessary improvizations and adaptations*

The Judging person marks "a," the Perceiving person "b."

Suppose we added two more possibilities again.

c.     *In a structured way with periodic revisions*

d.     *Flexibly until I can detect a new structure*

The four choices can be tabulated as in Figure 2.6. Once again choices "a" and "b" are exclusive of the other, while choices "c" and "d" culminate in carefully considered judgments. It is still possible to identify a dominant type, but now one of two types is given priority in an integrated sequence. We do not contend that one priority is

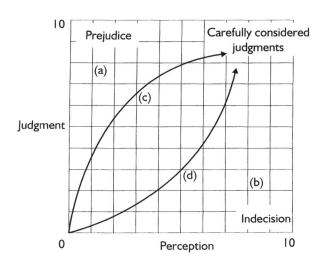

**Figure 2.6**    ITI – Judgment versus Perception

better than another. These depend on one's culture and personality. We *do* contend that integrated responses anticipate better managers, better performers, and better leaders, especially the latter.

It is important to grasp that while either/or responses cannot reveal that a personality or culture is developing, even if it is, integrated responses suggest that a person both thinks more effectively and feels more deeply, judges more accurately as well as basing that judgment on more acute perceptions. We also discover the candidate's sequence of types and their thought processes.

By combining answers from a series of questions, it is possible to get a profile of a person or a group, as shown in Figure 2.7. The relative shapes and sizes of the four blocks can tell us to what extent the opposite ends of the four functions have been reconciled. Are candidates able to move from perceiving to making judgments, from generating introverted thoughts and ideas to then expressing these openly to others in an extrovert way? This capacity to move to and fro on the four continua is much more valuable to the organization

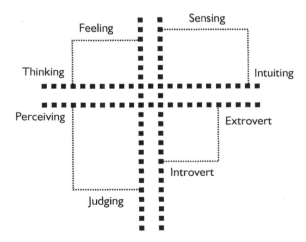

**Figure 2.7**   Individual/group profile

than getting stuck at one end or the other. You cannot usefully process information from a fixed position.

If each variable is scaled from 1 to 10, then we can arrive at an integration score for a whole group, department, or company, thus:

$$(\text{Introvert} + \text{Extrovert}) + (\text{Sensing} + \text{Intuiting}) + (\text{Thinking} + \text{Feeling}) + (\text{Judging} + \text{Perceiving}) \div 4 = \text{Developing Leadership Potential.}$$

## Reconciliation: a new paradigm for leadership

When you are faced with a contrary type with which you must deal, it is not very useful to insist on having your own way and running over the opposition. Nor is it wise to abandon your own position in favor of the contrasting type. If you do this you cannot draw on your past experiences and you lose your integrity.

The significance of the integrated approach we use at THT is that it enables us to determine the propensity of an employee to reconcile dilemmas, or value contrasts. We call this capacity *trans-cultural competence*. Here "culture" is defined widely to include different nations, different departments, different disciplines, different genders, and different personality types. We believe this to be a robust model, capable of being generalized, capable of leading diverse people to work with each other.

To this end we have created an Intercultural Leadership Assessment profile that measures reconciliatory capacities. This has already been tested on 4,000 international managers and leaders. Looking at a sample of 21 "outstanding" leaders (about whom we wrote a book, *21 Leaders for the 21st Century*), we found that they scored significantly higher in reconciliation than our general average.

But let us now return to the reconciliation of the four functions in the MBTI. Among the challenges we face is reconciling change with continuity. We want to continue the MBTI as much as possible, preserving Jung's genius and many people's past records, and we wish to change it significantly, so as to estimate trans-personal and trans-cultural competence. Let's take each of the four functions in turn. What kinds of questions would not only test for type preferences, but also discover if the subjects could integrate their first preferences with the contrasting type? What kind of leader or hero emerges from values reconciled by alternative sequences?

## Extrovert–Introvert

These two types contrasted the sources of energy in different people, whether these were generated externally or internally. We ask:

*Which option best describes how you manage?*

a.    *Most of my personal energy comes from the people I meet and greet, but in quieter moments, what I experienced through them starts generating ideas within me.*

b.    *Most of my personal energy comes from ideas, feelings, and data generating sparks within me. But then comes the acid test, when I tell everyone what I have conceived.*

c.    *Most of my personal energy comes from the people I meet and greet. It is as if an electric current between us has charged up my batteries.*

d.    *Most of my personal energy comes from ideas, feelings, and data generating sparks within me. I need to be alone and free of interruption to self-organize my ideas.*

The integrated answers are "a" and "b." The polarized ones are "c" and "d." Note how the integrated answers move across the continuum, while the polarized ones stay put.

Who are the leaders and heroes who symbolize the integration of an Extrovert mode with subsequent Introversion? Donald Schön called these reflective practitioners, in his book of that title. They first practice in the real world and later reflect on that practice. Perhaps the world's first reflective practitioner was Hippocrates, a working physician in Athens whose experience culminated in the Hippocratic Oath, taken by doctors to this day and over two thousand years old.

This dilemma is illustrated in Figure 2.8. Note that the helix starts with extroverted conduct, visiting patients in their homes, trying sometimes desperately to save lives. It then learns from and codifies this experience, *ex post facto*. This is why the helix starts with extroversion, then moves towards introversion in a clockwise spiral.

Who are the leaders who symbolize the introverted style, ones who start in an interoverted way and who then act boldly and decisively in an extroverted fashion? Western history's most illustrious exam-

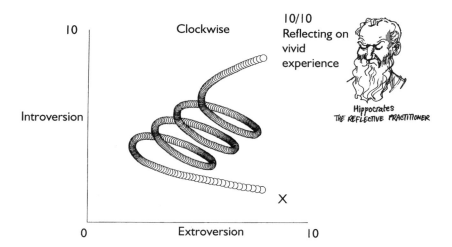

**Figure 2.8** Extroversion versus Introversion

ple is probably Martin Luther. That he was initially introverted is not in doubt. He was a monk, much given to prayer, reflection, and anguished confessions. He entered a monastery in 1505 and it was not until 1517 that he famously nailed his ninety-five theses to the church door in Wittenburg. We would have heard of neither Hippocrates nor of Luther had they not moved between types. In the case of Hippocrates, this was from extrovert practice to introvert codification. In the case of Martin Luther, this was from cloistered introversion to a famous act of extrovert defiance. Leaders lead by crossing over between types at the crucial moment. This is illustrated in Figure 2.9. Note that this helix winds the opposite way from the one in Figure 2.8, anti-clockwise, starting with introverted inner struggles and culminating in the Protestant Reformation.

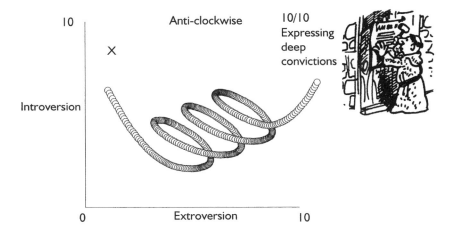

**Figure 2.9**  Extroversion versus Introversion

## Sensing–Intuiting

These two types are contrasting ways of processing information. Sensing looks at discrete, empirical facts and makes recorded observations. Intuiting looks into a whole phenomenon, interpreting its meaning and significance. Here we ask:

*Which option best describes how you manage?*

a.   *In solving problems I like to analyze the situation and look hard at the facts. I believe these speak for themselves and need no window dressing.*

b.   *In solving problems, I like to gain deep insights into the meaning of the issue. Once I have grasped this I test my supposition against all available facts.*

c.   *In solving problems, I like to gain deep insights into the meaning of the issue. Facts are dependent on context. Once I grasp the context the facts fall into place.*

d.   *In solving problems I like to analyze the situation and look hard at the facts, but then I start to draw inferences until the meaning of this issue is clear.*

The integrated answers are "b" and "d." The polarized answers are "a" and "c." In "d" the person starts with sensed facts and develops intuitions. In "b" the person starts with deep intuitions and tests these against the available facts.

A famous scientific leader of the sensing type was Sir Isaac Newton. He convinced three centuries of science to look first at the facts and only then to draw cautious inferences. The real world was neither what we wanted it to be, nor influenced in any way by our wishes. We must not let our beliefs or conceits stand in the way. Only after we have made sure of all the facts should we start to draw inferences. This approach to the physical world is illustrated in Figure 2.10, in the anti-clockwise spiral.

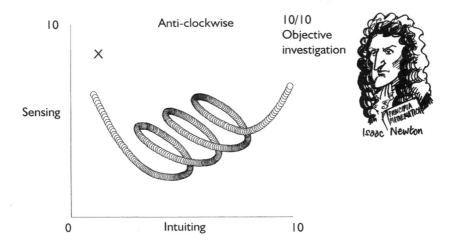

**Figure 2.10**   Sensing versus Intuiting

Yet science moves on and theoretical physics is quite another challenge, needing intuition to disentangle its puzzling anomalies. Albert Einstein was famed for his intuitive powers and would cut himself if an exciting intuition struck him while he was shaving. But this does not mean that he ignored the available facts. Having

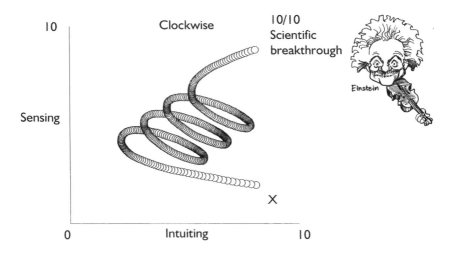

**Figure 2.11**   Sensing versus Intuition

gained his intuitions he proceeded to test them, an example of how one type helps to verify the conjecture of another type. The helix winding clockwise from Intuition to Sensing is illustrated in Figure 2.11.

## Thinking–Feeling

How do you promote such a concept as happiness? You can think about it, the conditions under which it is most likely to be manifest, or you can feel about it. Happiness is, after all, an emotion contrasting with misery, so it might help to experience both of these deeply before trying to promote the former. We ask:

*Which option best describes how you manage?*

a. *I like to subject a problem to rational thought and logical analysis. Wishing something were true does not make it so. Feelings are not "wrong." They're irrelevant.*

b. *I always ask myself what I feel about a problem, because my boredom, irritation, or excitement is an early clue to whether I can engage intelligently and find a solution.*

c. *I always ask myself what I feel about a problem, because "the heart has its own reasons which Reason knows not of." I seek to develop emotional muscles.*

d. *I like to subject a problem to rational thought and logical analysis. Yet feats of intelligence or folly arouse feelings within me, so these too guide my intelligence.*

Here the integrated or reconciled answers are "b" and "d," while the polarized answers are "a" and "c." In "b" the subject feels and finds these clues about how to think. In "d" the subject thinks but still uses

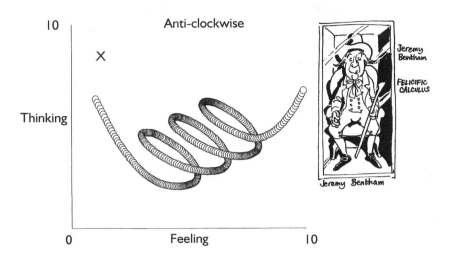

**Figure 2.12**    Thinking versus Feeling

feelings as a compass. "A" and "c" polarize thinking with feeling and feeling with thinking.

One of the great leaders of the thinking mode was Jeremy Bentham, British philosopher and originator of the felicific calculus, or "happiness equation," which was supposed to assure "the greatest happiness of the greatest number of persons." He clearly wished to benefit mankind, but he was more interested in thinking about this than feeling about it. Reconciliation with thinking as a clear priority is depicted in Figure 2.12 by the anti-clockwise spiral.

A man who began from the opposite pole of the same function was Martin Luther King. He began with the suffering souls of black people oppressed by segregation. "Suffering is redemptive," he taught. "Soul," the formerly resigned anguish of oppressed black people, could be turned into "soul power," the public demonstration of these injustices before the world's media, as evening after evening appalling pictures of nonviolent demonstrators being beaten into pulp by sheriffs' deputies were shown on television.

But there were brilliantly thought-out strategies behind these demonstrations. The demonstrators asked quietly and respectfully for their rights as citizens of the USA and were promptly beaten up with much of the world watching. Within months a horrified Congress passed the Civil Rights Act and who could behave civilly and who could not was proved beyond question. Black Americans made massive gains in the years following while the savage face of bigotry was unforgettably registered in the public consciousness.

The reconciliation wrought by Martin Luther King and his famous oratory, "I Have a Dream," is illustrated in Figure 2.13.

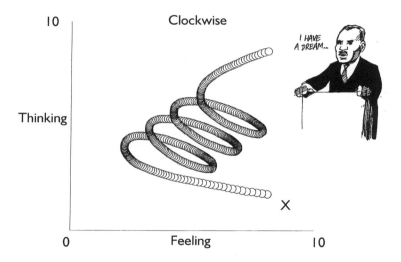

**Figure 2.13**   Feeling versus Thinking

## Judgment–Perception

This has to do with the relative salience of perceiving events and forming judgments about what to do concerning those events. Once you have made a judgment this tends to foreclose further perceiving because you will probably act on that judgment. Some people judge very quickly. Others always want more information and wish to go on discovering this. We ask again:

*Which option best describes how you manage?*

a.  *I like to be decisive since many of the problems I encounter cannot wait. They call for quick evaluation. It is when I decide and act that things start happening.*

b.  *I like to be decisive since many of the problems I encounter cannot wait. But when new information reaches me, I readily change my mind and alter course.*

c.  *I like to understand in depth and examine situations from different perspectives. Only then am I prepared to reach a firm decision in which I have confidence.*

d.  *I like to understand in depth and examine situations from different perspectives. The more I understand the less I want to evaluate and the more open I am to learning.*

Here "b" and "c" are the integrated answers and "a" and "d" are the polarized ones, in which judgment squashes perception and perception postpones judgment indefinitely.

Our examples of great leadership include Judge Earl Warren, head of the US Supreme Court, and Emile Zola, the defiant French novelist who exposed the army plot against Captain Dreyfus.

Earl Warren presided over the famous judgment of Brown versus the Board of Education, in which segregation of the races in the school system was declared unconstitutional. The remedy, desegregation, was to occur with "all deliberate speed." This places Judgment before Perception since the whole decision took place in the legal context of a Supreme Court ruling. Warren clearly regarded

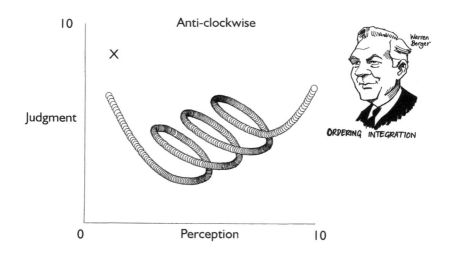

**Figure 2.14**  Judgment versus Perception

segregated education as unfair and perceived the need for remedy. He inserted this perception into an historic judgment. This is why the helix in Figure 2.14 winds from Judgment to Perception in a clockwise direction.

Emile Zola, as befits a French intellectual and a novelist, began with the powerful perception that the conviction of Captain Dreyfus, a Jewish army officer, was an anti-semitic plot by monarchists and Catholics in the army. He penned a furious article entitled *J'Accuse* and was tried for libel. After many years of official denial, Zola's stand was vindicated, Dreyfus was released, and all accusations were withdrawn. In Figure 2.15, then, we have an anti-clockwise helix moving from Perception to later Judgment.

Let's summarize our conclusions about the MBTI. Like most social science this scale attempts to measure object-like "things." Since Aristotle it has been held that two contradictory objects cannot occupy the same space at the same time and still be considered logical. The presence of Extroversion, Sensing, Thinking, and Judging is

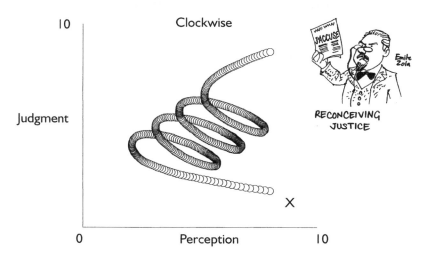

**Figure 2.15** Judgment versus Perception

thought to exclude Introversion, Intuiting, Feeling, and Perceiving. In fact, all human minds contain both types and they are not "things" at all but differences on a continuum with two poles, along which subjects continually move.

What is missing is any measurement of introversion that begets extroversion, intuition that truly guides sense impressions, feelings in close touch with thoughts, and acute perceptions that better inform judgments. We have shown that such connections between the types are measurable and characterize major leaders in world history.

## SHELL'S HAIRL SYSTEM

Another well-known system of corporate assessment is HAIRL, standing for

- Helicopter Quality (the power to encompass both details and the whole).
- Power of Analysis (the power to cut the problem into pieces).

- Imagination (the power to use a sense of creativity).
- Sense of **Reality** (the power to stand with both feet on the ground).
- Effective **Leadership** (the power to lead groups of people effectively).

These criteria were defined explicitly and used at least once a year in Shell to assess the potential of graduates (junior as well as senior), and give their Currently Estimated Potential (CEP) in terms of the job level they would attain at the summit of their career at approximately 50 years of age.

Shell's HR department has used this for over thirty years and many now at the top of the organization had their success anticipated by this instrument. In the early 80s, the Dutch author had an opportunity to study and use this instrument at the Amsterdam Laboratories where he conducted research. With statistical analysis he found that only three out of five categories correlated significantly with CEP. It was not very surprising that Helicopter and Power of Analysis correlated positively with CEP; the graduates worked in a R&D environment. But it was surprising, however, that Imagination correlated negatively with the potential of graduates.

Under the old logic it was assumed that the higher the power to analyze the greater the potential of the individual. We would not argue against this statement; it is a necessary quality but not a sufficient one. There is nothing against the power to analyze a larger whole into smaller pieces. In many complex situations it is very efficient to do so. However, once you have reduced a phenomenon to its parts it needs to be reconstructed into the larger whole which, in turn, changes its quality. If a person only analyzes there is the risk of getting into smaller and smaller details and losing sight of the larger context. The helicopter crashes down to ground level. On the other hand, Imagination can soar into the clouds and lose touch with the with the earth. Neither the bigger picture not the finest of details are sufficient in themselves.

Helicopter quality, a concept widely known, is defined as "Looking at a problem from a higher vantage point with simultaneous attention to relevant details." It is, in effect, the reconciliation of this dilemma. The helicopter can rise to see the big picture, yet descend once more to examine fine detail. Leaders must be farseeing yet not miss vital details. This was the type of helicopter that was available in the existing HAIRL system. In fact, it included the Power of Analysis criterion.

With the remaining three measures, Fons hypothesized that, taken separately, they would be substantially less predictive of later success than the Helicopter measure – and so it proved to be. Not only was the bigger picture paired with power of analysis in what became known as Helicopter 1, but also Imagination was paired with Realism, and Intuiting with Sensing. If only those with high scores in both pairs were considered, then predictions of future success rose sharply.

In other words, those reconciling the Big Picture with Fine Detail, or

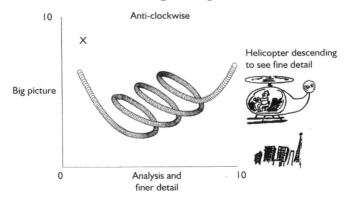

**Figure 2.16** Helicopter quality

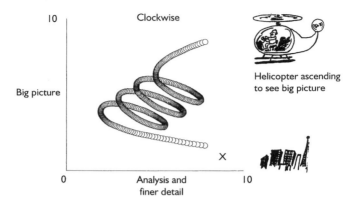

**Figure 2.17** Helicopter 1

Imagination with Realism, or Intuiting with Sensing were far more likely to succeed than those whose scores were uneven. Visionary Realism wins the day, not its separate components. Fons also found that a substantial number of Shell executives had been preferred despite being low on Imagination. This measure was the one least used in practice.

Fons then hypothesized that of all the measures, the three Helicopters – in Figures 2.17, 2.18 *and* 2.19 – would be the most predictive of later success. So it proved to be.

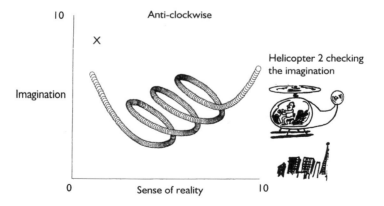

**Figure 2.18** Helicopter 2

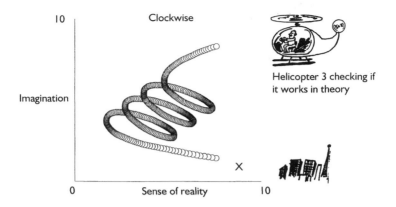

**Figure 2.19** Helicopter 3

## 360° FEEDBACK

This method is generally only used for self-assessment. There are problems, as we shall see, in making it fair internationally, or using it for selection. It consists of feedback from those above you, those below you, and those at the same level about what it is like to work with you. It is usually anonymous but need not be so.

From a dilemma point of view it is useful to contrast the verdicts of those above you with those beneath you. Are you currying favor with your superiors and bearing down on your juniors? Are you joining your juniors in rebellion against your seniors? If there is a discrepancy in your popularity with either status level, then some kind of political dynamic is in the making.

What 360° Feedback measures are the number and the success of your relationships, which is what the company pays you to create and build upon. It is dangerous to infer that criticism is the "fault" of either party. It is relatively safe to point out to someone that their poor relationships are well above average in number. To take one example, say a male manager is not getting on with female subordinates. You do not have to prove his sexism; you only have to point out that what you are paying him for – to build good relationships – is not being accomplished.

Whoever is more powerful in any relationship is the more responsible for it. Hence a boss earning three times the salary of a personal assistant is responsible for 75 percent of the quality of their relationship. With increased power and salary come greater responsibility. Some relationships simply do not work and parties can be reassigned. Over time, however, those relating poorly will emerge from any scrutiny of 360° Feedback and lack of interpersonal and intercultural competence can be safely inferred. Especially alarming is a relationship called "good" by a superior but "bad" by a subordinate.

However, 360° Feedback faces serious problems internationalizing, as in the capsule case opposite.

Cultures vary greatly in their willingness to lavish praise on fellow members, in making their criticisms known to strangers, in writing these down as opposed to first verbalizing them to the person, in being as outspoken as most questionnaires force them to be, and in answering in stark alternatives instead of soft gradations. There may be taboos against committing criticism to paper. In much of East Asia, for example, criticism is reserved for special face-to-face encounters.

Yet 360° Feedback remains an excellent tool for stimulating dialogue between people being assessed and assessors. It is these dialogues that will probably tell you the most about the person and how he or she regards differences in opinion.

## CAPSULE CASE
### Dilemmas of using 360° Feedback internationally

A major US investment bank was using 360° Feedback on managers from many cultures. They invited THT's opinion on whether the scores achieved should be used to select future leaders. One obvious problem was that American managers tended to rate each other and the foreign managers they knew much more highly than did groups from other cultures. The problem was not prejudice by Americans in favor of Americans but the tendency of Americans to be more lavish in their praise generally. This had the effect of pushing the ratings of the majority of Americans much higher than the ratings of all other cultures. The Americans reciprocated enthusiasm. The biggest gap, 18 points, was between the Americans and the French, followed closely by the Germans. The British, the Scandinavians and the Dutch fell somewhere between the two extremes.

We were asked why this had occurred and whether anything could be done to make the system fairer. To explain what had happened we turned to our four quadrants of culture.

Most US managers were in the Guided Missile quadrant, consisting of temporary teams of relative strangers. It is advantageous, in such circumstances, to be positive in the hope that your high opinion of fellow team members turns out to be self-fulfilling. If you treat them as talented, then they are more likely to become so. You are not with them long enough to know with any certainty how good they really are and so you opt for motivating them by your own encouragement and enthusiasm. Teams need to break the ice quickly and all-purpose cheerfulness is a good way of getting people to pull together and settle down to work. It is facilitative.

In contrast, the French managers tended to rate their work colleagues quite low, over twenty points below comparable ratings by Americans. This was because most French managers were in the Family culture quadrant. This consists of people coming from an elite background, in close and intimate long-term relationships. These conditions favor negative feedback, the kind from which people are most likely to learn. If you are very close to work companions, and you know and they know that you are all very good academically so that their quality is not in question, then appraisals can be far stricter. You do not need to cheer up such people; they actually want to be even better.

A term of high praise among French professionals is *"pas mal,"* said softly, or "not bad." You do not lavish praise on each other because you expect the other to be good; enthusiasm implies surprise and a certain *naïvité*. You are not afraid to be negative because family relations are strong enough to withstand it, while temporary team relationships are not always so strong.

Scoring both each other and foreigners relatively low were the German managers, although their scores were not as low as those of the French respondents. We believe that this is because many German managers believe themselves to be in an Eiffel Tower culture where the stress is on being dispassionate and objective. You are not lavish in your praise because hard measures of capacities are available. Your track record speaks for itself and making a fuss about it is superfluous. Experts are used to being experts and do not need to be praised for what they are; praise is for children not yet accustomed to high status. Nor should you be seen as showing off or encouraging others to do so. Anything approaching hype spells insecurity and deception. Do not just look good; you need to actually be good.

Having tried to explain how different cultures appraise and feedback internally, we turned to the issue of making 360° Feedback fairer internationally. We suggested that scores could have comparative value if each respondent was scored above or below the mean score given by fellow Americans, fellow French, and fellow German respondents. Hence if Americans gave an average of 66 points to those they evaluated and the French 48 points, then an American scoring 69 would rate 3, while a Frenchman scoring 54 points would rate 6. The tendency of cultures towards being negative and positive would be controlled. We also warned against using this method in most of Southeast Asia, where appraisals given on paper, without discussion, were often seen as disrespectful.

## ASSESSING AGAINST JOB DESCRIPTIONS: THE HAY SYSTEM

We have a final observation on all those assessment instruments that take as their departure point initial job descriptions. Colonel Hay of the US Army made this approach famous. Many point to its eminent fairness. People have applied for and been accepted for described positions; could anything be fairer than evaluating them according to what they promised to do if they were given the post? Has the incumbent performed as specified?

But like so many one-dimensional metrics, it sidesteps a key dilemma. Jobs evolve over time and their original descriptions are rarely up to date. Moreover, the changes incumbents make in their jobs tell us a lot about what leadership means. One of the ways in which you lead lies in the definition of your own job and where it is heading. Leadership includes the capacity to see what else is required, and starting to do this. Evaluating performance on a job description three to four years old is a recipe for stagnation. You are letting your job define you, rather than the other way around.

Today there are some 8,000 organizations worldwide which use the Hay Job Evaluation methodologies. The standard tool is the Hay Guide Chart Profile Method. Although customized tools are on offer, the standard core methodology remains the most popular.

## How does it work?

E. N. Hay and Associates developed Hay Job Evaluation in the early 1980s. It is a scheme that is based on the "points factor" approach, a common approach to job evaluation.

The process has the following basic progression. A description of the job is made, usually by management, including things such as the expertise required, accountabilities, experience required, functions performed, financial impact of the job, freedom to decide and act, number of staff supervised, preeminence of the position, influence of the position within the company, etc.

The various aspects of the job given in the description are usually split into categories. Hay's approach ranks jobs by the level of accountability they carry in setting and achieving organizational goals and objectives. They typically examine work content against several related factors including:

- Know-how: The total knowledge, skills, and competencies required in a job to realize its accountabilities and to perform the job in an acceptable manner. It consists of depth of knowledge/experience; breadth of management scope, and human relations skills.
- Problem solving: The level of the thinking process which a job requires, both in terms of initiative and level of complexity, in order to get the job done.
- Accountability: The measurable impact of the job on end results.

The last two scores result in a Profile, the number of steps (a certain range of points) between the Accountability and Problem Solving scores. (+4 is a profile with a maximum amount of accountability in view of problem solving, perhaps an operational manager, and –4 would be for a job where problem solving comes with minimum accountability, someone like a fundamental researcher.)

Other similar systems may have different sets of criteria. For example, the OCR system uses the following categories:

- Knowledge, Skills and Experience
- Reasoning and Decision-Making
- Communication and Influence
- Accountability and Responsibility

The description of the job is done under the headings given by the job grading system's categories.

## What do such systems assume?

For what kinds of culture are such systems designed? What do they take for granted? If we go back to our four cultural quadrants we can readily see that job evaluation is both task oriented and hierarchical, thus:

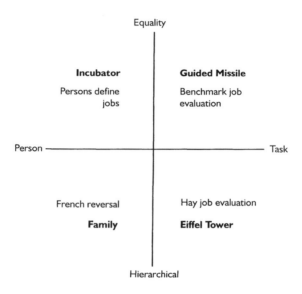

**Figure 2.20** Job evaluation by cultural type

What Hay assumes is something akin to a military hierarchy with tasks predefined and largely unchanging. Line managers are assumed to know, before tasks are undertaken, how difficult, how responsible and even how much initiative is required to complete the task concerned. These initiatives are not believed to alter the tasks in any way or to involve new complexities and responsibilities. In short, those who evaluate a job could perform it, hence their knowledge of what it takes.

Note that the task is put before the person. A "good performer" is the one whose work justifies and accords with the initial job description. In this way one performer can be compared to another where job descriptions are identical. Those who go outside or beyond their job descriptions create problems for the evaluation process and the culture may disapprove of them. It will very likely fail to recognize a contribution it has not foreseen.

Hay methodology tries very hard to be fair. If the specifications for a particular job have been set out in advance, and if an individual has applied for the job on the basis of that description, then if they work or fail to work according to the description, rewards, punishments, and preferment are readily justifiable. Employees know where they stand and why the institution supports them.

A refinement of the Hay system, used by Shell, is to create benchmarked job evaluations, as in the top right quadrant of Figure 2.20. These move over time, and job descriptions together with per-formances in those jobs are compared to what the industry is accomplishing as a whole. If competitors are improving their perfor-mance or redefining job requirements, then the company gets a wake-up call. In this quadrant teams gain the influence to redefine the responsibilities of their members. Tasks may become team responsibilities leaving members free to contribute in more than one way. There are two conflicting criteria by which to judge people: Have they well represented their function or specialty and have they contributed to the success of the team by "guiding the missile" toward customer satisfaction? Job evaluation loses much of its preci-sion if more than one rationale is used.

A complete reversal of the job evaluation methodology was observed at Shell Française when Marc de Graaf, who was responsi-ble for the benchmarked evaluation described above, presented his conclusions to the French subsidiary. Marc was congratulated for having moved away from "static" methods. Then the HR director asked him if he was interested in how they evaluated their jobs. He continued by saying to Marc that in his site the management team discussed which people were up for promotion every quarter. After fierce conflicts the team agreed, he explained. "So we then inform the boss of the person promoted and ask him to pass it on to the individual. The person chosen then helps us to describe the job he has been doing which justifies our decision. This is sent to The Hague where HQ is based and everyone is happy."

Note that this complete reversal, indicated at the bottom left quadrant of Figure 2.20, transforms a Task culture into a Person culture yet retains a hierarchical bias. Now those to be promoted are chosen by political patronage and influence, typical of a Family culture, with decisions justified *ex post facto* by the job descriptions demanded by the Dutch HQ. This approach puts intuition ahead of rational thinking and perception ahead of judgment.

The final quadrant at top left is the antithesis of everything job evaluation stands for. In highly creative organizations, individuals redefine, even invent, the job they are doing. The person makes the job rather than the job making the person. The problem solvers select and define the problem to be solved. The creation of new products create new problems, new opportunities.

Is there any way of mediating between these culture quadrants? Can we evaluate people in a way that changes and evolves over time? We believe this is possible and that Peter Drucker's approach to Management by Objectives shows the way, though we prefer to call it Management by Bold Aspiration. The first step is to evaluate all performance by two criteria, the degree of aspiration and the degree of attainment.

The supervisor and the supervisee together define the coming period's aspirations, before comparing the last period's aspiration with actual attainment. The bolder the aspiration is, on a scale from 1–10, the greater the possibility of subsequent attainment. Yet those with modest aspirations, scoring say 6 out of 10, can only subsequently attain a score of 60. The Aspiration is equivalent to a co-defined job description, while the attainment measures what the person assessed agreed to in advance. The dilemma is shown in Figure 2.21.

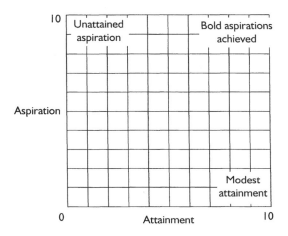

**Figure 2.21**   Aspiration–Achievement

One big advantage of this method is that both the organization and the persons assessing and being assessed learn. The assessed person learns the appropriate level of boldness to aspire to; the assessor learns how much challenge to issue in order to encourage. The corporation learns what dreams are locked away in the souls of its people and how to realize these.

The same approach also reconciles the task orientation on the right of the cultural diagram with the person orientation on the left, as in Figure 2.22.

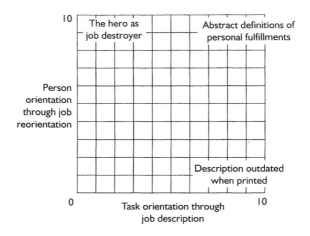

**Figure 2.22**   Reconciling Tasks with Persons

In Shell Fons discovered that you could describe jobs quite abstractly in ways that people could fulfill by various methods and through the exercise of autonomy and discretion. By looking at what researchers actually did in Shell's Amsterdam Laboratories it was possible to evolve three types – the Creator, the Integrator, and the Applicator. These would be at home in the Incubator culture, the Guided Missile culture, and the Eiffel Tower culture respectively. But perhaps the most important discovery was that each found personal fulfillment within an abstract description of their job. The job was described at an abstract level, yet was interpreted at a personal level. The description was the context that left the individual free to write the text.

In short, in this chapter we have examined various tools of assessment and have found them to be seriously incomplete rather than wrong. They take crucial aspects of mental functioning and turn these into pseudo-objects. They then assume that two contradictory "objects" cannot be present simultaneously and deny the importance of the less preferred value. They miss, almost entirely, the capacity to mediate between contrasting values, a crucial capacity that we call trans-cultural competence, a capability enabling the individuals to grasp values diverse from their own.

At THT we have created an International Leadership Assessment tool that measures reconciliatory capacities and has successfully identified outstanding leaders. Such leaders ceaselessly move between value differences to encompass these. This involves bridging all four quadrants of corporate culture. Among these resolutions are job descriptions and the people performing these jobs, aspirations and attainments, abstract descriptions and concrete fulfillments.

But we do not need to substitute our own instrument for those in current use by HR functions. With minor additions and modifications it is possible to convert existing instruments into measures of reconciliation, thereby assuring continuity with past results.

CHAPTER 3

# Training managers to attain strategic goals

n the previous chapter we looked at ways of selecting and assessing employees for their leadership potential and high performance. Yet the measures were largely one-dimensional values, with human endowments as exclusive options. The capacity to integrate diverse values was almost entirely absent. There were also doubts about exactly what HRM should be measuring.

So why not attach HR metrics directly to a company's strategic goals? It is up to top management to decide its own strategic objectives. It is then up to HRM to identify, celebrate and reward the appropriate behavior. Of course, we need to be very clear about a company's strategy in order to do this, and such clarity is not always forthcoming, as we shall see. We will now examine the following propositions:

- Does all strategy end in paradox?
- Designed versus Emergent strategies
- The Balanced Scorecard
- Global convergence versus Localization and diversity: The seven dimensions of difference

We shall show that it does end in paradox, that designing strategy upfront must confront the fact that new strategies keep evolving and emerging at the grass roots level. We will ask whether strategies can somehow be balanced off against each other. Finally, what happens when your regions have different values from your global HQ?

## DOES ALL STRATEGY END IN PARADOX?

It should be easy to discover the company's strategy and for HRM to discover to what degree goals have been attained. It should be possible to reward all employees for their success in meeting strategic goals. Yet in practice formidable barriers stand in the way. The greatest of these is arriving at a definition of what an organization's strategy is or should be. This is nothing like as simple as many believe.

Two academics from Erasmus University, Bob de Wit and Ron Meyer, have argued that all current strategies end in paradox and seeming impasse. You are told to do one thing by a strategic thinker and then promptly told to do exactly the opposite by another strategic thinker. If we were to create a metric for the attainment of strategies in the left-hand column below, this would clash head on with strategies in the right-hand column.

| | |
|---|---|
| 1. Strategy is **rational thought** (Kenneth Andrews) | 1. Strategy is **generative** (Kenichi Ohmae) |
| 2. Strategy is **preplanned** and deliberate (Balaji Chakravarthy and Peter Lorange) | 2. Strategy is **emergent** and incremental (Henry Mintzberg and James Quinn) |
| 3. Strategic reengineering must **obliterate** the **old** (Michael Hammer) | 3. Strategy should **refine** and **preserve** the old (Maskai Imai) |
| 4. Strategy must be **market** driven (Michael Porter) | 5. Strategy must be **capability** driven (George Stalk, Philip Evans, Lawrence Shulman) |
| 5. Strategic business units constitute a **portfolio** (Barry Hedley) | 5. Strategic business units constitute a **core competence** (C. K. Prahalad and Gary Hamel) |
| 6. Strategy is predominantly a **competition** among discrete business entities (Gary Hamel, Yves Doz and C. K. Prahalad) | 6. Strategy is predominantly **cooperative** among networked interdependent entities (Gianni Lorenzoni and Charles Baden-Fuller) |
| 7. Strategy is **evolutionary** with companies surviving through natural selection (Michael Porter) | 7. Strategy is the **creation** of new industries with new, innovative rules of the game (Charles Baden-Fuller and John Stopford) |

8. Strategy is the triumph of leadership **control** with organization following strategy
(Roland Christensen, Kenneth Andrews, Joseph Bower)

8. Strategy is the fruits of **chaos** from which a new order later emerges
(Ralph Stacey)

9. Strategy should be driven by the **global convergence** of markets
(Theodore Levitt)

9. Strategy should be driven by the **localization** and **diversity** of markets
(Susan Douglas and Yoram Wind)

10. Strategy should be tied to **profitability** and serving **shareholders** above all
(Alfred Rappaport)

10. Strategy should serve all **stakeholders** and **optimize** their different interests
(Edward Freeman and David Reed)

There is a tendency for strategy to follow culture. Hence strategy as rational thought bound by rules belongs in the Eiffel Tower culture, while strategy as generative belongs in the Incubator culture. Pre-planned strategy is also Eiffel Tower while emergent strategy is a mix of team process and incubation. Strategy as leadership control belongs to the Eiffel Tower while only Incubation and creativity can wrest order from chaos. Strategy as profit maximization is Eiffel Tower thinking, while strategy as stakeholders sharing would require a whole team to Guide the Missile.

This list of ten strategic paradoxes – and we could come up with many more – underlines the difficulty of rewarding employees for the attainment of strategic goals. Should you reward each business unit head in your portfolio separately, according to that unit's profitability, or should you reward efforts to forge a core competence out of separate units and celebrate what this has done for customers and other stakeholders? Should you reward rationality or generativity, rapid change or strong continuities, competing or cooperating, exercising unilateral control, or embracing chaos the better to understand its hidden order?

It is at least likely that high scores on the first of each of these dimensions would entail low scores on its contrasting dimension. Is this what we really want?

To try and examine these difficulties more closely, let's look at just one paradox mentioned by De Wit and Meyer, that of designed or preplanned strategy versus emergent and incremental strategy. Henry Mintzberg himself has most cogently addressed this topic in *The Rise and Fall of Strategic Planning*, and his views are instructive.

## DESIGNED VERSUS EMERGENT STRATEGIES

A difficulty in attaching assessments to the attainment of corporate strategic goals is that only some of these goals have been preplanned and designed into the system. Others are in the process of emerging from the ongoing tasks of serving customers. In theory, top management comes out with a battle plan and the troops have their marching orders, except that it rarely works that way. Often strategy has not been spelt out and even where it has been, customers may be asking for something else.

Where companies insist that their own strategic goals are the greatest priority, opportunities to serve customers and innovative responses which were not foreseen when the strategy was designed will be discouraged, if not punished. The company could become fatally inflexible, seeing only its own categories, not those of the customers it hopes to serve.

Many of these day-to-day, ad hoc responses to what customers ask for may prove profitable, yet remain outside the company's strategic vision. This raises the issue of why these effective and responsive initiatives are not part of the company's strategy.

In *The Rise and Fall of Strategic Planning*, Henry Mintzberg distinguished between designed strategy, which is preformulated, and emergent strategy – good moves or tactics which, when imitated by other business units, are on the way to becoming strategy in the future.

Many companies start to do things in new ways without ever calling this "strategy." They simply follow customers' requests and the new patterns emerge. This was typical of the Dutch international bank ABN AMRO. Its designed strategy was overtaken by events as the economy entered recession and customer needs shifted. (See capsule case.)

So if Designed versus Emergent strategy is our dilemma, how can the attainment of two such different phenomena be rewarded? After all, asking people to be innovative involves them in creating new services not envisaged in the original strategy. If we only reward strategic attainments we may kill innovation; we may punish anything that surprises us.

The recommendation made by THT to ABN AMRO was working backwards from success to strategy. If any business unit made surprisingly good returns we asked why. What customer dilemmas had been reconciled to achieve that result? We looked at up to a dozen excellent results and asked what strategic pattern was common to all of them.

From this point of view top management creates strategy out of successful tactics by ceaselessly studying what is working for customers and what is not. The customary problem of selling your strategy to business units, getting these to own the strategy and then blaming them for not properly implementing your "brilliant" plan tends to disappear. This is for the simple reason that one or more business units have already demonstrated that the strategy works

## CAPSULE CASE
### Investigating genius

ABN AMRO, the Amsterdam-based multinational bank, developed a bold strategy of rapid expansion in 2001. The Wholesale bank, concentrating on large corporate accounts and investment banking, was to take the lead, challenging the hegemony of US investment banking and paying the kinds of salaries which high performers in this field demanded. The Retail bank was to play a supportive role.

Two years later this strategy had gone into total reverse as world recession gripped the international economy. The Retail bank with its access to capital now held the most decisive advantage. Opportunities in the Wholesale sector had largely dried up. It was now told to back up the Retail sector and its senior staff were paid bonuses to institute radical cutbacks. "Dancing with bulls" had switched to "dancing with bears."

Dilemma-type thinking had been introduced to the bank via leadership training programs and had, for the most part, been well received. Yet doubts had been expressed by some as to whether this "fancy" type of thinking was relevant in a time of such stringency and economy. People were just "too preoccupied" to take on board a new way of thinking on top of everything else; besides, the strategy instituted as recently as 2001 had now been completely revised and there was reluctance to put much faith in models of any kind.

Charles Hampden-Turner proposed that he study successful emergent strategies, those initiatives that had surprised the bank by being even more successful than had been anticipated.

If dilemma theory was correct and practical, he should be able to discover dilemmas that had been successfully reconciled within those success stories. Were these to be written up in dilemma format, their instigators would get the credit they deserved and a dozen or so of the bank's finest achievements could be explained within a common framework.

Perhaps those who had accomplished these feats might adopt the explanations as their own. Perhaps some virtue that would otherwise be attributed to "genius" or "good judgment" could now be mapped, assessed and built upon by others. Perhaps all the successful strategies shaped a theme which could tell something about changing markets. Could a strategy be designed out of initiatives that had recently delighted customers, thereby increasing the likelihood of success?

At the time of writing the company's surprise successes are being written up in booklet form as a series of successful reconciliations to be used in leadership training. Dilemmas are prominently featured on the bank's website. We await events...

and it is as much "theirs" as "yours," as much the customer's strategy as that of your company.

None of this is to disparage the designing of strategy, which top managers, armed with their skill and experience, have every right to do. But they should design strategy out of proven and successful business unit initiatives and tactics. A strategy is far more likely to work if, taken singly, its constituent elements and tactics have already worked. Mintzberg (1994) argues that strategies arise spontaneously, individual success stories arising from the ashes of relative failure, like so many phoenixes. Top management should not be trying to build a mechanical phoenix but be content to learn about what is working and not working, what new patterns of success are arising from customer's new demands.

Figure 3.1 illustrates this dilemma . Note that there can be no objection to top management "bird watching" and letting all business units know how the best of them are doing, why this is and what strategic patterns should be imitated and generalized to other units. What is more important than "assessing" – which suggests that you already know what should be done – is learning about new patterns rising from successful initiatives. Top managers need to keep up with the evolution of success at the grass roots, to be the first to see the significance of new accomplishments. Mintzberg sees himself as a Darwinian evolutionist amid "creationists" and "Bible scholars," attributing semi-divine powers to the corporation's leaders.

The motivation of employees and the rapid preferment of the more successful would take care of itself in a situation where top manage-

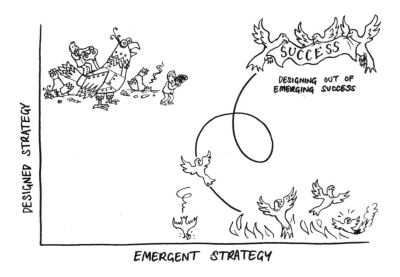

**Figure 3.1** Designed versus Emergent strategies: interpreting success

ment genuinely studied and admired the most innovative success stories and channeled extra resources to these. Designing strategy is not a battle plan drawn up in advance, reminiscent of Alexander the Great and his imposing phalanx of spears and shields; it is an ongoing process of learning from what customers demand.

## THE BALANCED SCORECARD

While we have stressed how difficult it is to judge human attainments by contradictory strategic objectives, it is by no means impossible. One approach is simply to accept the presence of polar standards and measure both sides of the polarity.

One of the most striking of all recent approaches enabling HR professionals and management to integrate value is the Balanced Scorecard, developed by Robert Kaplan and David Norton. Recognizing some of the weaknesses and vagueness of previous measurement approaches, their scorecard provides a clear prescription to management of what should be measured to balance the dominant financial perspective so apparent in the late 80s and early 90s.

Kaplan and Norton summarize the rationale for the Balanced Scorecard as follows:

> The balanced scorecard retains traditional financial measures. But financial measures tell the story of past events, an adequate story for industrial age companies for which investments in long-term capabilities and customer relationships were not critical for success. These financial measures are *inadequate* for guiding and evaluating the journey that information age companies must take to create future value

through investment in customers, suppliers, employees, processes, technology, and innovation.

Many experts claim that the bottom line is all that really matters. A company's mission is to make a profit, end of story. Perhaps so, but present profitability is a culmination of events occurring over a long historical period, in some industries thirty to forty years. Profitability does not necessarily mean that you are operating effectively now; present mistakes could come home to roost in several years' time. Steering a company by its current profitability is like steering a motor launch by the wake left several miles astern. The feedback comes too late, however accurate and precise it may be. You can hold the CEO responsible for current profitability, but that does not mean that a CEO actually is responsible. A lot of the desperate short-term expedients, by which employees are laid off in large numbers, come from this insistence that present incumbents are responsible for past errors and must somehow atone for these, or make others do so.

This is not to deny that the financial perspective is vital. Of course it is. But it is not enough. Anything that carefully records the past needs to be balanced by measures oriented to the future. Once again we have a dilemma. Can we look forwards and backwards at the same time? We can, and we must.

Kaplan and Norton contrast the Financial Perspective with the Innovation and Learning Perspective or the past with the future. They go on to contrast the Customer Perspective, which involves facing outwards, with the Internal Business Perspective, which looks inwards to benchmarks, standards, and so on, as in Figure 3.2.

There are in this circle a number of contrasts or, from our perspective, dilemmas:

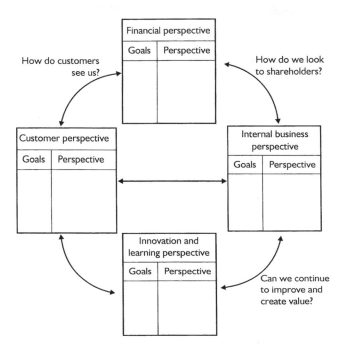

**Figure 3.2**   The Balanced Scorecard links performance measures

- Shareholder perspective–Learning Perspective
- Customer perspective–Internal perspective
- Shareholder perspective–Customer perspective
- Internal perspective–Learning perspective

All of these perspectives need to be understood and their constituents enhanced. Any one failure will affect the whole. For example, customer dissatisfaction may not immediately affect shareholders, but in time it will, unless the company is alert to its customer scoreboard. Maximizing returns to shareholders by cutting back on learning will at first pay off but the price must be paid when the company loses its knowledge leadership.

The procedure recommended by Kaplan and Norton is to state realistic goals and then specify the measures by which achieving these goals will be calibrated. The ideal is to reach a balance.

For example, a company has many Internal Business Perspectives in the shape of benchmarks and industry standards. It needs to keep its eye on Best Practice. If you fall behind your competitors you are in trouble. But benchmarks, like financials, tend to be historic. So you must also adopt the Customer Perspective and ask, "Does the customer still want what the benchmarks deliver?" Are new benchmarks now called for?

Similarly, a company can get high on its Innovation and Learning goals. Several companies have deployed Nobel Prize-winning innovations, notably EMI's Magnetic Resonance Scanner and Long-Term Capital Management's hedging equations. But these lost hundreds of millions of dollars in the case of EMI and billions of dollars in the case of LTCM. There is, alas, no guarantee that innovative excellence will make money. New, "sexy" technologies, as in the dot-com boom, lost shareholders millions. Unless you keep your eye on all the scoreboards you may court catastrophe.

The Balanced Scorecard is a management system (not simply a measurement system) that enables organizations to clarify their vision and strategy and translate these into action. It provides feedback around both the internal business processes and external outcomes in order to improve continuously strategic performance and results. When fully deployed, the Balanced Scorecard transforms strategic planning from an academic exercise into the nerve center of an enterprise.

Although we regard the Balanced Scorecard as a major step forward and infinitely preferable to any imbalance, it still retains an unstable quality. If the Financial Perspective goes right up, the Learning and

Innovation Perspective necessarily goes down by the same amount, but must this happen? Why would not faster and more innovative learning push financials up? Why would not some of these profits be invested in further learning? The seesaw balance is an inadequate metaphor. All four scoreboards have the potential to form a virtuous circle of improvement.

## The (proposed) Integrated Scorecard

In order to make this management system more effective in the new paradigm of the customized workplace, we would like to see the Integrated Scorecard evolving. We therefore need to reconcile the two major cultural dilemmas that underlie the original Scorecard – The Past (Financial) and the Future Perspective (Learning and Growth) dilemma and the Internal (Business Process) and the External Perspective (Customer) dilemma.

The point is less to "balance" past financial performance with future learning goals than to use those financials to learn, that is to reconcile growth with financials. In the Finnish organization Partek we found that key financial surpluses were reserved for the next year's learning budgets, while the learning fed into the financial results to improve them.

Next we need to improve the internal processes through the involvement of customers. Co-development programs, where suppliers align strategically with their clients, are a great example. Applied Materials, as one of the main suppliers of microchips, has used this approach very effectively. Their survival is completely dependent on co-developing systems with AMD and Intel. This is quite different from balance. It supposes that value is not added by having high scores in each of the four perspectives and then adding them up. No, rather it needs a win–win solution that derives from the integration of past and future, internal and external values.

The Integrated Scorecard gets around a major problem faced by those advocating the Balanced Scorecard. Corporate cultures often refuse, point blank, to value both ends of these polarities equally. You cannot order to them to do so. You can show that learning goals subsequently improve financials by a specific amount.

Some of the perils of "imbalance" and the benefits of "balance" are depicted in Figures 3.3 and 3.4.

A company can be paralyzed by analysis or by "lean and mean" cost cutting (top left in both Figures 3.3 and 3.4). It can indulge itself in subsidized seminars and become the customer's creature, ignoring its own internal standards (bottom right of both Figures). Or it can grow as a result of these balances. Such growth requires more than balance. It requires a fusion and reconciliation of contrasting values.

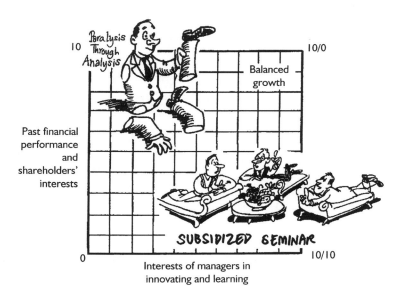

**Figure 3.3**   Financial versus Learning

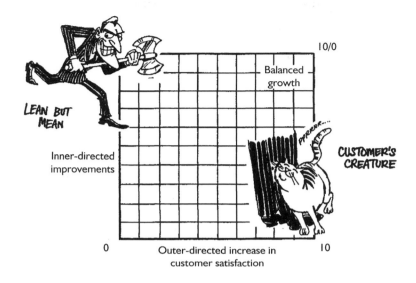

**Figure 3.4**   Internal processes versus External customers

## GLOBAL CONVERGENCE VERSUS LOCALIZATION AND DIVERSITY: THE SEVEN DIMENSIONS OF DIFFERENCE

One of the paradoxes identified by De Wit and Meyer was the issue of whether the world was converging in its tasks towards one global standard or whether new diversities were arising with thousands of local differences between markets. Should we try to be "global" like IBM and McDonald's, or "multilocal" like the Hong Kong and Shanghai Bank and Unilever?

This is an issue which we have addressed for most of our working lives and like so many other issues addressed in this book it is a dilemma. We are all in some respects different and in other respects the same. The question is how to integrate or reconcile this paradox.

We will now summarize these dimensions of difference. Yet the very existence of dimensions of difference reveals an underlying unity. These are contrasting ends of single dimensions, different yet somehow the same. We will see just how far apart are the peoples of this earth and in each case how these dilemmas were reconciled by one or more international companies. Many readers will be familiar with these seven dimensions, now featured in six books. However, we'll summarize these briefly for those who may be new to our work. The seven dimensions are these:

1. **Universalism**
(rules, codes, laws, and generalizations)

**Particularism**
(exceptions, special circumstances, unique relations)

2. **Individualism**
(personal freedom, human rights, competitiveness)

**Communitarianism**
(social responsibility, harmonious relations, cooperation)

3. **Specificity**
(atomistic, reductive, analytic, objective)

**Diffusion**
(holistic, elaborative, synthetic, relational)

4. **Neutral**
(dispassionate, controlled, detached)

**Affective**
(enthusiastic, responsive, passionate)

5. **Achieved status**
(what you've done, your track record)

**Ascribed status**
(who you are, your potential, connections)

6. **Inner direction**
(conscience and convictions are located inside)

**Outer direction**
(exemplars and influences are located outside)

7. **Sequential time**
(time is a race along a set course)

**Synchronous time**
(time is a dance of fine coordinations)

Let's consider these one by one, briefly explaining what the construct is, how it is measured, how different nations score, and how the reconciliation of this dilemma might be assessed by HRM.

## 1. Universalism versus Particularism

This is the dilemma when no code, rule, or law seems quite to cover an exceptional case. Should the most relevant rule be imposed, however imperfectly, on that case, or should the case be considered on its unique merits, regardless of the rule?

## How it is measured

We measure this with our now-famous dilemma of your best friend hitting a pedestrian with you beside him in the car. Is this one an occasion for truth telling in a court of law, or should you shade the evidence for the sake of friendship?

## How different nations scored

Figure 3.5 indicates the percentage of people in different countries who would not shade their evidence, but tell the universal truth as they witnessed it. Note that countries in East Asia, Southern Europe, and Eastern Europe are far more particularist than North America, Britain, and Northwestern Europe.

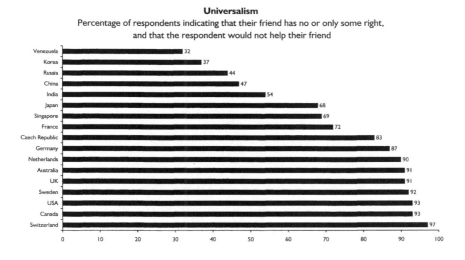

**Figure 3.5**  Percentage who would tell the truth

*How the reconciliation of this dilemma might be assessed by HRM*

For many years the strategy literature insisted you had to make your choice between universal product appeals like low cost and particular product appeals like premium products. It was either cheap Levis or haute couture from France. There were warnings, by Michael Porter especially, about being "caught in the middle": trying to sell "fashionable jeans" which were neither genuinely cheap nor genuinely fashionable.

Recently, however, these taboos have broken down. Levis are so customized that their Original Spin jeans offered 750 choices of internal fit and style, a process called mass customization, with the universalism of "mass" and the particularism of "customization." According to Joe Pine, mass customization is now very common, especially in the auto industry. The Toyota Lexus brings its prices down by having a common "platform" (chassis and wheelbase) for all its Toyota cars and gets its premium quality up by creating a unique, customized superstructure for each vehicle, which is manufactured to order.

But perhaps the most brilliant reconciliation between low-cost universalism and premium quality particularism occurs in Dell Computers. Dell is really an assembler of computers, not a manufacturer. It orders millions of components from suppliers at very low cost and, because it sells directly to companies, it is able to customize several hundred computers and special software to inform that company's strategy. It sells not so much computers as IT solutions to a company's challenges. The huge inroads it has made on IBM, although Dell only began in the 80s, testifies to the fact that it is both the cheapest solution and the most customized.

There is nothing to stop HRM rewarding key employees for getting costs down as part of the mass components strategy and rewarding those who sell whole strategic IT systems to corporations for the tenacity and longevity of those relationships. Both are vital strands of an overall reconciliation. It would be more than a Balanced Score-card, it would truly be an Integrated Scorecard.

This integration of opposites can be illustrated as in Figure 3.6.

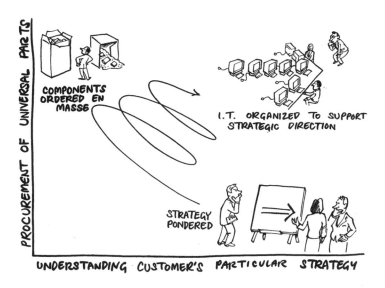

**Figure 3.6**  Dell's Optimal Assemblies

## 2. Individualism versus Communitarianism

Here the dilemma is whether it is more important to focus upon the enhancement of individuals, their rights, motivations, rewards, capacities, attitudes, or should more attention be paid to the advancement of whole communities, which all its members are pledged to serve?

## How it is measured

We measure this by asking whether the quality of life is improved by promoting more freedom or by taking better care of the needs of one's fellow human being.

## How different nations scored

Nations score as in Figure 3.7, with "Freedom" at the bottom and "Taking Better Care" at the top. Once gain the West and the recently-Communist Eastern bloc countries are the most individualist along with Israel, while East Asia, Latin America, and Southern Europe tend to be more communitarian.

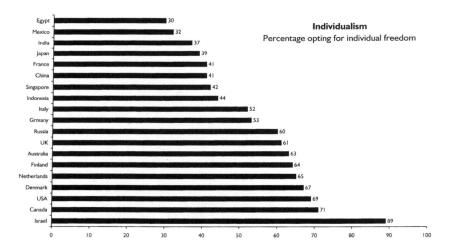

**Figure 3.7**  Percentage of people opting for individual freedom over taking care of others

## How the reconciliation of this dilemma might be assessed by HRM

Businesses and people within businesses have long been exhorted to compete with one another. Out of this fray there will emerge the better performers and resources will be redistributed from those who perform poorly to those who perform better, putting more resources under better management. Those countries which, for communitarian reasons, do not let their poorer businesses fail, such as Japan, seem to suffer long recessions.

On the other hand, people within a corporation, especially those in problem-solving teams, are expected to cooperate. Helping customers is largely a process of cooperation as is harmonizing different functions in the common pursuit of company objectives. Individuals die but the contributions they make to their families, their corporations, and their communities outlive them.

So should you compete or cooperate? Recently the hybrid term "co-opetition" has been used more and more. Is it somehow possible to compete the better to cooperate? Is it somehow possible to cooperate the better to compete? Many an HRM process does precisely that. One example is Motorola University's Total Customer Satisfaction competition. Only teams may enter and only teams who have "totally satisfied" identifiable customers can hope to get very far.

Once a team enters it must show off and promote its success vigorously. Heats are held throughout the world in countries where Motorola is located. The team that wins its national finals goes on to compete regionally, all the way up to the finals at the Paul Galvin theatre in Schaumburg, Illinois. In short, these teams are cooperating with customers and with each other in order to compete with other teams and float the best solutions up to the top of the company, where senior managers can discover them.

By inviting team members to exhibit their successes in public a premium is placed on individual flair and self-exhibition. You get up on the stage and show off, but of course you are boasting of the success

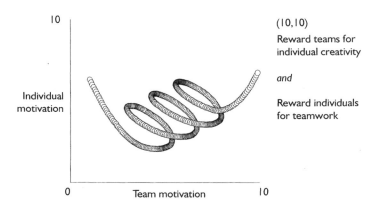

**Figure 3.8**  Co-opetition at Shell

of the whole team. This process combines the imperatives of helping customers and fellow team members with the arts of self-display and self-assertion.

The reconciled dilemma is illustrated in Figure 3.8.

Fons was able to combine team (or communal) rewards with individual rewards in Royal Dutch Shell. Half of the rewards for good performance were distributed to all team members, while the second half of the rewards were distributed to individual team members in accordance with the team members' estimates of relative contributions. Hence individuals received half the rewards but only if their co-workers deemed this to be just. Where individuals first contribute the winning edge to their teams, they are greatly enhanced in popularity and self-esteem by the gratitude of team members, so that the social system applauds their individual contributions and does not grudge their subsequent promotion.

If HRM is looking for new leaders, who could be more suitable than team members who have already "led" their teams towards enhanced performance? The informal leaders can thus become the formal ones, legitimized in their authority, and by their own superior contribution share rewards. Such people have already amply demonstrated their leadership capacities.

## 3. Specificity versus Diffusion

Are we more effective as managers when we analyze phenomena, reducing these to specifics, i.e., facts, items, tasks, numbers, units, or bullet points, or when we integrate and configure these into diffuse patterns, relationships, understandings, and contexts?

### How it is measured

Let's imagine a workplace where a trainee worker has made a serious error, costing the company considerable rework and loss of time. Is this the fault of the specific person, who made a specific mistake and should be disciplined, or is it a failure of the larger system, the procedures for training, supervising, and coaching new hires? Is it a failure of relationships within the team of workers?

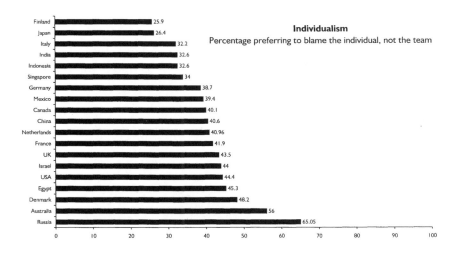

**Figure 3.9** Was the individual or the team to blame?

This is an important issue because firing the worker may not prevent such incidents from occurring again if, in fact, the system of initiating newcomers is at fault. "Firing" is a metaphor for pulling a trigger and making the problem disappear with the person, but will it disappear?

## How different nations scored

Nations score as shown in Figure 3.9. Note that Russia has now swung over to very high specificity. Otherwise the Protestant nations tend to be more specific than Catholic nations and those sharing the Confucian ethics of East Asia.

## How the reconciliation of this dilemma might be assessed by HRM

Time was when products and services stood mostly alone, a specific product commanding a specific price in the marketplace. Yet today products are more and more embedded in systems, systems of other products, systems of information, and systems of service. We do not just buy a specific product, we want to make good use of that product by putting it in an appropriate context. Now that Nokia, for example, can send pictures by mobile phone, is that company in the photography or imaging business as well as telecoms? Now that the direction finder in an automobile requires a satellite off which to bounce signals, what businesses are auto makers in? The system diffuses constantly.

The Swedish furniture retailer, IKEA, has achieved a wonderful reconciliation of the diffuse with the specific perspectives. The furniture is ordered in very cheap specific pieces: 100,000 glass ovals for a coffee table from a local glass works, 100,000 wooden bases from Poland on which the ovals rest. Yet the pieces are configured into elegant and tasteful designs, so that the whole is worth far more than the parts.

This whole–part equation operates at a number of levels. Perhaps some customers visit IKEA to buy table lamps, but once there they see a series of interiors, illuminated room designs that make them dissatisfied with how their own interior spaces are currently lit. Instead of buying one lamp, they create a whole new lighting system; instead of a chair they buy a whole suite of chairs.

Hardly is the purchase decision made, than the system switches back again to specifics. The illuminated living spaces are on the first floor, while the warehouse with the specific prepacked pieces is on the ground floor, so customers provide their own transport and do their own assembly work. Indeed, the boundaries between specificity and diffuseness move at the customers' bequest. Should they wish, their furniture can be delivered and assembled at an additional fee. This dilemma is illustrated in Figure 3.10.

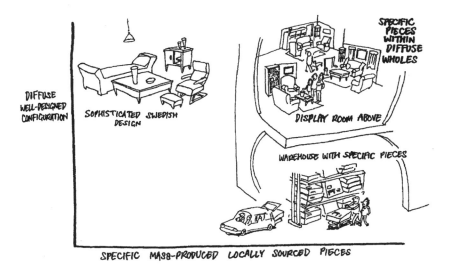

**Figure 3.10** The Modular Strategy of IKEA

The strategy of charging much more for the designed, diffuse whole, than for the specific cheap pieces is known as modularization. Pieces are created as "modules" capable of comprising a larger entity, which is much more valuable than the separate pieces, but less costly to produce.

If HRM wanted to encourage this process it could reward cheap procurement of pieces on one axis and high value-added (or value-reconciled) via good esthetic design on the other axis. It should be possible to calculate and reward large differentials between the cost of the pieces and the value of the whole result in the eyes of consumers. Good Design = (Price of Finished Whole) – (Cost of the Pieces). The really good designer does more with less.

## 4. Neutral versus Affective

Here the dilemma is whether we should communicate the full extent of personal feelings to other people (affective) in the course of engaging them, or whether we should behave "professionally" with an air of detachment and dispassion (neutral), so as to focus on the tasks to be completed.

### How it is measured

We ask this: "You are upset by something that happens at work. Would you reveal your feelings openly?"

### How different nations scored

Figure 3.11 shows how the nations scored.

### How the reconciliation of this dilemma might be assessed by HRM

This is quite a tricky question because the extent to which emotions

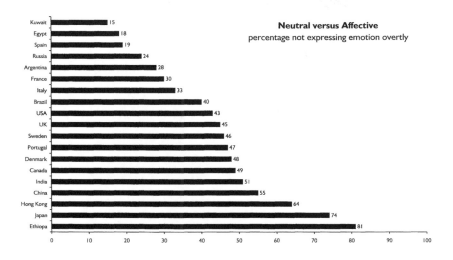

**Figure 3.11**   Percentage of those easily revealing their emotions at work

are publicly exhibited is not, unfortunately, a good indicator of how important emotions are to a culture. The Japanese, for example, are very neutral in their verbal expression, yet take subtle signs of emotional disturbance very seriously indeed and pride themselves on being attuned to one another.

Recently there has been a considerable upsurge in interest in emotional intelligence. Nick Georgiades, director of British Airways until the early 90s, presided over a highly successful culture change in which he lauded the emotional muscles of cabin staff, trapped at 30,000 feet with a cabin full of potentially disgruntled customers. He pointed out that cabin staff passed on to passengers the ways in which they were themselves treated by senior managers at BA. No wonder, then, that service standards collapsed following a bitter strike in the 90s.

Perhaps the clearest example of what HRM can do about emotional climates at work is to consider the dilemma first suggested by the linguistic anthropologist Deborah Tannen. She argued that a major difference between the cultures (not the biology) of men and women was the greater emphasis men put on report and women put on rapport. Reports are a detached and neutral account of the facts. In contrast, rapport is an affective bond between two people communicating. If you take neutral reporting too far, you can seriously offend the person to whom the report is being addressed, especially if its implications are negative. But if you take sympathy and "handkerchief holding" too far you may never get around to telling someone the hard truth of a situation. The dilemma is set out in Figure 3.12.

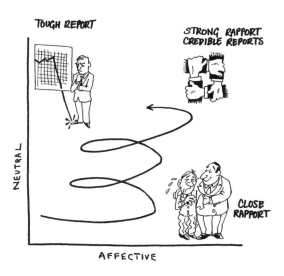

**Figure 3.12**   Neutral versus Affective

But there is an important reconciliation between these two axes. If there is sufficient rapport between two people each can tell hard truths and make tough reports and still be credible to the other. But if there is no rapport then honest reports may be ignored or be seen as personal attacks.

This issue becomes especially important when you are dealing with specific groups in the workplace, especially women and those from ethnic communities. We all make mistakes and those from minority groups make mistakes too. The real issue becomes one of the ability to be honest with them. Can we say to them, in effect, "I support and champion you and your future in this company (rapport), but I have to say that on this occasion you made a mistake and I would like you to learn from it"? (Report). In speaking like this we are criticizing in the context of affection.

One reason why minorities have so much trouble is that they are frequently given false reassurances. Superiors fear to criticize lest this is misconstrued as sexism or racism. People in minorities may be told that everything is fine but when promotion time comes around nothing happens.

HRM can easily check up on whether reports are being reconciled with rapport, by asking two simple questions:

1. *Has your boss ever criticized you or suggested you could do better in certain respects? Yes/No.*

2. *If "yes," do you believe, despite this criticism, that they are – and remain – on your side and are trying to help you?*

Unless the answers to both questions are "yes," the supervisor is not helping the subordinate to learn from correctable errors. A "no" to the first question is all too common. Many supervisors like to be nice and keep relationships smooth. But when we withhold criticism we impede learning and when we never get close enough to employees to dare to criticize them, we also impede learning.

## 5. Achieved status versus Ascribed status

Should we reward what employees have done and how they have

performed exclusively, or are other characteristics important, such as the employees' potentials, rights, seniority, ethnicity, gender, and so on?

## How it is measured

Here we ask such questions as this one: "The most important thing in life is to think and act in the manner that best suits the way you really are, even if you don't get things done. Do you agree or disagree?"

## How different nations scored

Figure 3.13 shows how the nations scored. Interestingly enough it is largely the English-speaking world which regards succeeding as more important than self-expression and self-discovery. The majority of all managers in nations surveyed regard the finding of "who you really are" as paramount.

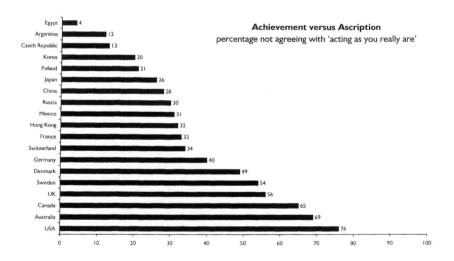

**Figure 3.13**   Percentage who prefer to act in the manner that best suits them

## How the reconciliation of this dilemma might be assessed by HRM

Employees have sources of personal identity, which are apart from whether or not they achieve at work. They want to be good parents, skilled professionals, loyal union members, "one of the boys" (or girls) among their friends, a good influence in the neighborhood or community, and many other things. HRM would be wise to respect and to facilitate all such identities, as the balance of home and work life has become a major issue.

Human development per se cannot start with achievement. Babies and young children achieve, in practical terms, very little. Development begins with considerable love and respect being shown to young people so that they subsequently achieve. The extraordinary success, academically and in business, of students from East Asia, especially those of Chinese parentage, testifies to the power of close-knit family structures.

An interesting change program was instituted at the Fairmont plant of Annheuser-Busch, the US-based brewer. An outside consulting team trained the top executive committee in personal interviewing skills. These interviewed their direct reports, who interviewed the level below them, all the way down to the hourly workers organized by the Teamsters Union.

Now the effect of interviewing is to ascribe status to each individual employee via that person's supervisor. The interviews were not about performance, achievement, rewards, or the objectives of the company. They followed the employees' own agendas, which included their families, their vacations, their hopes for the future and any subject which they cared to introduce.

The effects of interviewing were to substantially increase the amount of knowledge that employees possessed about each other. A lot of "irrelevant" information about Jim's fishing trips and Mary's father's by-pass surgery was included. The interviewing program lasted ten years or more and is to our knowledge still continuing.

Although "nothing to do with achieved status," and only focusing on personal lives and their importance, the program catapulted the Fairmont plant from being the worst in the USA to being the best, by very wide margins. On over forty indices of performance, the plant climbed inexorably year after year, although no other interventions had been made. There could be no clearer indications that ascribing to each individual employee the status of a unique identity creates a platform for subsequent achievement.

Explaining who you are is the best possible grounding for improving what you do. The more you know about subordinates or colleagues, the better the fit between their characters and the work needing to be done.

BUPA, Britain's largest private health insurer and provider, was able to create a powerful link between ascribed and achieved status. Those who staff call centers frequently take urgent and distressing calls from customers facing medical emergencies. The company stresses the preciousness of the one life we all have and insists that this be ascribed a status second to none. "Training" courses at BUPA are quite different from the norm, which aim to enhance performance. Those on the BUPA courses tell stories of personal bereavements, medical emergencies, and similar matters, then describe how they coped with these. One result of such courses is that a customer calling into BUPA can often find a person who faced a near-identical emergency and who can give sympathy, counsel, and bring quick medical attention to that customer's needs. In the face of death and illness we are all human, and the achievement of superlative performance is predicated on that underlying humanity. For years the customers have paid premiums; now they need you. Are you there for them in their darkest hours?

## 6. Inner direction versus Outer direction

Should we be guided by our inner convictions, our conscience, and moral compass, or by signals from the wider social and physical environment into which we must fit?

### How it is measured

We ask various questions about whether people's fates rest in their own hands or the wider human system.

### How different nations scored

Figure 3.14 shows how the different nations scored. One of these questions asked "What happens to me is my own doing. Do you agree or disagree?"

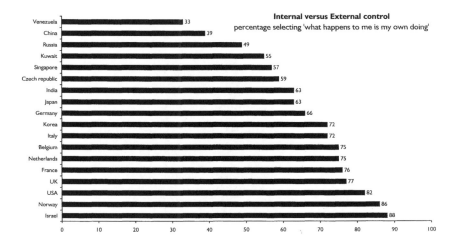

**Figure 3.14** What happens to me is my own doing (agree)

Again it is the USA and the English-speaking countries who insist on centering all sense of responsibility in the self, while other nations give a greater role to chance, fate, and the environment.

## How the reconciliation of this dilemma might be assessed by HRM

Inner versus Outer direction becomes a very serious issue whenever mergers, acquisitions or takeovers occur. For a time, at least, the company taken over is likely to lose all sense of inner or personal direction, which typically devastates morale. You are suddenly at the mercy of strangers who, in any restructuring, are likely to prefer their own. When you acquire a company you typically pay more for it than anyone else in the world is prepared to pay, so sudden crises of morale in the acquired company can lead to very serious losses.

With the benefit of hindsight the large number of senior management resignations that accompanied the takeover of Chrysler by Daimler-Benz, or the takeover by Vodafone of Mannesman, could and should have been avoided. Companies who are acquired may be less enterprising than their new owners but it is hardly a safe assumption. Federal Metals, the Canadian steel distributor, made it a practice to study all the US distributors it acquired. Several were judged to be more effective. Ahold, the Dutch retail chain, acquired Stop and Shop in the USA and reorganized itself completely according to the extraordinary retail effectiveness of the company it had acquired. You can run roughshod over your acquisitions but it is rarely wise to do so.

Small entrepreneurial companies especially may be almost worthless if their founders leave, or if their rare capacities to incubate new ideas are crushed in the giant bureaucracy of the acquiring com-

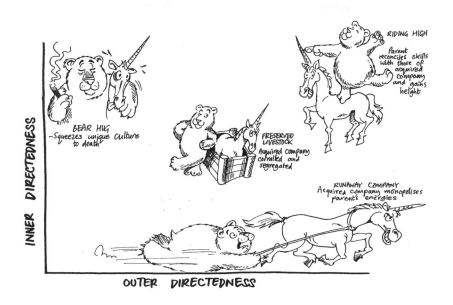

**Figure 3.15**   The bear and the unicorn

pany. Even where founders are legally required to remain, their genius may have died when their autonomy was curtailed.

The crisis of inner-direction following an acquisition is pictured in Figure 3.15.

An extreme of inner-directedness in a predatory takeover leads to a bear hug (top left) but this may happen even where a large company is trying to be gentle but expects to simply absorb a foreign culture into itself. Acquisitions do sometimes run away with their owners (top right), especially in cases where the acquired company is more sophisticated and knowledgeable than its owner. Barclays' acquisition of BZW was a disaster in the early 90s; the logic by which BZW operated its sales of derivatives was inaccessible to its parent.

Sometimes acquirers corral and segregate their new acquisitions to prevent these being hurt or hurting the rest of the company, but such imposed isolation rarely leads to effectiveness. A procedure we prescribe at THT is to learn everything you can from companies you acquire by intertwining their histories, dreams, and aspirations for the future with those of your own company. The most brilliant practitioner of that art whom we know of was Pierre Beaudoin of Bombardier, the French Canadian aeronautical company. We call him the Acquiring Scholar because, beginning with a skimobile company, he moved from relatively low tech to very high tech, acquiring by turns a train and carriage company and several aeronautical companies including Short Brothers and Lear Jet. This could not have been achieved without studious attention to acquisitions operating at higher levels of complexity than that to which he was used.

## 7. Sequential versus Synchronous time

Is it more important to do things fast, in the shortest sequence of passing time, or to synchronize efforts so that activities are coordinated?

### How it is measured

We have a series of questions about when the past, present and future begin and end for the respondent. High overlap in concepts of time equal synchronous time; discrete phases equal sequential time.

### How different nations scored

Relative preferences for sequential and synchronizing time are as shown in Figure 3.16.

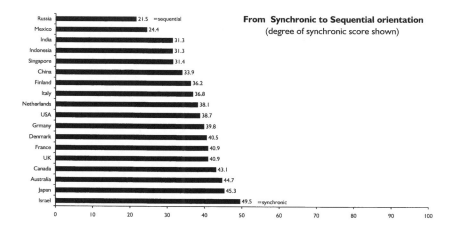

**Figure 3.16**   From sequential to synchronic orientation

## How the reconciliation of this dilemma might be assessed by HRM

Japanese automobile manufacturing in the shape of Toyota still leads the world, despite the continuing stagnation of the Japanese economy as a whole. This has been achieved by reconciling the American concept of fast sequences with the Japanese concept of just-in-time synchronization. The dilemma is set out in Figure 3.17.

At top left in Figure 3.17 we have the triumph of time and motion studies: "Racing with the Clock." This stresses ever-faster sequencing. At bottom right we depict the famous scene of Taichi Ohno, who first set up the Toyota assembly operation in the late 50s, kicking any pile of inventory he saw on the plant floor. He did this because piles of work-in-progress inventory are sure signs of poor synchronization. Inventory accumulates between workstations because operations are badly coordinated.

Both fast sequence and good synchronization contribute to speed of

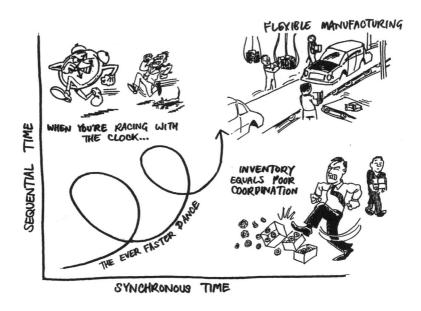

**Figure 3.17**  Time and Motion joins with Just in Time

operation in their own ways. Fast sequences will obviously run the course faster, but good synchronization shortens the "racecourse" by simultaneous operations, later integrated. Four parallel 20 ft assembly lines converging just in time will usually outperform one 80 ft assembly line operating in rapid sequence. Flexible manufacturing is achieved from both faster sequences and just-in-time synchronization. Both are measurable.

In conclusion, a seemingly "obvious" conclusion that HRM should discover the company's strategic goals, and assess and develop the skills required by these goals, is nothing like as simple in practice. Strategies rarely last long and may be qualified by contradictory advice within months. Customers need to be satisfied, whether or not that satisfaction is part of the company's strategy.

Moreover the culture at the company's HQ may be very different from the culture in different regions of the world. Seven dimensions

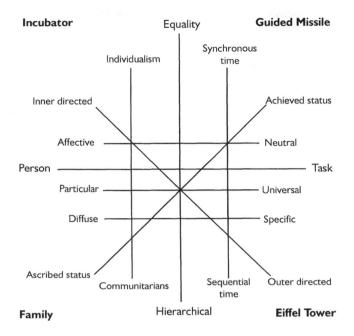

**Figure 3.18** Seven dimensions and four quadrants of culture intersecting

of culture were introduced to trace these differences. In each case a complementarity was discovered and reconciliation was wrought.

The seven dimensions intersect our four quadrants of culture, as illustrated in Figure 3.18.

The Incubator and the Family are more affective while the Guided Missile and the Eiffel Tower are more neutral. The Eiffel Tower is universalistic and specific, while the Family is particularist and diffuse.

Status is pre-defined and achieved in the role culture of the Guided Missile, while it is ascribed to you in the Family. Finally, sequential time began in the Eiffel Tower, but fast processes can only converge and be synchronized in the Guided Missile culture, with its destinations and rendezvous.

# CHAPTER 4

# How HRM can facilitate the problem-solving power of teams

Teams are of increasing importance to the success of a corporation, as this chapter will show. We'll address the following issues:

- Why teams are so important.
- How teams come into being.
- How teams manage information and help to create knowledge.
- What diverse roles must be played within a team to assure its success?
- How teams develop, help their members to develop and then dissolve; the secret of superlative performance.
- Are diverse teams genuinely more effective?
- Global teams as microcosms of the larger organization.

Where HRM knows how to mobilize team dynamics and make these more likely to succeed it will be in a far more influential position within an organization.

## WHY TEAMS ARE SO IMPORTANT

Teams were the heart and soul of the Guided Missile culture introduced at the beginning of this book. When teams heavily influence a corporation this is called a project group organization or a matrix organization. The matrix comes about because there are now two lines of authority. You are responsible to your Eiffel Tower functional head to fulfill the requirements of your discipline, and you are also responsible to your Project Group head to make sure that your group "missile" is being properly "guided" towards what it is that your customer needs. If your function is – say – safety, then you are responsible for the safe use of the finished product, but also for that product solving your customers' problems. Your responsibilities are both narrow and team-wide. You are in the business of total solutions.

Teams are largely responsible for getting viable ideas and prototypes up the organization from the level where the customer asks for them to the level where senior management presides. Single individuals are rarely as persuasive or generate as much momentum as a whole team. Teams tend to be egalitarian in their influence. Once formed, they grow autonomous and the group rapidly develops convictions of its own with influence coming from any or all participants. People enhance their standing by helping to solve problems, not through their prior positions.

As we've noted before, the anthropologist Margaret Mead once said, "Small groups have changed the world. Indeed nothing else ever has." Whether we are speaking of apostles, knights of the round table, communist cells, institutes of religion, literary circles, theoretical physicists, the seminarians of Socrates, or the acting troupes that performed Shakespeare's plays, the team becomes a microcosm and distillation of powerful ideas that carries within it the pattern of whole cultures. Teams carry within them the seeds of a new culture being born.

The team or Guided Missile culture plays a pivotal role in how the four quadrants of culture can be combined (see Figure 4.1). A new concept hatched in the Incubator culture is developed, championed, and pushed through by teamwork within the Guided Missile culture, which is also capable of team creativity, so as to influence innovation and incubation. Its own rules tend to trap the culture of the Eiffel Tower, unless teams are available to renew and to reengineer its operations to guide these afresh. Finally, the Family culture cannot properly become professional without the expert team to Guide the Missile.

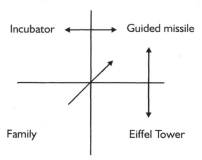

**Figure 4.1** Teams mediating between cultures

Teams must not be confused with committees, which have a deservedly dismal reputation. A committee delegates tasks to subordinates, which may or may not get done, and is anyway heavily rule-bound and procedural. Team members do "real work" themselves in fulfillment of promises made to their team and all its members. Teams have their own goals, visions, and even dashboards to monitor their progress towards these goals. The women in the Hawthorne experiment were a team and not a committee, as we saw in the Introduction.

Teams are a vital response to the fact that companies are more and more selling total systems of solution and satisfaction. A hi-fi system is not a pile of components but a complete musical experience. A lunar landing module is a vital part of a total mission and cannot be effective unless all other systems of flight and delivery work too. It was NASA that first made project groups famous as spacecraft were guided into space.

Modern systems are so complex that they require many different disciplines to encompass them. For highly complex assemblies only an entire team can suffice and it sometimes requires multiple teams, working on subassemblies of the larger system. Even Nobel Prizes are rarely won by lone scholarship these days but are awarded to team members. But teams are often expensive, so that the value they add between their members must be substantial.

## HOW TEAMS COME INTO BEING

Teams come about because an authority figure sponsors them or because members self-organize to solve a problem which is confronting and disturbing them. Less and less do top managers have the answers. The world is simply too complex for the person furthest away from field operations to know what should be done next and then issue orders for it to happen.

What senior managers do know are the issues or dilemmas facing the company. They know the problem a company has to solve in order to move on and they sponsor a team to find a solution. A typical sponsor must nominate team members or approve those who volunteer, give the team access to information, provide the team's remit, pay the team's expenses, and receive the team's final recommendations before implementing them.

The sponsor of a team faces real dilemmas. This is because the success or failure of the team reflects upon its sponsor and is a very public exhibition of good or bad judgment. Teams can go spectacularly wrong and if they do the mistake is costly and advertises the sponsor's error to all and sundry. A team that has worked hard on an impractical proposal is not easily silenced and is likely to blame its sponsor for non-implementation of its proposals. Because so much is at stake sponsors will sometimes cripple their own teams by over-control or make the opposite mistake of letting the team take over. This is illustrated in Figure 4.2.

As shown in Figure 4.2, a sponsor may try to create a Captive Team (top left) by seeding it with informers but such a team, full of people

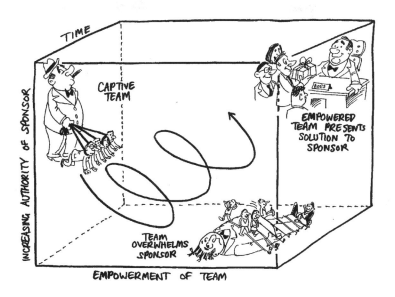

**Figure 4.2** The dilemma of team sponsorship

anxious to please the boss, is very likely to prove stagnant and unoriginal. What the sponsor fears is shown at bottom right; a team that runs away with the mandate given it and ties its sponsor in knots. Only with care and skill will the sponsor be provided with a creative solution of genuine novelty. Sponsors need to describe what a solution might look like and what it must accomplish. Only then can a newly empowered team present a solution to its sponsor.

Perhaps the most famous team sponsor was Jack Welch of General Electric. At the height of team processes at GE, Welch was debriefing four to five teams a week and taking team members' conclusions on board. He would implement as many as 75 percent of the suggestions he received. Sponsorship is no easy task. The sponsor knows the question, the issue or the dilemma but not the answer, and must be prepared to let the team be a source of enlightenment. Those who do know the answers are wasting huge amounts of money by asking expensive teams of experts to rubber-stamp their earlier decisions.

While sponsors should never spy on a team's deliberations, they should encourage team members to confer if they fear they are going beyond their remit into new territory. Sometimes an otherwise "good" solution will not work because of barriers of which the team is not aware. Sponsors must help their teams to surprise them.

Some teams self-organize around a problem they all find irksome and wish to solve. This spontaneous process is often very intelligent with members choosing those with the required skills. Here sponsors may decide to give backing to a self-organizing team if they approve its composition.

Ideally, a team starts with a problem needing to be solved. Let's say the Accounts Payable department is paying major contractors late but smaller contractors on time, and is getting rude phone calls and e-mails as a result. A group of people who are most concerned with the solution of this problem spontaneously organizes itself to remedy the situation. The team must care enough and it must have the requisite knowledge; usually those who care the most recruit those with the necessary knowledge. The team then looks for a sponsor and is on its way. The problem and solution in this case were simple. Invoices above $100,000 needed two signatures. Smaller invoices needed only one. It was taking two to three weeks to get both signatures for bigger contractors, but under the new rules signatures could be faxed.

A big advantage of the self-organizing team is that it comes out of the culture where the problem lies. Many consultant-based solutions fail because the tissue graft refuses to take. Consultants are seen as foreign: "Their solutions were not invented here." In the example above, in contrast, the team taken from Accounts Payable remained part of the culture and its solutions were generally welcomed.

## HOW TEAMS MANAGE INFORMATION AND HELP TO CREATE KNOWLEDGE

There are three levels of organizational understanding:

Knowledge

Information

Data

Teams are sponsored to study the data made available to them and turn this into information. If this information answers, or helps to answer, the vital issue that their sponsor has invited them to address, then their solution becomes knowledge. Top management decides what knowledge the company needs to succeed and throws down challenges for teams to meet.

This progression from data to information to knowledge is important because raw data tends to enter the organization at the customer interface or via technical advances, often adopted by relatively junior people. A way must be found of bringing to the attention of senior managers what these market or technological changes might mean for the organization. Teams and their debriefings are an important way of communicating these changes. What data are now needed to prove or disprove the propositions that top managers have in mind? Do the changing facts require new knowledge?

## WHAT DIVERSE ROLES MUST BE PLAYED WITHIN A TEAM TO ASSURE ITS SUCCESS?

Members of a team play different roles. These can be quite diverse, so that the team is full of potential conflicts and misunderstandings. Yet a team without a full complement of role-players is unlikely to be successful, however talented its individual members. If teams are going to come up with total solutions – and that is an important part of their mandate – then it is necessary for at least nine differing roles to be played.

A researcher who has spent a lifetime examining the roles played within management teams is Meredith Belbin, and his research is very helpful here. The breakthrough discovery came in the 70s at Henley Management College in the UK, where corporate executives came for short courses. One team consisted of members with such high IQs that Belbin christened them the "Apollo Team" in honor of the astronauts.

Since the business simulation the team played required high intelligence, he hypothesized that the team with the smartest members would win, a proposition so obvious that it seemed hardly worth testing. It was just as well he did test it, because the Apollo Team came last of six teams and in follow-up experiments was consistently closer to the bottom of the league than the top. What had gone wrong? We shall see in a moment. Suffice it here to say that team members must play several roles within their team. Highly intelligent people are too ready to use their critical powers; teams with very bright people tear each other's ideas into pieces. They are insufficiently constructive.

Teams with role diversity succeed best. Homogeneous teams playing similar and overlapping roles fall over each other.

## Belbin's team roles

These roles are self-identified by team members completing a simple questionnaire and include the following nine types.

The Plant is the idea generator and origin of the team's creative potential. Plants "think out of the box." A team may need only one

THE PLANT

or two Plants. If there are too many they compete for attention and quarrel with each other. Generating a good idea is only the beginning of the team's work. Other team members are needed to turn this into a reality.

THE SHAPER

Shapers get people to shape up around the new idea and drive it through. They are sometimes called Product Champions and put momentum behind the idea. Entrepreneurs are often Shapers and not necessarily Plants, but rather people with faith in an innovative project and the forcefulness to push it through.

RESOURCE INVESTIGATOR

A role that is often involved in innovative solutions is the Resource Investigator. These people may discover a new resource not employed before or may locate a crucial customer or rare opportunity, the window of which opens only briefly and through which the enterprise must dart if it wants to win. Resource Investigators operate on the boundaries of the system as roving ambassadors.

CO-ORDINATOR

New ideas are not automatically welcomed into a team, nor are these always placed at the top of the team's agenda. The person who opens the gate to include fresh approaches is the Coordinator. This team player must also mobilize the team around the new agenda and help them to run with it.

THE SPECIALIST

Most products on the leading edge of knowledge are the results of specialization and new disciplines. Understanding specialized members of a team is vital to gaining full competitive advantage from their advanced knowledge. Technical brilliance is often the key, but teams need to get behind this.

THE IMPLEMENTER

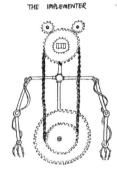

The sixth role is that of the Implementer. This is the person who gives the idea its embodiment as a product or service, who turns ideas into realities and gives practical utility to vision. Without good implementation, the real value of the original idea may be lost. With effective implementation the idea is born.

THE TEAMWORKER

This role is for the socio-emotional specialist, who maintains the morale and cohesion of the team by healing any hurts. Teamworkers encourage participation, facilitate team processes, and may even do running repairs on gaps or splits in the team. The best Teamworkers sense any incompleteness and supply the needed roles.

MONITOR-EVALUATOR

It was an excess of Monitor–Evaluators, or high IQ critics, that crippled Belbin's Apollo Team, but these are not always destructive. Monitor–Evaluators are useful when they kill ideas that are wasting the team's time and they may also improve ideas that require further work and elaboration, and help to turn these into viable projects. It is less expensive to be corrected by critics than by customers.

THE COMPLETER-FINISHER

The final role is the Completer–Finisher. Unfinished products are rarely much use to customers. There are few prizes for good tries. Completer–Finishers are the team members who edit, refine, and perfect the product. They are the detail people who take infinite pains to make the product user-friendly.

There is no inherent reason why team members may not play two, three, four, or all roles in a team. There is, however, a tendency to specialize and have role preferences. An unusually sensitive and aware team player will notice what is not being done in a team and then provide the requisite role. Some of us have all these potential roles within us, as aspects of our overall personalities, and are able to fill in and provide balance to the team.

All roles are really complementary so that an idea needs to be planted, shaped, and pushed through, with the right resources or opportunities. The "Renaissance Woman" illustrated in Figure 4.3 reflects all roles. She is a Plant and ideas generator at 12 o'clock, a Resource Investigator who uses her ideas to connect people, a Shaper with the confidence and strength to push her ideas through and a Monitor–Evaluator capable of criticizing and improving her own project. She maintains the morale of her team at 7 o'clock, acts as her own implementer, refines and finishes her own products and personifies one or more specialist disciplines in this process. Such a brilliant, versatile role-player would be very rare but is not beyond the bounds of possibility.

Belbin's Nine Roles have special relevance for the four cultures introduced at the beginning of this book. If the Guided Missile culture is to inform the three other quadrants to give and receive

ONE PERSONALITY, NINE ROLES

**Figure 4.3** The "Renaissance Woman"

expertise from these, then our nine roles occupy the positions shown in Figure 4.4.

The Plant is the incubation process. The Shaper, the Resource Investigator, and the Specialist are all crucial to getting a Project Team behind the idea. The Teamworker provides the Family atmosphere bottom left, while the Implementer gets the product ready for the Eiffel Tower production process with the Monitor–Evaluator inspecting and the Completer–Finisher signing off on the final product. The Coordinator tries to hold all four cultures together. While all nine roles are within the Guided Missile culture in one sense, in another sense the team also mobilizes the contributions of the other three cultures and helps these cultures contribute their best skills.

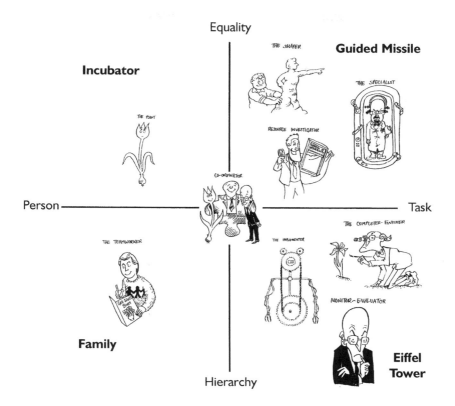

**Figure 4.4** Belbin's nine roles in the four cultures

Belbin makes a list of the team roles' "Strengths" and their "Allowable Weaknesses." The Plant, at best, is creative but can be dreamy, impractical, and self-absorbed. The Resource Investigator can be "out there" hunting new opportunities but can be easily distracted from the real business of the team. The Coordinator is vital in holding everyone together but may try to be all things to all people and patch contributions together in crude forms. The Shaper has commendable determination but can become politicized and may be a bully who turns people off. The Monitor–Evaluator has critical faculties, which save the team from serious error, but can also be destructive of ideas and of morale.

The Teamworker sustains morale but may indulge people and smooth over conflicts. The Implementer is highly practical and realistic but can lack the quality of subtlety and imagination. The Completer–Finisher is the master of fine detail and improvement, but can stray into obsession and compulsive perfectionism. The Specialist knows more about a particular discipline than almost anyone else, but may take narrow views of other specialists or be dismissive of non-specialists. In the figures that follow weaknesses are strengths pushed too far and championed too exclusively.

## The dilemmas of the creative team

How might HRM try to turn a company's team processes into a creative force? By examining some of the commonest dilemmas, which occur between the Plant, representing the process of incubation and creativity, and other key players in the team who represent the other three quadrants.

The reason for concentrating so much on the Plant was implicit in our Introduction. HRM must become the driving force for innovation or find its role reduced to that of an ambulance brigade picking up those wounded by technological advances. If the essential aspiration of a company is not deeply humane, its activities are unlikely to accrue to the benefit of employees or customers. Innovation must pervade all its cultures. The project team must test new products and services. The Eiffel Tower factory or bureaucracy must be capable of periodic renewal and reorganization.

The Family must nurture originality in its members. We now turn to this crucial interface between the Plant and the Shaper, the Resource Investigator, the Monitor–Evaluator, and the Specialist.

## The Plant versus the Shaper (or the ideal versus the real)

For a team to be innovative, creative ideas must be given shape. The Shaper is often a powerhouse and could not transform ideals into new realities were this not the case. But if the Shaper can make an idea into an innovative product or service, the Shaper can also break that reality and kill the idea.

The quality of the original idea is also crucial. Many people with the reputation of being brilliant and creative have earned that reputation by talking and visualizing, but not by realizing what they envision. So long as they stay at a level of abstraction and do not come down to earth, their reputations remain inviolate. But where their ideas are realized and fail, they will be found out. It can be quite a struggle to put ideas to the test, to put up or shut up. The Plant may resist. The Shaper may discredit the idea by the manner of

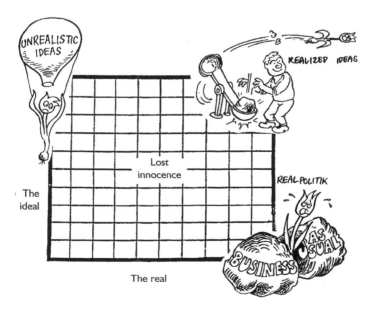

**Figure 4.5**   The Ideal versus The Real

championing it, making so many enemies by pressure tactics that the whole project becomes unpopular.

In the dilemma grid shown in Figure 4.5 we have unrealistic ideas at top left, a trial balloon that will not make it, and we have the Shaper's "business as usual" crushing the idea between immovable objects at bottom right. Perhaps the Shaper's "push comes to shove" misrepresents the whole tenor of the idea and team members resent being dictated to.

But at the top right the Shaper has succeeded in catapulting the idea and making it fly. The ideal has become real. The product is beginning to take shape. People are persuaded to give it a try. We are on our way.

### The Plant versus The Resource Investigator (or the concept versus the window of opportunity)

For a creative idea to work it must be matched not just with the resources available to do the work, but also with a window of opportunity in the customer environment. Innovation needs a sponsor and getting it may not be easy. Often windows of opportunity open quickly and stay open only briefly. Are we ready to dart through? It is largely a question of timing and getting activities coordinated.

In the dilemma grid in Figure 4.6 the window of opportunity has shut in the face of the new project (top left). The resources available from the customer came, but went before the team could respond. At bottom right the opportunity has presented itself again but now the innovative ideas are not sufficiently developed. We need more time. Perhaps if we better traced the evolving patterns of customer demand we could better anticipate what they would ask for next. Perhaps if we showed them what our new technology could do, a latent need for this could be aroused within one or more customers,

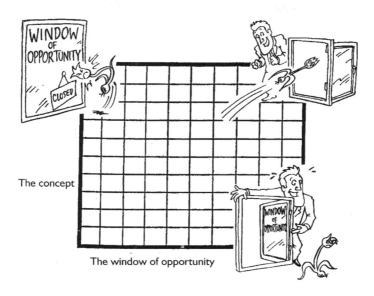

**Figure 4.6**   The Concept versus The Window of Opportunity

enabling us to dart through the window of opportunity immediately after it opens once more.

The new concept is inside the minds of team members. The external resource is out there in the environment. One way or another we have to coordinate our new initiative with shifting patterns of demand in the external world. The inward- and outward-looking team members must get their act together.

## The Plant versus The Monitor–Evaluator (or creative ideas versus critical appraisal)

Most genuinely creative ideas do not make money. For example, most patents to not make money for the company that has success-fully filed for them. This does not mean that they are fakes and not genuinely new; there may simply be no market for them. Their origi-nality may intrigue fellow scientists but not customers. While some

**Figure 4.7** Creative Ideas versus Critical Appraisal

people in a company will complain that their ideas are strangled at birth, others will respond that if many more ideas were strangled the company would not face the expense of discussing them, or building prototypes before projects were finally abandoned.

Critics or Monitor–Evaluators are rarely loved. No statue was ever erected to a critic. Yet the price of not shooting down bad ideas can be very high. It is much more expensive when customers ultimately lodge complaints that should have been foreseen and remedied months earlier.

All Plants who generate new ideas and try to float them need constructive criticism if the innovation is to be improved. This is one of the reasons for a face-to-face team, so that ideas can be improved, without hurting the generator, in an atmosphere of mutual respect and cordiality.

In a potentially destructive atmosphere creative ideas tend to be "blue sky" (top left); that is, so far up in the air that critics cannot get at them. This seeming evasiveness can generate hostility among evaluators. Precisely what is being suggested? What will it cost? How great is the risk? Why won't these guys come down to earth and tell us what they are plotting?

When detailed proposals are finally made (at bottom right), those team members who are impatient to exercise their critical acumen and show healthy skepticism stamp on them immediately. Questioning is often hostile, as though the Plant were trying to deceive other team members, and when they shift ground to accommodate criticism it is seen as evasive and "sneaky": Now something else is being suggested. Often there is acceptance but it seems grudging, as if the critics resent their inadequate marksmanship.

What is needed is a refiner's fire (see the top right of the grid), a critical fire that burns the impurities out of an idea and leaves it stronger and without flaws. Good criticism can be extremely valuable to any innovative project, provided advocates and critics work together to refine it. Where they do this the innovative project is much more likely to succeed.

## The Plant versus the Specialist (or creative connections versus rival disciplines)

Most major innovation now takes place not within one discipline or specialization, where most of the connections have already been made, but between different disciplines or specialties. The extreme case of this development is NASA, where it took more than one hundred distinctive disciplines to land on the moon.

The issue here is not simply what each discipline can contribute but how their contributions are to be synthesized and reconciled to create a successful project and mission. No discipline can, by itself, tell us how to connect it to other disciplines beyond its own boundaries. Not the least of the challenges facing Plants and Coordinators is the cross-disciplinary synthesis of multiple specialties assembled in configurations that are innovative.

Our dilemma grid in Figure 4.8 details the hazards. Interdisciplinary studies often involve the clash of rival disciplines, each believing it has greater authority than other disciplines in this area and each planning to expand its own influence at the others' expense. When the Plant brings them into necessary contact with each other (top left) both specialists may resent this. Why has the other been consulted? All too easily both disciplines gang up on the Plant who has had the temerity to bring them together. Specialties tend to be "containerized" and they tend to punish those who breach the boundaries of their container. The Plant, who is neither of one specialty nor the other, is an obvious target of their wrath and may easily be crushed between them.

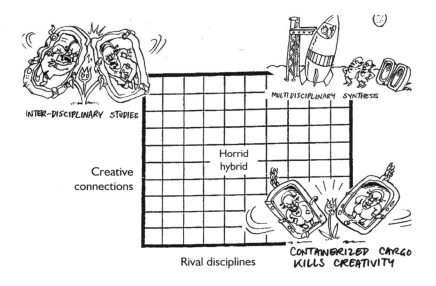

**Figure 4.8**   Creative connections versus Rival disciplines

Nonetheless it is possible to connect different disciplines in a multidisciplinary synthesis (top right) and at NASA and the European Space Agency, now both on their way to Titan, one of Saturn's moons, this has been brilliantly accomplished. These are Guided Missiles, literally as well as metaphorically, whose performance is wrought by project groups working across disciplines.

## HOW TEAMS DEVELOP, HELP THEIR MEMBERS TO DEVELOP, AND THEN DISSOLVE; THE SECRET OF SUPERLATIVE PERFORMANCE

In the history of corporations there are rare instances of really superlative performance. When a new innovation defies all the odds to produce an amazing result, in virtually all cases a dedicated team is behind these breakthroughs. These have been called "hot groups" by Lipman-Blumen and Leavitt because the excitement runs so high and the sense of accomplishment and destiny in reaching superordinate goals is palpable. What is going on in these small microcosms of excellence?

The psychologist Mihaly Csikszentmihaly studied this phenomenon, which he has described as a "flow" experience. This occurs in individual performers, artists, sportsmen, scholars, and creators, but also in small teams of problem solvers faced with a challenge which they are striving mightily to surmount. Csikszentmihaly takes the issue of Challenge versus Skill, and considers what happens when the skills of a team encounter a challenge that has yet to be met in order for the task to be accomplished. Figure 4.9 is a cartoon treatment of his chart.

We see that where the challenge is greater than the team's skill, the team is plunged into a vortex of anxiety (top left). Where skills are greater than the challenge the team gets bored (bottom right). But

**Figure 4.9** Challenge versus Skill

something much more interesting happens when skills and challenges are very closely matched. All of a sudden the two axes cease to subtract from one another and join together in one ecstatic, dynamic flow experience. A great whoosh of excitement carries the team along to higher and higher levels of performance. The challenge seems to have called forth all the hidden reserves of the team members, who now see themselves just a few tantalizing inches away from their shared goal and strain every nerve and sinew to get there, ransacking every corner of their collective memories.

Many respondents have now recalled these heady experiences, the thrill of the chase, the spontaneous outpouring of energies not seen before, the pride in joint ownership of a solution and the fulfillment of being admired for your contribution by close colleagues, whose lives you are helping to change. There is a shared sense of making history, of leaving a legacy for your company, of passing mental milestones you never dreamed you could reach. One company we know was so afraid that its whole team could defect to a rival that it prepared "golden handcuffs" to keep them loyal.

It is crucial to realize that teams may actually develop over time to reach peaks of superlative performance before once again falling away. This development of teams is quite apart from personal learning or development, although team members may have growth experiences as a result of teamwork. Teams develop as a result of filling up with information and knowledge about the skills and personalities of their members. Wilfred Bion charted the development of small groups at the Tavistock Institute. He described them as passing through stages 1 to 4:

1.  Dependence

2.  Fight/Flight

3.  Pairing

4.  Interdependence

The group of strangers were at first highly Dependent on those who convened them. What did their sponsor require of them? Their sponsor tells them that they are on their own; when the sponsor says "I want to know what the group thinks," the Fight/Flight pattern begins. Some wish to abdicate, some fight for leadership. The first signs of cooperation come in the form of Pairing, brief alliances between members, often against other pairs. The final stage is Interdependence, where team members now know enough about each other to cooperate in jointly desired outcomes. A richer knowledge about mutual proclivities brings ever more skilful interaction and communication; the team is taking off as a problem-solving entity. Its progress is charted in Figure 4.10.

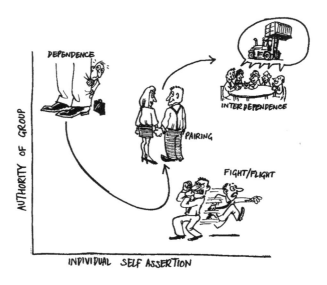

**Figure 4.10** Stages of group development

This is only one theory of team development. Other scholars have described stages of Forming, Storming, Norming, and Performing. There are at first cautious introductions, then fights for relative influence, then norms of proper procedure are agreed, and so the actual performance can begin. Inclusion, Control, and Affection are stages observed by William Schutz. Team members need to feel included before struggling with each other for control, and before coming through inquiring to appreciating one another. All these phase theories have common themes. The group must first create a microculture before it can proceed with work that is useful to the company.

The rapid growth of teams towards, on occasion, superlative performance does not last indefinitely. There comes a point when the team knows too much about one another and not enough about engaging their wider environments. There is only so much to learn about fellow team members and when most of this is communicated, learning slows. This is the time for the team to break up and for its members to address new challenges in newly formed teams. In this way, the challenges never cease, nor does the novelty of engaging new team members.

It is crucial to understand that the Guided Project Team is tempo-rary. When it has hit its target then its task is complete and it dissolves. Hence the Guided Missile culture is anti-bureaucratic in the sense that the Eiffel Tower is not. The GM culture is essentially time limited, moving from project to project, coming into existence because there is a challenge and passing out of existence when that challenge is met. It is perhaps the only corporate culture that resists the temptation of being an end in itself.

The failure to see small groups as temporary was responsible for the rise and fall of T-groups or Training Groups in the 60s and 70s. When the development of these groups was tracked over extensive periods their benefits were found to fade. What should have been looked at was their short-term impact upon enhanced team performance. Much the same disappointment accompanied the use of Quality Circle and Quality of Working Life Groups, which were both briefly fashionable until over-hyped. The challenge of generating hot groups remains. All such groups will decline beyond a brief period. These may not last, but what they create will last.

Off-site training sessions are a good opportunity to give new birth to teams who outlive the end of the training sessions. In our work at THT we ask for training seminars to be kicked off by a senior man-ager enumerating the greatest challenges facing the company. We then form teams and instruct these in dilemma resolution. On the final day of the seminar they present their solution to the leader who issued the challenge. Where the leaders are impressed by these solu-tions we ask for the team and its work to be preserved for several weeks, while it presents its conclusions to those most involved and finally to senior decision makers. This is a way of getting those in training sessions to consult back to their own organizations and apply what they have learned.

## ARE DIVERSE TEAMS GENUINELY MORE EFFECTIVE?

So far we have argued that roles played within teams are diverse yet essential to the optimal functioning of those teams, but what about diversity in general? Suppose teams are multinational, multi-disciplinary, and multifunctional, containing many different points of view? Role diversity is a necessary diversity, while the presence in the group of a middle-aged Portuguese ex-conjurer or a physically handicapped Masai warrior may be random and incidental to the team's purpose.

The research results on the relative performance of diverse versus homogeneous groups are, as we might have guessed, paradoxical. Nancy Adler found that diverse groups were both more likely to fail and to succeed in spectacular fashion. It depends on how good the group process is. Diversity creates obstacles that induce failure but if overcome, such obstacles contribute to outstanding successes.

Diversity is one more risk companies take when they set out to build a profitable enterprise, and like all risks it can succeed or not. Using homogeneous groups is less risky, less likely to fail, yet more modest in its potential attainments. The more diverse a group, beyond the roles that must be played in any case, the harder it is to manage well – but the higher the rewards for doing so.

There is a crucial relationship between diversity and creativity. You cannot be creative without connecting two or more ideas previously remote from one another, so one well-known test of creativity is the

**CAPSULE CASE**

**The Recovery Team at JPL saves the whole space mission**

The Cassini–Huygens space mission to Saturn and Titan, the largest moon in Saturn's system, was launched in 1997 and was well on its way when a potentially fatal miscalculation was discovered. The Italian subcontractor, who had supplied the high-gain antennae (which sends images back to Earth) had omitted to consider the Doppler effect. This is the tendency for communications to become scrambled when two objects in space, in this case the orbiter and the probe, are traveling at different speeds on opposite trajectories. If clear pictures could not get from the probe to the orbiter, then the latter would be unable to beam these back to Earth. Most of the scientific experiments focused on Titan would be lost.

The Recovery Team at the Jet Propulsion Lab at Pasadena took up this challenge. Thanks to some brilliant mathematics from one member, it was still possible to alter the trajectories of the orbiter from the ground by reprogramming its instructions. The question was, could the trajectory be changed so as to minimize or even eliminate the Doppler effect? It meant recalculating and redesigning the orbiter's entire set of rotations around Saturn and through its rings, so that the two vehicles could communicate without distortion. The math involved was prodigious and the solutions were highly creative. Yet the Recovery Team as a whole pulled it off, and the life work of a score of space scientists was rescued from oblivion. This is a remarkable example of what a team can accomplish.

Remote Associations Test. If newly connected ideas were previously remote, then the sources from which these ideas came are very likely to have been diverse also. The chances of success would be quite remote, but the quality of the solution, if successful, would be very high, so that when creativity is involved, there is a high-risk, high-gain equation operating. In the JPL Capsule Case the super-lative math of a team member was used to redesign a complex orbit of trajectories around the planet Saturn – after the spacecraft had been launched.

## GLOBAL TEAMS AS MICROCOSMS OF THE LARGER ORGANIZATION

The great advantage of global teams, with members from various countries, is that they are capable of creating an atmosphere of social intimacy in which cultural miscommunications between units in, say, Japan and the USA can be understood and worked through.

A Japanese national with extensive experience in America and with Americans can quickly grasp and explain the conflicting assump-tions of two business units talking past each other on the Internet. Because the team, but not the units, have had time to establish trust and mutual respect, these virtues can be used to work through potentially dangerous disputes and explain these to the respective nationals. The solution wrought by the team can be used as a model to establish new patterns of communication between Japanese and American protagonists.

There is not the time, nor the budget, to have two large business units talk through their misconceptions about each other. Yet a team can diagnose their problems and know from its own experience that Japanese and American executives can inform and enlighten each other.

HRM must first try to describe the global dilemma which has arisen between two units convinced that one is "right" and the other "wrong." What are these arguments about? Let's say they are about models of inventory control, which the Americans expect the Japanese to adopt, utilize, and report back to Chicago. A Global Team would include not just Japanese and Americans with experience of each other's culture, but experts on Japanese-style mathematics and accounting conventions, as well as on comparable American conventions. These would work through procedures that convert the way one culture thinks about numbers into the way the other culture thinks and back again. No way is the mental arithmetic of a middle-aged executive going to change on request; you must translate one "language" into the other, showing that they lead to the same results by different means.

Once members of a team get to know each other intimately, they can, for a while, comprise a virtual team, joined electronically. But the memories of each other's faces, jokes and gestures must never be allowed to fade, or they will start misinterpreting the "low context" messages they receive.

In summary, teams are like "knowledge genes" (sometimes called memes) within the body of the corporation. They combine ideas with solutions, with enthusiasm, with momentum. They reconcile the values of individualism with community because they are small enough to champion personal creativity, yet large enough to get behind innovative projects and drive these through. Teams are not committees, but pledge to accomplish "real work."

Teams only work well if a diversity of roles is played by at least one member. They are living examples of the unity that can combine diversities. The greater their initial diversity, the greater is the chance of innovation arising from their solutions, but the greater too is the risk of breakdown.

Teams develop and under special conditions are capable of superlative performances and flow conditions that generate great excitement. Teams champion not only new projects but also the needs of customers. They are a major influence in making organizations flatter and more responsive to markets, and are of critical importance.

# CHAPTER 5

# Building a learning organization: a challenge to HR

n this chapter we will examine the feasibility of building a learning organization. Many HR departments have tried, but far fewer have succeeded. Learning is as full of paradoxes as was culture in Chapter 1, assessment in Chapter 2, strategy in Chapter 3 and teams in Chapter 4. Instead of trying to evade these conflicts we must confront them head on, and reconcile the dilemmas.

In this chapter we will first see why learning is now so important. Then we will examine some of the unresolved issues that swirl around the challenge of *what* needs to be learned. Let's proceed as follows:

- Is all corporate activity learned?
- Should we gather facts or pose questions?
- Should we strive to be right first time, or make errors and correct these quickly?
- Do we learn explicitly or tacitly?
- How does change relate to continuity?
- Should a company open itself to the world or protect its proprietary secrets?
- Is social learning different from technological learning? Can we achieve both?
- What is the role of standards and benchmarks? Should we meet these or transcend them?
- How do we centralize learning reaching us from decentralized locations?
- What is "merit" in a world of diverse values?
- How do we build a culture of innovation?

## IS ALL CORPORATE ACTIVITY LEARNED?

Learning is like the lens of a new pair of eyeglasses. Given this lens, all activities are learned. We saw in the Introduction that turning the assembly of telephone relays into an experiment on how relays could better be assembled boosted productivity and transformed the workplace. There is no inherent reason why anyone doing a job should ask whether there are better ways of doing it. To paraphrase Socrates, "the unexamined workplace is not worth operating." This process has been called action learning. You act and then ask yourself whether the results might be improved upon. The amount of knowledge, which finds its way into products and services, is known as knowledge intensity. The term usually indicates high tech, which substantially underestimates the role of social experience but is still useful.

Knowledge intensity can comprise a powerful competitive weapon. If your company is at the leading edge of some knowledge vital to supplying a satisfaction, then that satisfaction will be scarce and will command a premium price. If it takes scarce knowledge to manufacture, distribute, sell, maintain, and use a product then the entire community of users and providers may grow in intelligence and wealth as a result. Whole nations in Southeast Asia like Singapore, Malaysia, and now China, are trying to capture markets for high end products that educate their people.

Knowledge intensity is a strong barrier against new entrants to an industry. Most countries have chronic shortages of newly developing skills and lack the educational infrastructure to supply these quickly. Hence there are scarcities not simply of innovative, patentable products and services but of the skills necessary to manufacture and distribute these. Malaysian factory workers making Pentium chips need to be able to use computers and mathematical models. Skilled labor of this kind is precious.

Almost by its nature, knowledge comprises a system in which products and services are deeply embedded. What customers want are not so much things as solutions to their own problems. You buy a computer for what it can do for you. You buy lighting for what it illuminates. You may use information technology to monitor your strategy. These are all internally coherent knowledge systems designed to deliver satisfactions.

Where you make whole knowledge systems proprietary, you are selling the processes of thinking themselves. You set the standards and protocols that whole industries must follow. The payoff for knowledge generation is thus infinite. Could there be a more important mission for HR to champion? Yet this field is full of traps for the unwary, as we shall see.

## SHOULD WE GATHER FACTS OR POSE QUESTIONS?

The answer to this and all the questions in this chapter is "both," but we have to start with a world where gathering facts from everywhere is almost an obsession.

Science began with astronomy that fixed its telescopes on distant stars whose existence was entirely independent of our beliefs, our religion, and our conceits about being the center of the universe. It moved on to physics and once again the world was seen as a celestial clock, wound up by God and ticking onwards. Things of the mind (*res cogitans*) were left to religion. Things "out there" (*res extensa*), in the language of Descartes, were left to science.

For this reason the persistent habit of objectification of almost everyone and everything has grown. Information, while originating with human beings, gets cut off from them to hang in public space like so many planetary objects and solar systems. Knowledge is thought to exist as independent of human beings, as something objectified, commoditized, abstract, decontextualized, and representational.

Some dangerous fallacies arise from this. It assumes, for example, that the more information we have the better. It is like any other resource: money, property, real estate, and, of course, "human resources." We prosper by accumulating it in large amounts. That masses of data might confuse us and overwhelm us is not properly understood. We have all the "facts" yet we cannot extract useful knowledge from them.

Objectification is especially dangerous when applied to values. If people think values are things, that the more they have of such values the "better" they are, then risk-taking, aggression, tough-mindedness, and cutting pay rolls knows no limits. We must profit by any means available because profiting is a "good thing." When two groups in any dispute believe that they value contrasting "things" and that it is logically impossible for contradictory "things" to coexist, then the scene is set for the clash of civilizations. Was 9/11 the overture?

Values are, as we have seen, processes in the mediation of differences. A corporation risks its money so that it can secure additional monies. Risking–securing are on two ends of a continuum; with enough skill more money is risked and more is then secured and therefore more risked, in a spiraling process of wealth creation.

It follows from this that real knowledge is not an accumulation of facts bursting from giant databases but answers to the questions we have posed. Information becomes knowledge only because we first asked questions and because the answers are important to our purposes.

No one familiar with modern corporations could claim that they lack data. Rather they are awash in objectified information whose relevance to their particular problems is quite doubtful. They do not even know what to do with the statistics generated by their own operations. Is it relevant that the company sold X packets of fish-fingers in store Y on June 13? What should be done with such information, now deemed "objective" because it has emerged from a computer? The problem is not that we lack answers. It is the good questions capable of organizing those answers that are in short supply.

When asked why they collect such hoards of data, corporations typically say because "it is there" and that they "always do so." Besides, bar codes and similar technology make it available. One of these days they are going to data mine everything they have.

There are also, in any corporation, many people faced with challenges who need help. They have questions but have little idea of whether somewhere, buried in the mass of data collected, are the answers they seek. Lots of data without questions and lots of questions without answering data do not constitute knowledge, just a mess. Instead of leaving employees to beg for help from other employees, senior managers should be posing questions to which employees as individuals or as teams should be supplying the answers. Questions form the context to which answers and data are the text. What knowledge consists of are questions, hypotheses, propositions, and conjectures to which customers, or those dealing with customers, provide the answers.

Corporations should be asking some of these questions: Does our new way of serving customers provide more or less satisfaction? Is it really possible to cut late deliveries by half? Can three successes by three different business units be generalized to other units and scaled up across the board and, if so, why are they not acting on it?

Has our formal strategy learned from these successes and is it being modified?

A learning organization worthy of the name is, above all else, an inquiring system. This means that top managers, far from knowing all the answers and issuing orders on the basis of those answers, are rather chief inquirers. They know what questions are crucial, what dilemmas need answering, what customers need to be won back, but they do not know, in most cases, how this should be done. After all, they are some distance from the action and from personal engagement with markets. What they can and must do is preside over the ongoing processes of inquiry and derive vital knowledge from it.

An inquiring system belongs at the top of our culture quadrants because it is relatively egalitarian. If you are asking questions you need to show respect and appreciation for the answers. Theory cannot be "better" than data, nor are conjectures superior to refutations/confirmations. Those asking questions and those answering them need each other to make sense and engage in dialogue to do so.

In Chapter 4 we considered the sponsorship of teams, whose task it was to get to grips with complex issues, devise solutions, and report back to their sponsors. This is one form which inquiring systems can take.

Some seemingly humdrum activities can be given added meaning by turning these into questions. Suppose you have to deliver many gallons of heating fuel to contractors each day. This is pretty routine work, not enough to keep the mind alive. Yet you can turn it into a question: "By deliberately varying my delivery route, can I find the quickest and most economic way of delivering fuel? Can I save time by calling ahead so the depot is ready to receive me?"

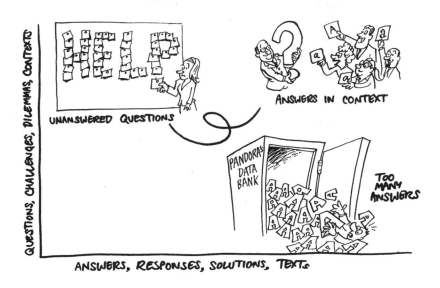

**Figure 5.1**   Dilemma A – Questions versus Answers

The process of questions and answers is shown in Figure 5.1. At top left we have employees (vainly) asking for help with the requisite answers irretrievable from the mass of "objective" information. Perhaps it is somewhere, but where precisely? And does it fulfill our purposes? At bottom right we have Pandora's data bank, a massive box of answers to which no one has  questions and for which the original questions are lost.

Genuine knowledge is portrayed at top right. It consists of strategic questions answered by employees and customers, or texts within contexts. The whole process of continuing inquiry unwinds in a helical pattern of ever-more-probing questions answered by the most up-to-date operations of the company, which culminates in vital knowledge about the corporation and its environment.

## SHOULD WE STRIVE TO BE RIGHT FIRST TIME, OR MAKE ERRORS AND CORRECT THESE QUICKLY?

The knowledge easiest to objectify is the self-sealing technique or predicted result, which can be tested and replicated by others before being sold in the marketplace. This is what most people mean by the Knowledge Revolution – a mass of discrete tools, which are thoroughly tested and are right the first time they are installed. It is this type of knowledge that is idealized by universities and academics.

But there is quite a different kind of learning, very widely used in business and everyday living. It is learning by successive approximations. We make errors in our earlier attempts but quickly correct these. Getting to know customers, learning languages, trying to love or to help someone, crossing cultures to engage foreigners, and virtually all entrepreneurship and innovation consist of trial and error.

But trial and error does not simply occur with inexact ways of inquiry in softer subjects, it becomes very important when issues grow complex and never making mistakes is an impossible demand. Here is where model making and simulations come in. You correct errors in simulation so that you do not have to make them in reality. Knowing that mistakes are inevitable and needing to learn from mistakes, you set up simulations and dry runs. Once you have eliminated errors one by one, you employ this technique in real situations.

This process has been called Serious Play. The play occurs when inexpensive errors are made in simulated environments. The seriousness occurs when the perfected techniques are put to use in real situations. As an added precaution the techniques themselves can be cybernetic and self-correcting, so that "Houston, we have a problem" can be put right after it occurs. You build into a system the capacity for retrieval.

In order to stay competitive business often has to act before all the data can be gathered; hence decisions must be made on imperfect information and the situation rapidly retrieved. The famous method of Case Learning introduced at the Harvard Business School, and long used in British and North American law schools, recognizes that every case is unique and that the precedents may not be clear until after a decision has been made by a judge or by a business executive. We can then consider whether or not that decision was erroneous or correct. This dilemma is shown in Figure 5.2.

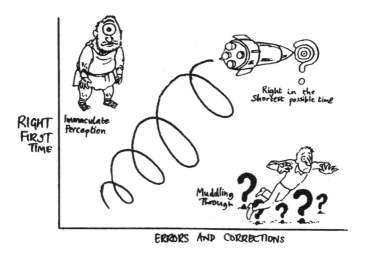

**Figure 5.2**   Dilemma B – Right the first time versus Error and correction

Note that those who insist on their own immaculate perception may be denying the possibility of serious error. Like one-eyed giants, they tend to blunder on in absolute certainty (top left), punishing mistakes and so driving these underground. Yet people forever tripping up and never grasping the truths over which they stumble are little use to us either (bottom right). Business succeeds by getting it right in the shortest possible time using the logic of the Guided Missile described earlier.

## DO WE LEARN EXPLICITLY OR TACITLY?

Another way of distinguishing "objective" information from personal knowing is via a distinction made famous by two Japanese researchers, Ikujiro Nonaka and Hirotaku Takeuchi. They contrast explicit, codified knowledge with tacit knowledge, shared intuitively between people. The latter is inseparable from the personalities of its creators, although it may later be turned into a codified technique and separated from its originators.

Tacit knowledge may be metaphorical, as in the case of an aluminum beer can which gave a team the idea of building a cheap, disposable drum for a home copying machine, or it may be a form of manual dexterity, as when the hands of master bakers twisting dough were filmed and then copied by engineers designing a dough-mixing machine for home baking. The tacit knowledge was in the bakers' hands, which the machine made explicit, just as the analogy was in the empty beer cans, which the disposable drum codified and objectified. This work is important because it reveals that the origins of new knowledge and creativity lie in cultural relationships between people; see the dilemma illustrated in Figure 5.3.

The buried treasure lies in a shared meeting of minds (bottom right). This may in time become (top left) explicit intellectual property to which the owner has the key, in the manner of Microsoft. Knowledge moves from being tacit to being (in part) codified and explicit, although the process of actual creation – along with its tacit understandings – may not be shared, so that what is made explicit has

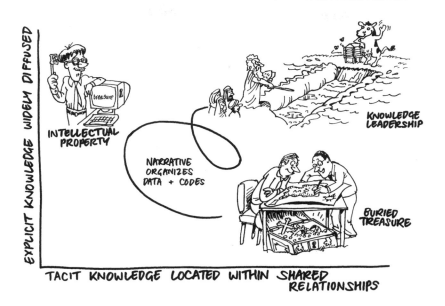

**Figure 5.3**   Dilemma C – Explicit knowledge versus Tacit knowledge

been torn from its roots like a flower put in water and then sold as an object, soon to wither since its roots are lost.

Corporations flourish by interweaving the tacit with the explicit. This is sometimes done by use of a narrative or a "learning journey" in which knowledge is generated and made explicit. Here we have used the example of Moses leading the Children of Israel across the Red Sea. On the far side is the land flowing with milk and honey. A stirring narrative with explicit and tacit meaning holds the experience of an entire ethnic group together. The story has the effect of eliciting new meanings until the end of time. You never know quite what the story "means" because it is there to help you create new meanings. Knowledge Leaders embark on journeys of endless discovery, sharing and codifying as they create knowledge. John Sculley of Apple wrote *Odyssey* about his time with the company. His slogan was "the journey is the reward." Like Odysseus, he saw himself on a wandering adventure without end. Computers were "the wings of the mind" navigating through seas of knowledge. You never finally arrive but you keep inquiring. Sculley called himself the Chief Listener.

## HOW DOES CHANGE RELATE TO CONTINUITY?

So far we have not discussed how the knowledge a corporation needs is to be organized internally over time. It has recently become fashionable to talk about knowledge "genes." Within each of our human cells is not just information about their specialized functions – the heart, kidney, liver, lungs, etc. – but coded instructions about their growth and place in the whole assembly. If knowledge behaves like "genes," or its cultural equivalent "memes" (systems of cultural information), then these logics endlessly replicate themselves to create a unique human being, very similar to other humans but in crucial ways dissimilar.

The dilemma we face here is that corporations need to change over time, if only because markets and customers are also changing, but that continuity is also vital. The organization must in several respects, remain the same; that is, it must generate profits, act professionally and ethically, maintain its brand before its customers, hold or gain market share, and so on. Yet in other respects it must change. Indeed unless a corporation changes to reengage its customers and renew its appeal, it will not remain profitable, professional, etc. Change relies on certain continuities and these are maintained by periodic changes.

Is this just a dance of abstract ideas? If we examine a company like Microsoft and its astounding success, we see that it has real relevance to this dilemma. Microsoft is not in the conventional sense the most innovative of companies, although we shall see that in one important respect its ingenuity approaches genius. Windows, for example, was an acquired technology, not home grown. There are no Nobel Prizes in the offing for what Microsoft has wrought, perhaps because its strength lies in mobilizing creative breakthroughs by other programmers, not creating these itself.

We cannot account for Microsoft's record of profitability without taking continuity much more seriously as a knowledge and strategy generator. The company's extraordinary success lies in the invention of a "language" or "genetic code" that is used over and over again to generate additional products. Every time these codes are redeployed they make new products and new profits for the company, whose core competence is resynthesized in fresh combinations. It is as if writers paid a wordsmith for the use of his vocabulary.

Adrian Slywotski has called this process, illustrated in Figure 5.4, "cornerstoning." You begin with a computer language, in this case BASIC. You add to this MS-DOS that reuses BASIC in altered forms.

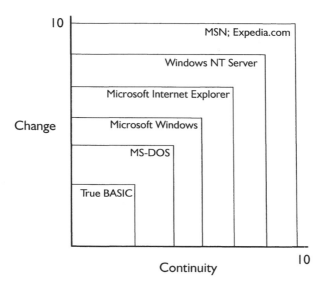

**Figure 5.4**  Dilemma D – Change versus Continuity; cornerstoning

You superimpose over this Windows, which once again rearranges and resells BASIC and MS-DOS. Using Windows as a common platform, you invite the most creative people you can find to design applications that must reuse your accumulated logic and knowledge, so that you have combined their changes with your continuities to reap the benefit of many new programs mounted on your platform.

From here you create or co-create successive cornerstones: Internet Explorer, Windows, NT Server, and whole online businesses like MSN and Expedia.com. The competitive advantage of building up products that rest upon each other is that your successive logics constitute much of an entire industry and that you overwhelm your competitors by tying in one cornerstone with the next one as your strength accumulates.

Of course, cornerstoning is more easily pictured than actually done and the judgment needed is particularly acute. But at least we have a potential question to put to the next proposed cornerstone: "Will this make the maximum use of the language and knowledge accumulated thus far by reusing our continuity, and will it constitute a quantum leap in significance by using the world's most creative program designers?" If the answer to both these questions is a confident "yes," then you have a prime candidate for your next cornerstone and your organizational culture is learning and developing in important ways.

While Microsoft itself has dealt largely in proprietary, codified, explicit, and objectified knowledge, it has very cleverly built a platform on which software designers and entrepreneurs can create and generate new knowledge, an opportunity that enables Microsoft to change. But is a move coming that might dethrone the company?

## SHOULD A COMPANY OPEN ITSELF TO THE WORLD OR PROTECT ITS PROPRIETARY SECRETS?

A continuing debate is now occurring between "open" and "closed" innovation. Closed innovation is represented by the R&D labs of major corporations: Xerox PARC; Bell Labs; GE's Global Research Center in Niskayuna, Japan; Glaxo Labs; Du Pont's central research labs – all are famous examples. If your R&D is not proprietary, others will steal it; you innovate behind closed doors. The limitations of this "closed" model is that all creative connections are first developed in-house. The advantages include hiring some of the best and most creative scientists in the world and so maintaining your lead in your discipline. The downside is the notorious Not Invented Here (NIH) Syndrome whereby discoveries made beyond the confines of the corporation are deemed irrelevant and are often seriously underestimated.

What "open" innovation does do is create novel connections between the corporation and a myriad of other players in the industry environment or even in other industries. Proctor and Gamble's Connect and Develop Program exemplifies this. A Director of External Innovation heads it. P&G's $5.00 electric toothbrush – the Spin Brush – is not the product of its own labs but that of four entrepreneurs in Cleveland. P&G even offers the innovations of its own labs to outside developers where the corporation has not utilized them within three years.

Whereas funding for innovation used to come from a corporation's R&D budget, there are now innovation investors and benefactors focused on novel enterprise. There are venture capitalists and SBICs (Small Business Investment Companies), all moving ideas out of universities and corporations into markets.

Opening up to find new combinations in a "marketplace of ideas" is clearly the more innovative solution, but also a more perilous one. Imitators will be quicker to spot what you are doing. It puts a premium not only on speed, but also on a succession of rapid innovations, each building on the other.

An analogous conflict is going on about closed and open source software. Microsoft largely dominates closed source software while a new social movement towards open source software is informally organized around Linux and its Finnish founder. The PRC has recently announced an open source national strategy and China has a market large enough to change the game. It may yet highlight a crucial difference between US and other market cultures and their approaches to the electronic knowledge revolution. What open source software promises, but has not yet delivered, is a faster pace of innovation for the whole industry.

With closed source proprietary software the vendor sells the finished product and its functions but withholds the source code – the logic by which the software was initially programmed. This code is inaccessible to the user who buys the result, not the programming itself. Huge profits have been made by Microsoft and other vendors who have a near monopoly of various software applications and have "cornerstoned" these in the manner explained in the previous section.

But suppose that along with the software we were to sell the source code, so that the buyer received our coded instructions for making the product that we sold. The price could be substantially higher because what we have sold is considerably more valuable. What customers now have is a "platform" on which they could mount their own customized solutions, varying the product to their requirements. This is illustrated in Figure 5.5.

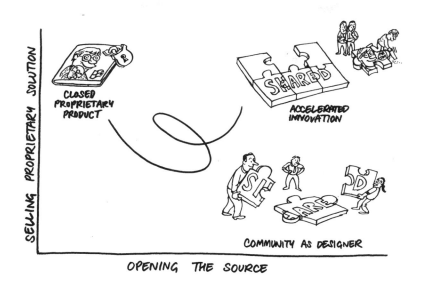

**Figure 5.5**  Dilemma E – Closed versus Open source

This move is not without hazards. You have sold the secret of your success. You have greatly shortened the period in which you could enjoy monopoly profits. Anyone to whom you have sold the source code might decide to compete against you and cut into your margins. But they might not, especially if the market were developing fast. What they are more likely to do is leapfrog you and supply your basic source code plus their own special refinements. This would have the effect of vastly accelerating innovation. Inventors would essentially share their tacit, cultural, error-correcting logic with the wider community and everyone would be free to build swiftly on each other's achievements.

Open source software was in fact how the industry began before Bill Gates and others locked it up in intellectual property. As the pace of innovation speeds up, might it return to this mode? Gates says he will share in this new phase although it is too early to test his sincerity. Early Internet entrepreneurs gave away their source codes, simply asking for donations from those who found these useful. Several became millionaires through the gratitude of users. It is not beyond the bounds of possibility that we have found a way of greatly accelerating the pace of innovation.

## IS SOCIAL LEARNING DIFFERENT FROM TECHNOLOGICAL LEARNING? CAN WE ACHIEVE BOTH?

Another way of distinguishing "objectified" information from cultural information is to note that the first is technical and the second social. The second can include the first, but the first typically excludes the second.

Learning about technology requires "technical reason," sometimes called means–ends rationality, while social learning about other living systems, human beings especially, requires the kind of paradoxical logic outlined in this book. We do not really "cause" anyone to behave, because they have conscious purposes of their own with their own needs and goals. We trigger responses from others, all of which are consistent with their agendas. These agendas include the techniques they use.

We can, on occasion, get total obedience from another individual, but to do so we must behave coercively and marshal a threat system. The history of slave labor suggests that coercion is not just wrong but stupid. We need employees to exercise judgment and discretion. Obedience can be programmed into machines more easily and cheaply than human beings can be exploited.

Unfortunately, there has long been a split in our educational system between the Sciences and the Humanities or Liberal Arts. C. P. Snow called these "The Two Cultures." He doubted publicly whether a first class honors graduate in the humanities had the slightest idea of how a button was manufactured, while scientists spoke of reading Dickens as a great feat. There are similar splits in business organizations between those qualified to understand machines, largely engineers, and those claiming to understand people, HR, Sales, etc.

Robert Blake and Jane S. Mouton measured this venerable dichotomy. They tracked the development of managers on two "opposed" axes, Concern with Task (or technology) and Concern with People. The first requires the "I–It" logic of manipulation. The second requires the "I–Thou" logic of dialogue and mutual respect. In short, technical and interpersonal competences are distinct.

In Blake and Mouton's Grid Seminars participants rate each other on both dimensions comprising a grid. Hence a task person may discover that they are considered incompetent with people, while a people person may discover that their contribution to completing tasks is rated close to zero. The aim is to create a synergy of both types of learning.

This logic of grid seminars is applied below to the notorious cultures of many call centers. These are often cost-saving technical innovations located in places where land and labor are cheap, many miles distant from the things being discussed in the telephone calls, so that bookings for Swiss Air may be routed through India. Call centers are often windowless, regimented, and austere, with employees needing permission to visit the bathroom. The work can be isolating and stressful. Hence we see, in Figure 5.6, that high concern with task leads to a sweatshop at top left, while high and exclusive concern with people leads to a country club at bottom right. But there is no inherent reason why these two skills should not be combined at top right, where concern with productive people combines technical with social logics. The optimizing of the socio-technical system has

**Figure 5.6**   Dilemma F – Concern with task versus Concern with people

long been the mission of the Tavistock Institute of Human Relations in London.

## WHAT IS THE ROLE OF STANDARDS AND BENCHMARKS? SHOULD WE MEET THESE OR TRANSCEND THEM?

Most learning seeks to approximate the standards or benchmarks authorities have specified. "Good" students get straight As by answering questions posed by their instructors. Top marks are reserved for answers similar to those conclusions that their teachers have already reached. In industry there are benchmarks, professional standards, codifications of "best practice," and tools like Six Sigma on which targets are preset. In Chapter 3 we asked whether HRM could not simply assess people against the company's strategic goals. Employees either "come up to the mark" or they do not.

The difficulty we encountered was that strategic goals were themselves constantly evolving and changing. If it takes three years to get an employee performing to the highest standards, whereupon those standards must change, then where are you? One reason standards and benchmarks become obsolete is that they are typically one-dimensional. You achieve them and then wish you had not; you have sacrificed one side of a dilemma to the other.

Peter Senge tells of an insurance company that rewarded a "low pending ratio," that is the number of insurance claims still waiting to be processed. It was assumed that expeditious work would keep this ratio down and so, up to a point, it did. Unfortunately, settling claims "quick and dirty" over the telephone, and failing to take witness statements of accidents or needed repairs, considerably raised the costs of settlement and provoked additional litigation.

It took some six years for litigation to wind through the American court system. Only then did the company discover, to its horror, the hidden costs of "quick and dirty" settlements. Juries awarded punitive damages against the company, which, in several cases, had not bothered to discover the full facts of heart-rending tragedies. The bill reached $150 million – many times the actual harm suffered by claimants and many times the costs saved by speeding up settlements.

If strategy does reside in paradox and impasse, as we argued in Chapter 2, then measuring and maximizing one axis of a dilemma will seriously unbalance objectives. Hence, British hospitals given incentives for low death rates in perinatal units shipped out their dying infants to perish in specialized units with their desperate parents in tow. There are virtually no single measures of learning or of attainment on which we cannot, with ingenuity, cheat.

You have to ask two questions alternately. "Have our people lived up to our standards?" and "Have our standards lived up to the aspirations of our people?" Chris Argyris calls this Learning I and Learning II or, taken together, "double-loop learning."

We can characterize living up to standards as doing things right. This is highly explicit, codified, and objective. We can characterize our standards living up to our noblest aspirations as doing the right thing. That is tacit, uncodified, impressionistic. At top left on Figure 5.7 we achieve organizational goals but have little confidence in those goals. At bottom right we make a bonfire of benchmarks deemed unworthy of customers or creative employees. But how are we now to rate ourselves?

**Figure 5.7** Dilemma G – Doing things right versus Doing the right thing

Only at top right can we reconcile both values by creating ever-moving goalposts as our people come up to standards, which must themselves be critiqued and changed as the environment shifts. This is very much a Guided Missile culture.

## HOW DO WE CENTRALIZE LESSONS REACHING US FROM DECENTRALIZED LOCATIONS?

A consistently vexed issue is about where information originates and where it should be stored for greatest effectiveness. If a global corporation is to communicate its knowledge, from whence should it travel and to where? Should it move bottom up, top down, outside in or from inside to outside? Arguments about centralizing versus decentralizing never seem to end and are rarely settled. For several years on end the watchword has been "decentralize!" But those with memories can recall that "centralize!" was once the cry. Will we ever make up our minds or is the concertina with us to stay?

One way of avoiding contradiction and reconciling the seeming dilemmas is to make sure that what is decentralized is subtly different from what is centralized. The slogan "Think Global–Act Local" gives us a clue. What we should decentralize are corporate activities across the globe. What we should centralize is knowledge *about* these activities. The company has a central nervous system to which impulses about its diverse local activities travel, to become knowledge and to be stored centrally. If we take the dilemma step-by-step it looks like the five boxes in Figure 5.8.

We first polarize centralizing with decentralizing as in most debates, pulling now towards one pole and a few years later towards the other. We then create a dual axis, using the same piece of rope. We now have a culture space in which to work. We next create a learning loop in which decentralizing activity is followed by centralizing knowledge about that activity. We then turn our loop into a helix. A helix is part circle, part line, since it winds in either of two directions. As such it models centralizing information from decentralized locations.

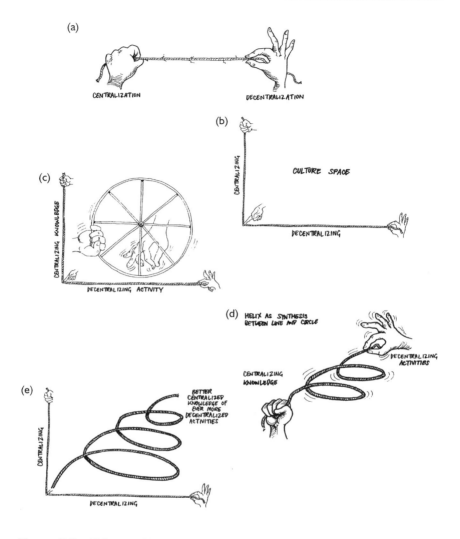

**Figure 5.8** Dilemma H – Centralize versus Decentralize

We next have centralizing and decentralizing axes, but the first controls the second. Decentralized activities must be kept in check by the vigilance of central authorities. The system still lacks enough local autonomy. The final stage gives full reign to decentralized initiatives, provided always that the center is informed of these in good time. What we have is the most highly effective centralization of the most highly decentralized and autonomous activities. There is no inherent reason why both axes and both values should not increase in salience.

Actually there is another phase, in which centers of excellence are themselves decentralized. Ideally countries of the world should be allowed to specialize in what they do best. Hence Apple Computer's center of excellence for skilled assembly and manufacturing is in Singapore, because this location is the best for this function. Motorola's center of excellence for software is in Bangalore; Sony puts its software center in California; AMD's star Fab is in Dresden, East Germany; ABN AMRO's East Asian call center is in Malaysia, where the population speaks more languages than in any other location.

The "center" does not have to be in one place in a system. Different functions may look to their own centers of excellence.

## WHAT IS "MERIT" IN A WORLD OF DIVERSE VALUES?

How is a corporation to promote and reward its employees by merit in cases where there are diverse views on what constitutes merit? The idea of meritocracy has much to recommend it. HRM prefers not by education, nor class, nor ethnicity, nor gender, but by sheer unadulterated performance. What could be fairer? What could be better for the corporation and its shareholders?

But it is not that simple. Who gets to define merit? Business conduct deserving praise in one country may not be appropriate in another country. Meritocracies lead to league tables and hierarchical orders of excellence. People may compete as equals but very soon a pecking order emerges with half of all contestants found to be "below average." The problem with ranking people is that most find themselves outranked by a significant portion of fellow employees, much to their dismay.

Chris Argyris describes "defensive routines" used by superiors during assessment interviews. They do not want to tell their subordinates that they are in the bottom half of some league table and so finesse the encounter. What Argyris blames on personal "defensiveness" we regard as a major defect of any ranking system. Most people believe themselves to be "above average." This comes about because they rate those things in which they excel as being more important than those things in which they do poorly. In short, their talents are diverse. A brilliant Mandarin scholar wastes little time bewailing his incompetence at swimming, while an Olympic swimmer does not rate herself low because she plays a poor game of poker. Rank ordering different forms of talent makes no sense at all.

But unalloyed diversity can end in a colorful Mardi Gras parade where no one standard is accepted by any other group and everything and everyone is relative. Where a corporation is located in many nations, which nations' standards should apply? If it is a French organization, should all national values be subordinated to French preferences? To do this might be very unwise and greatly undermine the strength of local cultures.

This dilemma is illustrated in Figure 5.9. Failure to respect diversity will end in narrow hierarchies of predefined "merit" in which thousands of people are made to feel inferior (top left). Diversity with no concept of preferred conduct ends in anarchy and the Tower of Babel (bottom right). What is needed is a "heterarchy," sometimes called a plurality of elites, where outstanding performers from local cultures meet to compare different forms of excellence and learn from these.

A "heterarchy" is an egalitarian exchange of varieties of excellence,

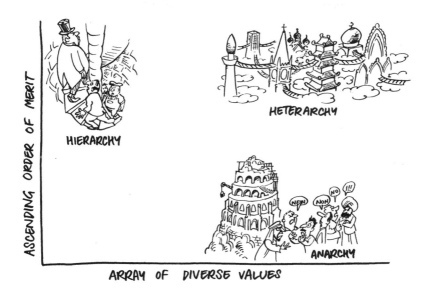

**Figure 5.9** Dilemma I – Merit versus Diversity

since every person in these pluralities of diverse talent has something others lack and could learn from. You listen not because you deem your own talents inferior but because the excellences you confront are incomparable to your own. These people have "made it" in very different circumstances and deserve respect. Learning in such situations is the source of trans-cultural competence.

## HOW DO WE BUILD A CULTURE OF INNOVATION?

Much of Chapter 4 was about this topic. Here we would only add one very important perspective. There appears to be a creative response to the dilemma of Universalism versus Particularism.

Let's recall what these words mean. To universalize is to ask what all successful businesses have in common. What principles, if any, can be generalized across the globe? To particularize is to ask which are the unique value propositions that different cultures, different corporations, and different business units offer their customers. Both values are crucial to wealth creation. Universalism is crucial because the universe is our ultimate market, because the more people who desire a product the more widely it will sell. Particularism is crucial because a unique relationship to a special customer is irreplaceable and has no real competitors. If your offering is incomparable in quality then your position is very strong indeed.

Yet both these values fail without the other, as we see in the dilemma illustrated in Figure 5.10. The insistence that everyone else in the world "be like us" (or be like the US) ends in particular cultures dressed in Mickey Mouse ears (top left).

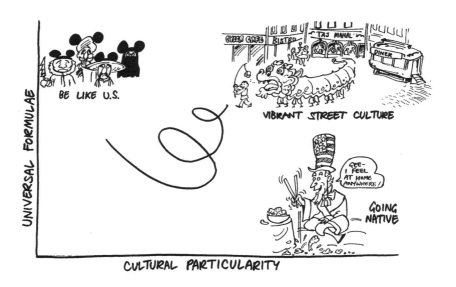

**Figure 5.10** Dilemma J – Universal formulae versus cultural Particularity

The attempt to go native (bottom right) also fails. It takes most of a lifetime to truly appreciate a culture diverse from your own, and tourist-type knowledge and superficial assimilation will not suffice.

## CAPSULE CASE
### Individual dignity and entitlement at Motorola

Under the leadership of Chris Galvin, grandson of the founder of Motorola, the concept of IDE (Individual Dignity Entitlement) was born. It was designed to create "a perfect match between individual needs and the survival of the institution." The program required every supervisor, every quarter, to discuss six questions with the individuals they managed, whereupon the company would act on the information emerging from these dialogues. The six questions, which were printed, framed, and hung in prominent places in most offices, were the following:

1.  Do you have a substantive, meaningful job that contributes to the success of Motorola?

2.  Do you know the on-the-job behaviors and have the knowledge base to be successful?

3.  Has the training been identified and been made available to continuously upgrade your skills?

4.  Do have a personal career plan, and is it exciting, achievable, and being acted upon?

5.  Do you receive candid, positive or negative feedback at least every 30 days that is helpful in improving or achieving your personal career goals?

6.  Is there approximate sensitivity to your personal circumstances, gender and/or cultural heritage so that such issues do not detract from your success?

Perhaps the most important aspect of these six questions, which were written and responded to by the supervisee, was the dialogue that ensued. Among the early benefits was an increase in job retention, higher job satisfaction scores, lower complaints, fewer lawsuits and a closer alignment of personal ambitions with the needs of the business. Management also received important clues to the climate of morale in different parts of the business. It was not possible to attribute financial success to IDE because Motorola's trading position deteriorated sharply for quite other reasons, following the failure of the IRIDIUM satellite project.

The six questions facilitate several of the learning dynamics discussed in this chapter.

- The company sets out to learn from its own activities.
- It does so by posing questions and acting on answers.
- It makes errors, corrects these quickly, and so perfects supervisory processes.
- By face-to-face interviewing it tries to make the tacit explicit.
- The questions provide the continuity while the answers provide the changes.
- The learning is social but includes technical issues.
- It asks not simply whether the supervisee is up to the job but whether the job itself is meaningful, i.e., worthy of the person.

In short, Motorola's six questions include many kinds of learning and monitor them all. The IDE program was generally popular within the USA, but ran into some difficulties globally, especially in East Asia.

On a visit to Malaysia we found the Managing Director poring over a Mandarin–English dictionary. "There are no Chinese words that convey Individual Dignity and Entitlement," she told us. "The word 'entitlement' is especially difficult here. We do not regard an employee as entitled to anything until work has been performed. We try to treat employees well, so they will repay us, but they are not 'entitled' to such favors so much as 'obligated' to us. I can't explain this entitlement concept to our people. There would be a riot!"

One problem with IDE in East Asia was that nearly all subordinates said "yes" to nearly all questions, scoring at least 20 percent higher than in Europe or North America. An instrument that failed to differentiate good relationships from bad between bosses and subordinates was not fulfilling its function. At the same time the instrument itself was much praised in this region of the world; they were saying "yes" to the instrument too!

What the designers of the instrument had failed to grasp was that many cultures in East Asia say "yes" to a relationship, while saying "no" to the specific question being asked. "No," their job is not meaningful, but "yes" they respect and wish to support their supervisor. When you force such people to say a bold "yes" or "no," you prevent them making this subtle distinction between support for their supervisor and disagreement with the question. Because a "no" had to be written down before the interview, supervisees were reluctant to write anything about their bosses that might injure their reputations in the company. In this culture, negative feedback, if delivered at all, should be expressed face to face in the context of mutual respect and should also be constructively framed. This misunderstanding arises because the USA and most of Western Europe is specific – yes/no – while East Asia is diffuse – yes to our relationship; no to your question. We looked at this in greater detail in Chapter 3.

The situation was greatly improved when an alert HR official in Shaumberg changed the "yes/no" system in Korea, and subsequently in other East Asian cultures, to a sliding scale where "yes" could be on a scale of 1 to 10. This allowed bosses to grasp that even a 90 percent "yes" meant "no" concerning one or two key questions. These fine, diffuse gradations, so important to the originators of "fuzzy logic," allowed supervisees to support their supervisors while making them (gently) aware that the objectives of the six questions had not all been met. Useful dialogues followed.

But we strive to combine many diverse particularities and to search among these for underlying rules and principles, something very interesting happens. We begin to build cultures of creativity. As we noted in Chapter 1, Richard Florida's recent book *The Rise of the Creative Class* is a study of those parts of America that have contributed to the recent surge of innovation. Some 85 percent of all US innovation comes from only 15 percent of its major population centers. All of these are characterized as cosmopolitan urban settings with vibrant street cultures. They include Manhattan; the San Francisco Bay area; parts of Los Angeles; the Boston–Cambridge area; Silicon Valley; Boulder, Colorado; Seattle, and several others. They are all characterized by a rich ethnic mix, high toleration for diverse lifestyles, egalitarian norms, large foreign populations, a plurality of elites, and integrated neighborhoods. Highly creative corporations were described as being "like the United Nations" though with less diversity.

Diverse inputs appear to increase the chances that a new, creative combination will be found within this cultural variety. People from the far ends of the earth are more likely to discover new truths in the midst of their several contributions. In the end the real payoff for encouraging diversity is that it gives fresh impulse to innovation. This may be the most important lesson of all. American capitalism was almost being written off at the end of the 80s. Then there came a great surge of innovation from a handful of creative communities and everything changed. The lesson is instructive.

In conclusion, there are many ways of learning. The ways HRM selects depend upon what challenges and dilemmas the organization must surmount. What do you need to know in order to succeed? All your crucial activities can be potentially reframed as questions to which answers are then sought: "Is this the best way of distributing X?" If you tolerate and study errors you will learn faster. If you simulate events, the cost of errors is much reduced.

Those who create knowledge will find that it is at first tacit but is later codified. What have you lost through codification? Can you renew the tacit process? Knowledge is like a genetic code that keeps reproducing, changing within continuity, reusing the old for new purposes. Innovation is increased by opening up to the environment, by letting others use your logic to customize and build upon. Yet the risks are higher.

Learning about people requires a paradoxical logic, since they have their own values and purposes, while things can be manipulated by your purposes. Dealing with people always leads to a clash of logic at some point. Learning is mediated by standards to which learners must approximate; yet these standards are not necessarily the best and must in their turn be judged by people for their adequacy, a process called double-loop learning.

A corporation is a network seeking to know and act profitably, and as such it has a center and peripheries. It needs to centralize knowledge about ever more decentralized activities, another paradox resolved. You need to reward merit, but you also need a continuing, cross-cultural dialogue on what "merit" means. Amid all these differing meanings trans-cultural competence remains a sheet anchor.

CHAPTER 6

# Leadership development
# across cultures

Time was when great leaders were like stars in the firmament. Their nations faced crises and George Washington, Charles De Gaulle, Martin Luther King, and Nelson Mandela came up with answers tailored to those crises: "Cometh the hour, cometh the man." Leaders like these take a stance that does not change. When the tide eventually goes out they are left like great monuments on the beach.

Modern business leadership is very different in its requirements. Global corporations are not simply buffeted by the winds of change but stretched across nations and continents and expected to be effective in each one. As products grow more complex and become multiproduct systems, leaders find themselves amid a plethora of disciplines and specialties. The divisions of labor beneath contemporary leaders are vast and variegated. Hundreds of contrasting claims are made on their allegiances.

The view of leadership taken here and the view of leadership development, which is HR's responsibility, is that leaders find themselves *between* conflicting demands and are subject to an endless series of paradoxes and dilemmas. There are nonstop culture clashes and by culture we mean not simply the cultures of different nations, but those of different disciplines, functions, genders, classes, and so on. We will illustrate some well-known leadership dilemmas in this chapter, but their exact descriptions are less important than the capacity for trans-cultural competence or paradoxical problem-solving which underlies them all. These include:

- Authoritative, participative, or transformational leadership?
- Abstract, concrete, or "porpoise" leadership?
- Lord, servant, or servant leader?
- Demonstrating, following, or improvising leadership?

- The leader as authority, resource, or conductor?
- Directing, facilitating, or developing culture?
- Inner-directed, outer-directed, or navigating turbulence?
- Knowledge of the world, of self, or cybernetic wisdom?
- Command, control, or delegated autonomy?
- Shareholders' creatures, managers' champions, or wealth creators?

The above are an army of current challenges. Are leaders the authors of strategy and policy or do they orchestrate the necessary participation? Do leaders deal in high-level abstractions or in concrete details? Can a leader also be a servant? Such questions culminate in what is, perhaps, the biggest crisis of the day. Are leaders people hired by shareholders to channel the lion's share of profits in their direction, or do they lead a learning, developing community?

The answers to these dilemmas affect HR profoundly.

## AUTHORITATIVE, PARTICIPATIVE, OR TRANSFORMATIONAL LEADERSHIP?

James McGregor Burns, the American historian and biographer of Franklin Delano Roosevelt, contrasted transactional leadership with transformational leadership. In the transactional style, there is a simple exchange of work for money, or votes for representation. Nothing new is created and each party serves only self-interest.

In the transformational style the leader transforms the consciousness of those led, and those led, by their response, transform the consciousness of the leader. Each elicits a potential latent in the other and brings to fruition a yearning or aspiration of which they were not previously aware. Transformational leaders would include Franklin D. Roosevelt, Gandhi, Martin Luther King, Nelson Mandela, and those who led powerful social movements.

Transformational leaders are present in business. Pierre Beaudoin transformed Bombardier from a skimobile company to a transport company and then to an aeronautics company, a huge leap in complexity. Richard Branson leaves the mark of his personality upon his entire portfolio of Virgin companies. Sergei Kiriyenko, the youngest ever premier of Russia, transformed NORSI Oil from an apathetic, bankrupt organization, immobilized by fear, into one that was both vibrant and effective.

In Figure 6.1 we have expressed Burns' distinction as a dilemma. On the vertical axis is the authority of the leader, which becomes corrupted by the unilateral exercise of power from which the populace shrinks. As Lord Acton famously said, "Power corrupts and absolute power corrupts absolutely." On the horizontal axis is the degree

**Figure 6.1**  Transactional versus Transformational leadership

of participation, which can lead to lost or abdicated leaders whose authority is taken over by those they are supposed to lead. The incident pictured at bottom right actually occurred when Puritan pilgrims to the New World replaced their captain while at sea. Between this arbitrary and failed leadership lies the transactional leader, as a kind of compromise, tolerated because he or she provides the necessities of life, routine work for routine pay. At the top right is the transformational leader, whose followers "stand on the shoulders of giants" and are elevated through having experienced them.

Transformation is mutual, not unilateral. Leaders and followers resonate to one another. The experience of having thousands or millions of people pin their hopes upon you, identify with you, express themselves through you is profoundly significant for the leader, as it is for the led. A leader is collective determination writ large. The boundaries dissolve in a surge of human spirit bound together by shared purpose. When you come to think of it, authoritative leadership grows out of widespread participation. How can you represent thousands of people if you are not deeply immersed in their aspirations and desires? How can they resonate to you unless you articulate their innermost feelings?

## ABSTRACT, CONCRETE, OR "PORPOISE" LEADERSHIP?

Jim Morgan, the CEO of Applied Materials, created the phrase "porpoise leadership." It is similar in many ways to the Helicopter capacity described in Chapter 2. Just as a dolphin leaps and plunges, so must modern leaders move above the fray to see the corporation spread out beneath them, but they must also dive down deep to make critical examinations of details. You cannot always be at the top of the abstraction ladder at a distance from concrete reality. You need to get your hands on the day-to-day minutiae of organizational life, to walk your talk, and be seen to do what you have been articulating.

This capacity has also been called "zooming." As with the zoom lens of a camera you need to assure yourself that quality is being achieved to the most exacting standards. You need to stand where the customer will stand, product in hand, reliant on 100 percent delivery of what was promised. All too easily leaders confuse the abstraction ladder with the status ladder. Ladders deal in grand abstractions and noble ideals, leaving implementation to minions. But the porpoise leader is down there, where the tire meets the road, engaged in minute inspection. The dilemma is pictured in Figure 6.2.

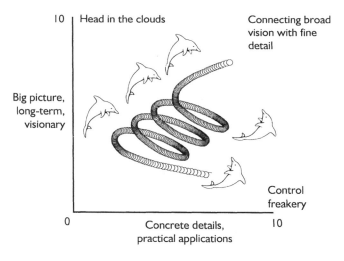

**Figure 6.2** Abstract, concrete, or "porpoise" leadership

## LORD, SERVANT, OR SERVANT LEADER?

Should leaders lord it over people, striking heroic poses, or act humbly? Is there another way, leading by giving service to others?

In business the servant leader is relevant wherever the mission of the company is to give service to customers. When leaders serve subordinates well, those subordinates can model how they should behave in the same way with their customers. If leaders are not too proud or too high to serve others, then why should employees not imitate them? Servant leaders are forever trying to give their status away, only to get it back again in gratitude and admiration. The more you serve the more you lead your fellow servers.

Servant leadership is powerful in East Asian cultures, especially Japan. The leader "gives" followers more than they could conceivably repay; they become obligated as a result and more compliant to the leader's wishes. Servant leadership is a highly ambiguous concept, since we typically associate service with subordination. We depict it in Figure 6.3.

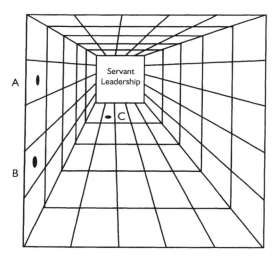

**Figure 6.3** Servant Leadership

Is the servant leader at the bottom of a deep shaft, or at the apex of a truncated pyramid? The answer is both. The leader has reversed the organizational hierarchy and is serving subordinates as if they were superiors.

Servant leadership was importantly involved in the radical upgrading of cabin staff service on first SAS and then BA. Nick Georgiades, BA's HR director in the early 90s before service again declined, emphasized that staff serving customers should pass on to those customers the way they were themselves treated by supervisors. It is this that makes servant leadership so important. Staff, who like both each other and their supervisors, will spread their *esprit de corps.*

The modesty of this style of leadership is especially important in East Asia. Those who have weight do not throw it around. Indeed they behave as if they were eager to learn from you, as if they had nothing to boast about. People with high status exude modesty which enhances their status; they have nothing to prove. HRM must be very careful not to underestimate servant leaders.

## DEMONSTRATING, FOLLOWING, OR IMPROVING LEADERSHIP?

Certain kinds of leadership are not a permanent possession. They have to be earned and re-earned. This is especially true of leading Incubator cultures in the process of innovation. You can only lead in such a culture by having your creative ideas applauded by others. John Kao of San Francisco's Idea Factory calls it "Jamming" in his book of that title. Roger Harrison, the Berkeley-based consultant, has likened the process to an improvisational jazz band. Any member of the band can try out a new beat or number and the other players will follow the leader if they like it and leave the leader hanging if they do not. Improvised tunes are "bids for leadership" which are accepted or rejected. The band wants to be led not by any identified person but by novelty and improvisation as values. Leadership may change as new ideas and approaches come to the fore. You are "only as good as your last tune."

Improvisational leadership is crucial to self-organizing groups or teams. These have come together to create and whoever proves most innovative becomes the informal leader, whose future leadership will rise or fall depending on the fate of his or her innovation. Entrepreneurs are often improvisational leaders, who sometimes cannot afford to pay employees but offer to share the fate of their companies with them. The employees who join such companies are often there for the sheer thrill of inventing their own futures, balanced on the knife-edge of wealth or catastrophe.

Improvisational leaders have certain key characteristics. They are "hands on," throwing the dice themselves. They are often very reluctant to delegate and may precipitate a succession crisis because they have not had time to mentor or nurture successors. They are often consumed by their own creativity and neglect other organizational functions. The Polaroid Corporation collapsed not long after its charismatic founder, inventor Edwin Land, retired. It lacked alternative leadership and had relegated to obscurity all contributions save those of its brilliant founder.

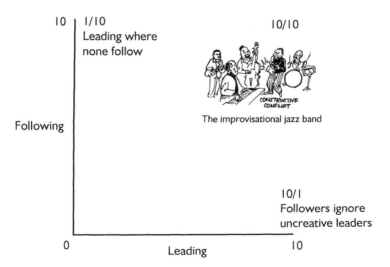

**Figure 6.4** Leading versus Following

In the dilemma shown in Figure 6.4 the jam session reconciles leading with following in the improvisational jazz band where would-be leaders vie for temporary leadership.

## THE LEADER AS AUTHORITY, RESOURCE, OR CONDUCTOR?

Does a leader teach the culture of the organization about how it should behave or does that culture use the leader as its optional resource?

Theories of leadership have changed substantially as a result of the central importance taken on by corporate culture. Increasingly culture is seen as the secret of an organization's success, a phenomenon almost impossible to imitate and very fragile in the hands of those who would acquire it, yet accumulating vital knowledge and learning from ongoing experience. More and more, a skilled leader is seen as managing the values of a culture, while the culture performs the actual work of the corporation as a semi-autonomous living system with its own direction and purpose. How is such leadership exercised? Two metaphors spring to mind, that of the conductor of an orchestra, and the film director or narrator of an ongoing saga.

Any leader who purports to teach subordinates so that they learn faces a serious dilemma. On the one hand they seek to be dynamic, articulate, incisive, commanding, and admired. Most of us have secret, or not so secret, fantasies of attracting wide acclaim. This perfectly understandable ambition is taken a step too far in the symbol of the Magician, or the Sage on the Stage; see the dilemma illustrated in Figure 6.5.

On the other hand, it is an important part of the magical arts that these are not shared with the audience. The aim is not to inform but

**Figure 6.5**  Authority, resource, or conductor

to impress; to make the audience marvel at powers that greatly exceed their own. The magician entertains and/or bamboozles and does not instruct or teach, quite the opposite. The audience must remain naive for the tricks to work. It has been rightly said that charisma is theft. When members of an audience worship the leader, they are "on their knees," literally or metaphorically. They feel unworthy and sinful in the sight of the Great Magician, who has succeeded in drawing attention but not to educating or eliciting from subordinates their latent potentials. Education is from the Latin *educo*: "to lead out." The magician has damaged those minds that needed to be led out.

The strong egalitarian sentiment against manipulative and "magical" leadership has unfortunately led to the opposite extreme, the so called resource person, who is offered to the group as someone to be used or consulted should the group feel fit. In Figure 6.5 we see him as little more than an umbrella stand, while his players "do their own thing," often with discordant results.

The reconciliation of this dilemma is the conductor, top right. This is not the composer, nor the commander-in-chief whose orders must be awaited before anyone acts. Members of an orchestra are professionals who know how to play their instruments better than their conductor does. They have the score in front of them. Each knows the part they have to play in the harmony of instruments as a whole. Note that we are speaking of harmony, not unison, the aesthetic blending of diverse instruments that nonetheless complement each other. The conductor does not tell people what to do but conducts the timings and the combinations of their contributions, conducting the culture of the orchestra. That culture does the rest.

On this topic there was an interesting experiment by Kevin Kelly on how one might best lead a connected network of professional persons, each needing autonomy. A computer game was projected upon the screen in which a submarine had to weave its way through an underwater minefield. Each member of the audience was given a

**Figure 6.6**  Steering the submarine

console that would direct the submarine port or starboard so as to skirt the mines and make it go faster or slower. It was found that the audience behaved like an "intelligent swarm" going the shortest way around the mines, given the current trajectory of the submarine. The system had been wired so that the concerted judgments of an audience of two hundred people would steer the submarine and for the most part they did this with consistent success.

But there was one important exception. In a few cases the submarine was heading straight towards a mine, and half the audience decided to skirt it by steering to port, while the other half of the audience decided to do so by steering to starboard. When this happened the weight of decisions cancelled each other out and the submarine crashed into the mine and was destroyed.

This situation was obviated if one clear voice from the audience announced the sequence by which this dilemma would be reconciled: "OK people, we steer left!" This is roughly the intervention of an orchestra conductor and has to do with timing and unanimous action. It well illustrates how cultures steer themselves, yet still respond to instructions.

## DIRECTING, FACILITATING, OR DEVELOPING CULTURE?

The film director is a useful metaphor for modern leadership because it is once again a model for leading highly competent professionals, actors in some cases earning millions of dollars. These professionals know, often better than the director, how – say – Scarlet O'Hara in *Gone with the Wind* would behave when trying to wheedle money out of Rhett Butler. Such situations were probably in the experience of Vivien Leigh herself and, as a professional, it was her judgment that had to be employed.

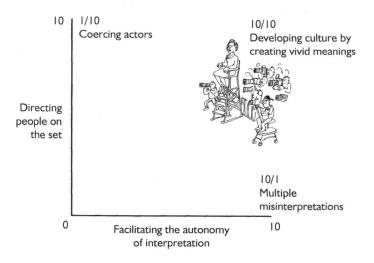

**Figure 6.7**   Directing versus Facilitating

The director sets the scene, retells the story and the place of this scene in the story, since a film is shot in small pieces with the continuity created later. The director decides whether the scene is good enough so that no more takes are necessary. In short, the director presides over the culture of the film set and makes sure that everyone understands the parts they are playing in the unfolding scenes.

Some directors use no script. They explain the situation to the actors and have them project themselves into the scene, using their own words and emotional responses. Actors may object to words or actions they are required to make: "I would never say that. It's not in character." A wise director listens and may change the words.

The film director steers an optimum path between the autonomy of interpretation and directing people on the set. Her job in Figure 6.7 is creating vivid meanings. The director has to steer between coercing actors at top left and multiple misinterpretations at bottom right.

It is the director's job to organize autonomous interpretations, guiding these with promptings and advice until vivid meanings emerge.

But so far we have had little to say about narrative. Every corporation is an unfinished story, which its leaders are trying to steer to a triumphant ending. Good leaders understand scenes, narratives and dramas. For example Richard Branson, a masterful storyteller, is featured in the following Capsule Case.

## CAPSULE CASE
### Richard Branson's virginity

Richard Branson of Virgin is in many ways the kind of leader portrayed in this chapter. Although a strong personality whose personal reputation is very much the brand which unites the disparate units of his empire, he remains a strong exponent of participation. Because of his dyslexia he must rely on others to supply the skills he lacks and explain complex operations. He is very much an "ideas man," yet we find him constantly at the sharp end – on one occasion dressed as a can of Virgin Cola in Tokyo's main railway station.

He is a strong exponent of servant leadership and when traveling on Virgin Atlantic, he serves meals with the cabin staff instead of relaxing in Upper Class. A great believer in ceaseless innovation he encourages staff in all his companies to come up with entrepreneurial business ideas, many of which he "spins out," using a mixture of his own equity funds and their own.

His motto is "have fun!" and business after business is built around colorful ideas like "Virgin Brides." He explains that when employees enjoy being with each other, a culture is created which customers enjoy. He systematically avoids bureaucracy by dividing companies that grow too big and having them compete against each other instead. He is a great believer in informal, intimate behavior.

He has a great nose for a narrative or story, whether he is bidding to run Britain's Lottery, fighting against British Airways, or rescuing a BA crew from Kuwait when they were trapped by the Iraqi invasion. He devised a plan to blow up land mines using blimps, in honor of Princess Diana's campaign. He defuses criticism by telling hilarious stories against himself, as in his autobiography entitled *Losing My Virginity*.

He deliberately courts controversy and turbulence whether he is aloft in his balloon, or trying to save Concorde from being mothballed. Again and again he emerges unscathed, even when his bid fails, as did his offer to run the UK National Lottery at no profit. He wins public sympathy. When he discovered that shareholders might prevent him being as generous to employees and customers as he felt appropriate, he bought back the shares and returned his companies to private ownership.

LEGO, which was voted "the toy of the millennium" in the year 2000, was conceived as a child's ongoing construction in front of a parental audience. It was, according to Christian Majgaard, a way of attracting admiration to early feats of construction and engineering. The family would participate in the child's learning; the toy was part of an ongoing project, an unfolding scene.

We have to be clear about how much more valuable an entire story is to everyone than the separate things or elements within the story. We see this if we examine the spin-off sales of blockbuster movies. Garments, figurines, lunch boxes, toys, games, and computer games have a hard time appealing to customers, even with high quality graphics. But place the images in the context of known stories like *The Lion King, Sesame Street*, the *Lord of the Rings,* or one of the Harry Potter movies and every image takes on narrative power. This dilemma is illustrated in Figure 6.8.

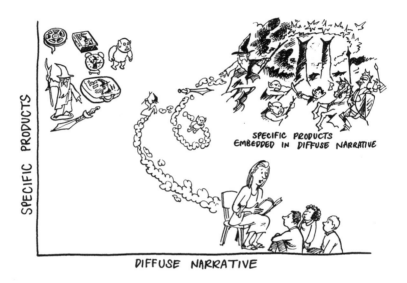

**Figure 6.8** Narrative power – Specific products versus Diffuse narrative

What we sell are specific items, but a known narrative gives to them a diffuse meaning and joins them to one another in a reenactment of remembered scenes.

If stories sold to consumers have so much power, it seems a pity that relatively few business leaders have woven stories around their own progress, although there are notable exceptions. Steve Jobs of Apple, Donald Burr of People Express, Jack Welch of GE, Richard Branson of Virgin, Jan Carlzon of SAS are a few that spring to mind.

It is perhaps not wise to assume a heroic pose; some of those listed are now fallen. Sharing an ongoing sense of adventure with your own people and giving them a sense of destiny, like that felt by the women in the Hawthorne Experiment, is highly advantageous.

## INNER-DIRECTED, OUTER-DIRECTED OR NAVIGATING TURBULENCE?

Should leaders plough courageously through the waves like the Titanic, or spend most their energies dodging icebergs and responding to hazards?

Japanese executives in the 70s and 80s liked to call themselves "the white water men." There is a cross-cultural background to this experience. Japanese culture is overwhelmingly outer-directed; see the seven dimensions in Chapter 3. Japan found itself competing in a capitalist system, invented elsewhere, and preponderantly fast following strategies in the West, earning its profits from more effective manufacturing and from the refinement *(kaizen)* of techniques invented in the West.

All of this convinced Japanese leaders that they were river rafting or otherwise navigating a raging river of world turbulence. Paddles out, they desperately sought to steer between rocks and continue riding on the flood tide of economic events. It is most important when leading an organization not to exaggerate your own powers of inner-direction. This is a clear example of "rearranging the deck chairs on the Titanic." The ship was going down but very few of the passengers could believe it; several boats were lowered half-empty before the "invincible" ship's doom became apparent.

In modern business you can fail because you are so super-efficient that the environment cannot sustain you. Europe's fishing fleets are being ferociously cut back not because they catch too few fish, but because they catch too many and the more effective the nets the fewer fish there are to breed the next generation. Increasing the capacity of your factory could lead to disaster, simply because fifty companies have done the same at the same moment and there is now chronic over-capacity. All leaders have their calculations knocked sideways by what is happening elsewhere.

However much a culture admires inner direction and self-determination, which as we saw were very pronounced in the cultures of North America, Northwest Europe, Australia and New Zealand, it is necessary to be realistic. No leader is the master of his own fate in a fiercely turbulent ocean, yet drifting helplessly waiting for someone to rescue you is no answer either. The dilemma is set out in Figure 6.9.

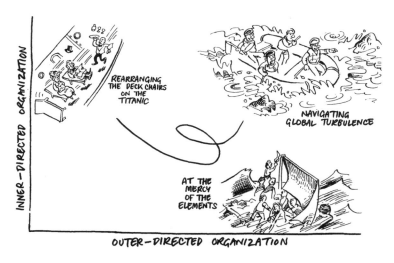

**Figure 6.9** The Inner-directed versus Outer-directed organization

Both Anglo-American inner-direction and East Asian fatalism can spell disaster. The leader in a modern economy has to come to a clear realization of the limits of power. What has happened is that business is now permanent white water; highly turbulent, highly cyclical, and growing worse.

It is this conviction that makes us believe that leadership is *cybernetic*, a word coming from Kybernetes, the Greek for "helmsman." Leaders are constantly setting their compass only to realize that unexpected turbulence has driven the corporation off course and that the compass must be reset. The cybernetic loop faced by a leader in a turbulent environment reads as shown in Figure 6.10.

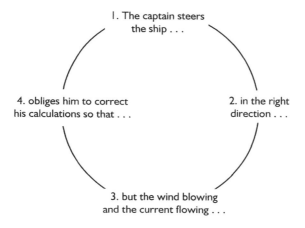

**Figure 6.10** Cybernetic loop in a turbulent environment

To what extent the leader fulfils expectations and to what extent fortunate or unfortunate events wash up in the vicinity of the ship is an unknowable equation. Leaders have to be ready to plan, yet improvise frantically when those plans go wrong, becoming white water navigators.

## KNOWLEDGE OF THE WORLD, OF SELF, OR CYBERNETIC WISDOM?

In the Golden Age of Greece, between approximately 460 BC and the outbreak of the Pelopennesian War against Sparta forty years later, Athens "invented" most of the Western world's civilized arts. That period saw the development of history, poetry, tragic drama, medicine, philosophy, democracy, the rule of law, magnificent architecture, and equally magnificent statuary. This very brief period of history inspired the Renaissance and many later flowerings of creative genius.

So what did Athens have that so many subsequent leaders lacked? The well-known story of Oedipus is told in Figure 6.11. He knew much and solved the Riddle of the Sphinx, who killed herself when her dilemma was resolved. But he did not know who he was, having been abandoned as a child on the mountainside and given to the neighboring Prince of Corinth by the shepherd who found him. Not knowing any of this he killed his real father in a fracas, was crowned king, and married his own mother.

When a terrible plague struck Thebes, a punishment for incest and patricide, Oedipus pledged himself before his subjects to find the truth and banish the "unclean thing" from the city. He was the chief

**Figure 6.11**    Knowledge of the world versus knowledge of yourself

inquirer, the knowledge leader, and even when personally imperiled by what he was discovering, he doggedly completed his quest. When the true horror of his crime was revealed, his wife/mother killed herself, he blinded himself and decreed his own exile.

Oedipus has tried to command events and has failed. He settles for knowing about his place in the world. At the end of Sophocles' *Oedipus Rex* the blinded hero exits the stage tapping the ground before him with a stick. This is a very potent metaphor. Oedipus's final realization is that no person can predict the future or know what triumph or disaster it will bring. The most any leader can do is lead people in the process of learning about their shared environment and this is done by "walking on three legs," the third of which ceaselessly probes the way ahead, constantly testing the leader's assumptions and receiving feedback from outside.

Oedipus exits the stage as a living system, which will never cease to test its environment, a flawed man who has learned to live with the inevitability of error and the need to correct his aims.

## COMMAND, CONTROL, OR DELEGATED AUTONOMY?

Thus far we have acknowledged no insuperable barriers to business leaders being as good as their capacities can make them. We have argued that leaders must develop themselves and learn but we have not identified any limits to that learning. There are dilemmas, of course, differing from one industry to another and from one culture to another, but with enough skill and enough power are there any reasons why leadership should not develop indefinitely? Cannot HRM develop leaders with a clear conviction of being on the right lines? Above all no serious limitations to a leader's power have been assumed. Such limitations have recently arisen, and they bode ill.

In recent years there has arisen a significant threat not only to business leadership, but to the future, if any, of the learning organization. HRM must face this challenge if it is not to find its function seriously diminished along with the humanity of the workplace. We refer to the rise of shareholders to power, a group notable – as Fons has often pointed out – for its failure to share.

The Canadian psychiatrist Elliot Jacques was the first to point out an important aspect of leadership. Those with good leadership potential have a very different orientation to time. Their "time-span of discretion," that is, the period of present to future time for which they seek responsibility, is much longer than that of other managers. Jacques found that Pentagon generals, for example, accepted responsibility for the next ten to twenty years, even where they would be obliged to retire long before that.

Investment in technologies vital to the future has a long time-line. If to lead is to be out in front, then great leaders are concerned to gain and hold that lead for decades, to commit their lives to long-term goals. Jacques found he could predict leadership potential in quite young people, by looking at how far ahead they envisioned their plans and actions.

Jacques argued that "felt fair pay" for work correlated consistently with the time span of discretion, how long you were left alone to get on with your job without being supervised. In business we all have to be supervised by those who are directly responsible to shareholders *and* we all want as much discretion and payment for that discretion as we can get. Those with strong leadership potential are especially keen to be supervised at more infrequent intervals. In dilemma terms it is a simple contrast between responsibility on the vertical axis and autonomy on the horizontal axis, as in Figure 6.12.

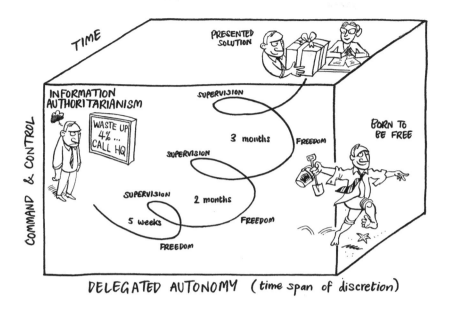

**Figure 6.12**   Leadership and time

The degree of autonomy has to do with the distance between the rotations of the helix, since every time the helix turns up again the manager is supervised. Every time it turns down, another interval of autonomy has begun. All leadership must depend on the amount of autonomy granted to persons to exercise leadership. They are "free" within their time-spans of discretion.

## SHAREHOLDERS' CREATURES, MANAGERS' CHAMPIONS, OR WEALTH CREATORS?

Over the last few years there has been a dramatic power shift at the heart of American capitalism, which threatens to have a dire effect upon corporate leadership and its all-important sense of time. For much of the twentieth century the managerial corporation was more powerful than those who owned shares in it. The shareholder was paid dividends but the power to direct the company remained with senior managers, who ran that company mostly for their own bene-fit, buying off union pressure with higher wages. In *The Modern Corporation and Private Property* (1932), Adolph Berle and Gardner Means chronicled this somewhat unequal relationship.

But with the Reagan–Thatcher revolution of the 80s and 90s, the pendulum swung back. The diagnosis of slow growth in the USA and Britain was blamed on insufficient attention to the supply side of the economy, that is, to insufficient rewards to equity share-holders and those who supplied capital. What was required to right this situation was a heavy dose of profit maximization on the share-holders' behalf. This change signaled a major rise in the power of financial markets and the predatory acquisition of underperforming companies.

Unfortunately, the financial markets are exceedingly short term in their outlook. In fact their interest in the performance and survival of particular companies in the longer term is almost negligible. Whether companies succeed or fail there are profits to be made from the process of one taking over another.

Many shareholders, perhaps most if those participating in Pension Funds are included, do not even know in which companies their money is invested. They are "absentee landlords" with no participa-tion in the wealth-creating communities they "own," if only for a week or a few hours before their shares are traded. A system in which absentees have more rights than those present, especially those who have dedicated a lifetime to a company or industry, plan-ning years ahead how best to serve it, is deeply troubling.

Nor are we talking about ownership that is only abstract. Consider two phenomena which should give us pause. When a company declares a plan for redundancies the share price typically jumps, not always but in the vast majority of cases. If this was a judgment on the effectiveness of the cuts we might expect a mixed verdict. Sometimes management would cut out the fat, sometimes the muscle. Verdicts would go both ways.

That the verdict on redundancies is overwhelmingly positive has another meaning, we suggest. Shareholders believe that wealth is being transferred from employees' pockets to their own. Now this has an effect on bonus payments to senior managers, which are often tied to cost-cutting targets or to the share price. If you cut jobs and the share price rises then you are getting incentives to axe fellow employees from your shareholders.

Consider a second phenomenon. The salaries and bonuses for chief executives have recently gone through the roof. They have also lost all connection to the success of the company. Pay for performance is for subordinates. Top executives arrange to be paid off whether they succeed or fail and getting rid of them is especially expensive.

The mystery is why the Pension Funds tolerate this. They have the votes, in most cases well over 50 percent, to bring self-serving CEOs to heel. Individual shareholders have voted their indignation many times. We believe that the reason Pensions Funds do not stop this is quite simple. CEOs are extravagantly rewarded for failure and success alike because their real function is to redistribute corporate wealth from employees, with whom they work, to shareholders. Since they live day-to-day with employees, forming natural bonds, it takes major incentive payments to pull their allegiance towards outsiders.

Now, if this is true, and we fear very much that it is, then what price the learning organization and the capacity of its culture to generate knowledge? If you lose one person in ten through redundancies, then this is nine relationships, in which, as we have seen, information is stored. The corporation is soon as full of holes as a colander. With 30 percent turnover in the branches of a bank we know, almost no one is left after three years to remember what the objectives once were.

But perhaps the severest impact is on leaders upon whom shareholders impose their own short-term orientation. If leaders' remuneration is based on the share price at the time when their contracts end, then investments made in the company years before they came are unfairly credited to their brief tenure, while any investments made in the future of the company are credited to their successors. Leaders are unlikely to make these investments if their eyes are on their own payoffs.

They are very unlikely to invest in learning, or training, or better serving customers because all their effects are very indirect. Employees must first learn, then improve, then perform. Better service to customers pays off in the next contract round, perhaps a year away. In contrast, cost-cutting has immediate impacts, improving the balance sheet at once. This is precisely the policy to follow if you are thinking of immediate payoffs.

All this raises very serious problems for the HR department, because its chief role in the corporation may become the declaration of persons as redundant. In this event HR becomes feared, even hated. In the early 90s HR began to locate security departments within its function. This is useful in a situation where employees have half an hour to clear out their desks and return their parking permits; security stands over them to stop them sabotaging their computers in their anger. We should remember that such redundant employees are not being fired for good cause; we have simply discovered that we should not have hired them in the first place. Their anger is justified.

It is no use uttering slogans about growth, empowerment, diversity, learning, culture, relationships, and transformation if your chief reputation is that of a hatchet person, if a call from HR on Friday afternoon means doom.

So far we have talked about reconciliations, but reconciliations have to fight with the process of splitting and disintegration. Henry Mintzberg has argued, at the McKinsey consultants' annual meeting in Cambridge, MA in 2002, that shareholder sovereignty and its replacement of the older system of multiple stakeholders attempting to help each other is causing splits or fissures right through economy and society. Figure 6.13 is an elaboration of the presentation he made to the McKinsey consultants.

In Mintzberg's view there is a "syndrome of selfishness," or what we would call uneven valuing of Egoism–Altruism. This drives a wedge of disparity down through the culture in the shape of grossly unequal shares of wealth. The lean and mean organization spreads discontinuity by multiplying redundant persons, the heroic leader with an astronomic salary disconnects from the humble employees who actually create the wealth, the shareholder disengages from – yet overpowers – the manager. Economic man lords it over social man and society as a whole is fatefully split.

In the Introduction we traced the birth of HRM back to a protest movement against the excesses of Taylorism, which treated human beings as mere adjuncts to machines. We suggest that the reasons for these protests have not yet gone away. Every generation produces the old excesses in a new guise. Where once were the abstractions of all-conquering machines, there now are the abstractions of Finance

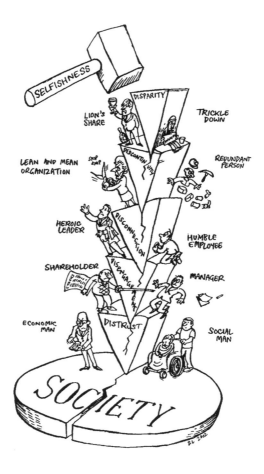

Capitalism and its treatment of human beings as just one more disposable resource.

Without a revived sense of justice and fairness our companies will
not see dilemmas, only people to be disposed of, jobs to be cut. To
see a dilemma in the first place you must see that there are two sides
to an issue and that one side cannot be allowed to ride roughshod
over another side. The most important part of HRM is our humanity
and we believe it to be imperiled by current trends.

# CHAPTER 7

# From personal diagnoses to web-based assessments

**M**ost of the previous six chapters have relied upon diagnosing what the underlying dilemmas in an organization are. Once we know this, then better strategies can be crafted, better teams organized, and the requisite knowledge can be generated. We have challenges against which to develop leaders. But how do we discover the salient dilemmas in the first place? If we misdiagnose a situation nothing else will go right. Let's consider the detection of dilemmas under the following headings:

- The Researcher's and the Informant's models.
- Personal interviewing to elicit dilemmas.
- Single-principle imperialism: The killer questions.
- The seven dimensions and their family resemblances.
- Explaining success in retrospect.
- Feeding the client's dilemmas back to the client.
- Web-based assessments.

Our argument is as follows. The informants, those interviewed, have their own models of reality, models that are good enough to earn them leadership positions in companies more prominent than THT. As researchers we have no right, and would anyway be unwise, to substitute our models for theirs. In fact, we accept the contents of what they perceive, altering only its structure or pattern. This is also the basis of techniques such as client-centered therapy, appreciative inquiry, scenario planning, ethnographic studies, and much consulting practice. The client's perceived world is accepted by the researcher or consultant and these mental models are studied or modified with their owners' permission. In this way clients are left firmly in charge of the realities they perceive, which they modify at their own discretion. What follows describes how we approach this in our own organization; it is, of course, more widely applicable.

At THT we interview to elicit dilemmas because the more informants take any conflict into themselves the easier it will be to reconcile. Even so some informants refuse to admit to any doubts or hesitations and place themselves on one side of a social or institutional conflict. We accept this reality while insisting on the existence of another legitimate perspective. We call those who insist on their own views exclusively single-principle imperialists and we have questions designed to elicit countervailing principles and discover unintended consequences.

Another important way of combining the Researcher's model with the Informant's model is to note family resemblances among dilemmas. The Researcher's model is typically more abstract, while the Informant's model points to a number of concrete manifestations of an abstract principle. Hence both we, at THT, and our clients can share a major dilemma while perceiving this at a different level of abstraction and using different – yet analogous – vocabularies.

Another way of discovering dilemmas is to examine recent successes enjoyed by this or that business unit within the company. Sudden and unexpected success indicates that a major dilemma has been reconciled. It helps to know what this was to give due credit to those who showed leadership.

Without exception, the clients or informants must be fed back the dilemma they supplied to us and must approve the way we have framed it. In our experience clients enjoy seeing their own convictions placed in new contexts and are frequently converted to our context. We finally explore the feasibility of using the web to assess dilemmas.

## THE RESEARCHER'S AND THE INFORMANT'S MODELS

All people have models of social reality, most of them very approximate and loosely held. Without models we cannot organize or classify our experiences. The problem for staff departments or support functions like HR, and the problem for external consultants is that their models are typically different from the models of those who are engaged in day-to-day operations in a company.

Whose model should you use? This book is full of concepts, many of them unfamiliar. Are we insisting that readers abandon their own models and accept ours? Do we advocate change agents doing the same? We do not. Indeed those trying to introduce change greatly limit their effectiveness unless they operate through their informant's models rather than their own. Once we start to demand that others "think as I think" then resistance to change is mobilized. Why should they think as you think?

We happen to believe that the seven dimensions of culture outlined in Chapter 3, the strategic models outlined in Chapter 4, the team roles described in Chapter 5, and the leadership models described in Chapter 6 are all good ways of thinking. But this does not mean we dismiss the way in which someone earning $400,000 a year has learned to think. We could hardly diagnose our client's culture if we did this. We should take our informants' models seriously. How is this to be done?

The first point to grasp is that the dilemma approach is not, first and foremost, an orientation to content, but an orientation to pattern or structure. We are not championing Freud in claiming that the super-ego is in a battle with the id, or championing Jung in claiming that the collective unconscious battles with the libido, or championing the split-brain researchers in claiming that the left and right brain hemispheres compete for dominance. Nor do we disagree with Freud, Jung, and split-brain researchers. They are all our informants as well, and very brilliant too.

What we note is that while all three have different mental models, all three see dilemmas and believe that their patients must somehow resolve these. We leave to these luminaries the exact description of the dilemmas they have encountered, and concentrate instead on how the bifurcations they experience might be reconciled.

What we try to do at THT is frame the dilemmas our informants tell us about, using our structures of dilemma (or bifurcation) and reconciliation. We let them provide the content, while we put that content in novel, non-intrusive configurations. This allows and encourages our informants to maintain their current initiatives and to further their convictions. We are trying to help them achieve their chosen ends by qualifying the ways in which those ends are formulated. We do, of course, alter their formulations by how we frame these, but very rarely are there any objections to this process. We leave them substantially in charge of their own models of reality.

This is a very important point and goes to the heart of participant observation, appreciative inquiry or "listening with the third ear." If you wish to change a person or an organization you must go with the momentum of their own purposes. They are there to achieve their aims, not yours. Together you may be able to construct a new social reality.

## PERSONAL INTERVIEWING TO ELICIT DILEMMAS

Personal interviewing one-on-one is expensive and time consuming. However, it may be the only way of eliciting dilemmas that are latent within the organization but not widely discussed by its members. Many organizations have not got a handle on their sources of dissatisfaction. They know something is not working but they do not know why, and they hesitate to identify a problem for which they have no solution. To do so may seem "negative."

At THT we do not usually ask informants to give us their dilemmas; this sounds too much like muckraking or searching for something that is wrong. We conduct client-centered interviews while thinking "dilemmas" in our own minds. If you do this you will swiftly detect any ambivalence, qualification, hesitation, inner conflict, or conflicting testimony with other informants. It is very important to move any conflict from a place between people to a place within the individuals concerned. We can often reconcile the conflicts we have internalized, but we may be incapable of reconciling conflicts where we have already taken sides and pledged our support to one faction.

If, in your style of interviewing, you can make it acceptable for your informants to feel conflicted, then you will learn more and more about these inner conflicts as they come to trust you. Interviews should last at least an hour or more, since it takes time for trust to build. Many informants believe that to be conflicted or feel ambivalent is a sign of weakness and indecision, so you must strive to show interest and approval of any doubts expressed by your informant. Interviews must be confidential on the subject of who said something while being open about what was said. You begin to discover the culture of the organization as these patterns repeat themselves. If three or four informants sense the same tensions, you know you are on to something.

Clues to the dilemmas of the organization are often found in humor, stories, dismissals, and metaphors. Let's discuss each one. Humor in the form of jokes, cartoons pinned on the walls of cubicles, or even graffiti will, by definition, feature the sudden clash of two very different perspectives. "JFDI" (just f***ing do it). "BOHICA" (bend over, here it comes again) are jokes about situations in an organization that cause people distress. JFDI is about the clash of one's own convictions with those of superiors. BOHICA is about the surfeit of change programs that merely cause inconvenience.

Corporate stories are often more significant if they are *not* funny. A much-repeated unfunny story is intended to teach you something about the organization rather than entertain you. For example, a story was circulated during the British author's time at Harvard Business School. Three students submitted identical essays to the young women who graded written analyses. They received three very different grades, which was supposed to show how arbitrary and unfair the grading system was.

But the administration promptly put its own spin on this story. The three students submitting identical essays were caught "cheating" and dismissed. There is a dilemma within each story and another dilemma between these stories, which have dramatically differing interpretations of the students' motives. If you try to expose the unfairness of the system, you lay yourself open to accusations of plagiarism. Perhaps the real dilemma was that young women just out of college were often grading the work of more experienced men. What is genuinely wrong may not be admitted by any of the disputants, mired as they are in politics.

Any good story has a succession of crises, which are happily or tragically resolved by protagonists breaking out of dilemmas. Hence stories are good gateways to discovering dilemmas and to studying the kinds of reconciliations of which that culture approves. If the hero simply slays monsters or negotiates solutions agreeable to all parties, this will illustrate what the culture most admires about its leaders.

A recent, unexpected dismissal of a prominent employee may give you important clues to the norms of the organization since it is likely that the person violated those norms and that the drastic action of dismissal was deemed necessary to maintain and emphasize that norm. Studying such phenomena has the added advantage of reminding you where the land mines are, so that you do not step on them yourself. Norms are often invisible until violated, at which point the culture acts to protect itself.

Metaphors used in interviews are important clues to dilemmas, since a metaphor draws attention to the likeness between unlike characteristics. A metaphor is in some ways the same and yet also different from its reference point. One interviewee told THT: "We have some really good machine tools on this floor, oases of excellence in a sea of chaos." According to this metaphor there were small sections of the plant that were excellently tooled but the plant as a whole had logistics that were turbulent and chaotic. Such phrases lend themselves easily to mapping, as in Figure 7.1.

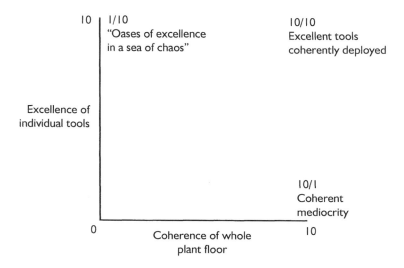

**Figure 7.1**   Excellence of individual tools versus coherence of whole plant

Note that we use the Informant's model in the shape of our client's own metaphor. Yet at the same time we frame it with two axes. The excellence of individual tools is on the vertical axis and the coherence of the whole plant floor is on the horizontal axis. In this way the Informant's model and the Researcher's model are joined like picture and frame. We also discover what the problem is, not enough coherence and logistics to match the quality of some tools. In all probability, work-in-process inventory is piling up on the floor.

## SINGLE-PRINCIPLE IMPERIALISM: THE KILLER QUESTIONS

What do you do when the person you are interviewing thinks in straight lines? Most people, as we have seen, regard values as things or "goods" (good things). Just as it is better to have $1 million than $500,000 so it's better to have more courage, more perseverance, more get-up-and-go. When you interview such people you find that they do not like dilemmas very much. They are "doing their thing" and you are casting doubt on how worthwhile this is.

What you get in such interviews is single-principle imperialism. The company does not just do well on industry benchmarks, it does *magnificently*. Indeed, such informants see better scores on higher benchmarks stretching up into the blue yonder. Last year they took 20 percent off the costs of two business units and suddenly realized that these cuts were just the beginning of a campaign of slash and burn. Next year they will save $60 million, not $30 million. The financial markets are delighted.

These people speak as if higher standards and cutting costs could go on indefinitely. They are charging down one-way streets, shouting, "more, better, best!" But it rarely helps to tell such people they are wrong. In fact, they are half right. Benchmarks are very useful and often worth attaining. Costs can usually be pruned even further.

We ask ourselves what the other side of these one-dimensional virtues is. Were you to beat every benchmark in sight, what might you miss? In an orgy of cost cutting, what contrasting values might be overlooked? It is this that leads to the "killer question." Knowing that enthusiasms tend to be one-dimensional, you inquire about the other end of this continuum. Of the rabid cost-cutter you ask: "But what about quality? Aren't you afraid that it might suffer if you go on cutting costs?" Of the avid bench marker you ask: "But do customers still want what these benchmarks measure? In the last year how many benchmarks have you originated out of new customer needs?"

There is often a long, awkward silence following such questions. Your informant has beaten benchmarks because they were "there." It never occurred to him to question their relevance to customers. He cut costs because this showed up in his performance contracts, while loss of future quality could be years away, after his retirement.

But, of course, killer questions restore the dilemma you were looking for, even if your informant does not initially see it. Now the issue is Cost versus Quality, Benchmarks versus Customers. The Informant will usually agree that quality and customers are important, so that you have turned one-dimensional values into two dimensions.

Most single-principle imperialisms are hidden within the latest tools used in the HR department, or made into a "deliverable" by consultants and sold as a sure-fire technique. Hence Managing for Value, now used by many banks, measures the economic profit each manager has made, which is part of his or her performance contract. This is, of course, important but it measures what the manager has received, not what they have contributed to other business units. Often a cheap loan is extended to a customer on condition that mandates are also given to other business units for higher-margin work.

Under Managing for Value the beneficiaries of such arrangements would prosper at the expense of the main contributor who extended scarce capital.

Nearly all performance indicators are likewise flawed. British hospitals can "cut their waiting lists" if a very short interview with a junior doctor precedes a longer wait for a consultant, although patients have simply been transferred to another (unmeasured) waiting list. As previously noted, some British hospital units assessed by the number of child deaths occurring in their wards ship out those near death to specialist units so that they die in another jurisdiction. None of this has anything to do with improved medical practice and can be very hard on parents.

Many psychologists and psychiatrists speak of the unconscious. Many of the core assumptions of culture are not fully conscious but latent or tacit. We believe that the so-called unconscious is created by the fear of dilemmas and contradictions. Because people do not think you can be morally pure and erotic at the same time, the erotic tends to be repressed where it turns nasty, thereby "proving" its impurity. Similarly, many managers do not believe that they can be certain and doubt, determined and flexible, a strong leader and encourage participation, a competitor and cooperator. One in each pair of these values has to be subordinated to the other. It is, alas, a short step from repressing one side of a dilemma within you to oppressing that same value in other people. You must control your personal views, and there they are, expressed in a politically incorrect joke; you must control your own compassion, or you won't be able to fire people – and there it is personified in that pathetic subordinate trying to ingratiate himself with you. We attack in others what we reject in ourselves.

# THE SEVEN DIMENSIONS AND THEIR FAMILY RESEMBLANCES

Each of our seven dimensions, detailed in Chapter 3, have a host of "family resemblances," that is, corporate dilemmas, familiar to managers, but less abstract. There is no inherent reason why we, as researchers, should not have one of the seven dimensions in the back of our minds, while our informant tells us about a more concrete example of a dimension that has occurred in their own workplace. Let's look at the seven dimensions in this light.

## 1. Universalism versus Particularism

This seeks to discover one's prime allegiance to rules and rule-bound classifications or to exceptional, unique circumstances and relationships. Within a corporation the conflicts are typically as follows:

| | | |
|---|---|---|
| Low cost strategy | versus | Premium value strategy |
| Economies of scale | versus | Economies of scope |
| Legal contracts | versus | Loose interpretations |
| Developing core competences | versus | Closeness to customers |
| Standards and benchmarks | versus | Latent needs |
| Emphasis on globalism | versus | Emphasis on localism |
| Taylorism or Fordism | versus | Job-shop, Hand-crafting |
| Common "platforms" | versus | Optional variety |
| "One best way" | versus | "Several cultural paths" |
| Americanism | versus | Regionalism |
| Level playing fields | versus | Changing the game |
| Human rights | versus | Special relationships |
| Extending rules | versus | Discovering exceptions |
| Grand strategies | versus | Unique services |

Universalism versus Particularism is great if you are a sociologist, but most managers are interested in one or more of the "family resemblances" beneath. Should your strategy aim for low cost (the universal appeal of cheapness) or for premium value (the advantage of particular scarcity and uniqueness)? Are you after the economies of scale or the economies of scope? Will emphasizing higher standards and universal benchmarks make you more competitive or should you be searching out the latent needs of ever-changing customers? Will you do better by extending your rules to cover more cases or by noting exceptions? This is the stuff of dilemmas found through interviews. The Informant's model is typically less abstract than the Researcher's model, but there is no reason why both people should not share both perspectives, so that the two models illumine each other.

## 2. Individualism versus Communitarianism

This measures the extent to which managers see the individual employee and shareholder as paramount, their development, enrichment, and fulfillment; or to what extent the corporation, customers, and the wider community should be the beneficiaries of all personal allegiances. This leads to the following conflicts of opinion:

| | | |
|---|---|---|
| Profit strategy | versus | Market share strategy |
| Rivalry | versus | Mutuality |
| Competition | versus | Cooperation |
| Rights | versus | Duties |
| Self-assertion | versus | Self-negation |
| Egoism | versus | Altruism |
| Personal gains, promotion and income | versus | Group support and social stimulation |
| Responsibility for self | versus | Responsibility for others |
| Dissent | versus | Loyalty |
| Identifying best practice | versus | Disseminating best practice |
| Originating ideas | versus | Refining useful products |
| Winner takes all | versus | Winnings shared |

Once again, your interviewing skills will increase if you recognize that the twelve dichotomies above are all variations on Individual-ism versus Communitarianism. Hence, profit strategy champions the individual shareholder while market share strategy, popular throughout East Asia, considers how much has been done for the community. Competition weeds out the best individual or unit, while cooperation sustains the less capable and helps to improve them. Your rights are what you demand from others; your duty is what you give.

Individualism and Communitarianism may be more abstract and hence inclusive of other variations, but they are not better nor truer than other dilemmas. It is usually best to deal with the dilemma as your informant sees it. If the work group is worried that loyalty is being defined as not voicing dissent, then this is the problem for that group. Their thinking has made it so and the interviewer must accept this.

## CAPSULE CASE
### The Cooperating Individualists of the Saturn/Titan space mission

THT were interviewing several space scientists engaged on a mission to explore Saturn and Titan, both at their conference in Venice and at the Jet Propulsion Lab in Pasadena. As research-ers, we were struck by how very individualist they were and yet, paradoxically, how reliant each person was on the rest of their scientific community. Unless the spacecraft reached its destination and operated as was intended, decades of work in many scientific disciplines would be wasted. They had been working for twenty years or more on the experiments that would be performed in space.

"We are latter day Argonauts," said one interviewee. "If you remember your Greek myths, the Argonauts consisted of heroes and princes from more than thirty City States, who joined together to sail into the Black Sea in search of the Golden Fleece, but more prosaically in search of trading rights. All Argonauts secured these rights for their cities."

From such statements we quickly guessed that there would be several operational issues with "family resemblances" to the dilemma of Individualism versus Communitarianism – and indeed there were. The following statements were highly pertinent as to how this dilemma was being resolved in different forms.

"Yes, we know who made the mistake. It was an Italian sub-contractor but no, we don't cast blame on any one unit. We constantly review each others' work and all our reviews missed this crucial error. So it's everyone's responsibility. We should have looked out better for our partners. Blame helps no one. Being alert to each others' problems is the answer."

"We review, and review, and review each others' work, squeezing out the doubts and imperfections. Peer review is the name of the game."

"All our Principal Scientists are heroes in their own fields. In each case their life's work is riding on this one spacecraft and its various instruments. But we also have Interdisciplinary Scientists, whose job is to weave the experiments together to find whole-system solutions. In fact, it takes multiple perspectives from several sciences to arrive at solutions to planetary puzzles."

"All scientific experiments aboard the spacecraft originally negotiated with NASA on cost, volume, and power requirements. But when the instruments had been perfected some wanted more power, some wanted more costs to be allocated, and some wanted more space. Rather than arbitrate between these demands, a trading system was set up with a common 'currency.' Those with too much money could trade this for power or space. Those with more space than they needed could exchange it for greater power or cost allocations. Rising prices signaled scarcities. The various units self-organized into a coherent whole."

"When we realized that a serious error had been made, but that it was still possible to reprogram the orbiter from ground control, the Recovery Team went into action. Never have so few, working closely together, saved the scientific reputations and working lives of so many. That team saved the whole mission!"

"I guess we are all pioneers and explorers, but unlike our predecessors we have to work together. The meaning of thousands of lives hangs in one perilous package hurtling through space. I have never felt so exposed as an individual, yet the efforts of my companions are infinitely precious to me. We're all in this together. The real breakthroughs will come from comparing the images evoked by different instruments."

"To me this is the culmination of the European venture. For centuries we fought for personal advantage, nation against nation, now we are discovering together. It is just as exciting and infinitely more enlightening."

"Who would have guessed that seventeen nations, three space agencies, governments, universities, and private enterprises could all have cooperated to pull this off? What about the Tower of Babel, the League of Nations, the 'impotence' of the current UN? Something very important is happening here. Against all odds nations are cooperating as never before. What can we learn from this?"

These statements are all "family resemblances" of the highly abstract, Researcher's model of Individualism versus Communitarianism. It seems that this project has found a number of workable solutions to how (usually) rival disciplines, cultures, nations and institutions can work together on a superordinate goal which dwarfs their petty divisions, yet unites their separate interests. Interviewing for dilemmas can produce insights of high quality.

The Researcher's model and the Informant's model can be arranged as follows:

| Researcher's Model | Individualism | versus | Communitarianism |
|---|---|---|---|
| Guiding Metaphor | The Argonauts | versus | Quest for the Golden Fleece |
| Informants' Models and Family resemblances | Mistake made by one unit | versus | Oversight by all units |
| | Individual opportunity | versus | Review, review, review by peers |

| | | |
|---|---|---|
| Principal scientists | versus | Interdisciplinary scientists |
| Individual negotiations | versus | Trading system |
| Serious error | versus | Recovery Team |
| Pioneers and explorers | versus | Reliant on one common project |
| Multi-culturally diverse "Babel" of individuals | versus | One superordinate goal and new world order |

## 3. Specific versus Diffuse

This measures the tendency to analyze, reduce, and break down the field of experience, or to synthesize, augment, and construct patterns of experience. The conflicts are as follows:

| | | |
|---|---|---|
| Text | versus | Context |
| Bottom line | versus | General goodwill |
| Bullet points | versus | Connotations |
| Piecework incentives | versus | Social rewards |
| Statistical breakdowns | versus | *Esprit de corps* |
| Letter of the Law | versus | Spirit of the Law |
| Data, codification | versus | Concepts and models |
| Making reports | versus | Establishing rapport |
| Get to the point | versus | Circle the issue |
| Results-oriented | versus | Process-oriented |
| Objective | versus | Intuitive |
| Facts | versus | Relations |

Very few bosses speak of Specific versus Diffuse. They are much more likely to show their specificity in other ways, saying things like "Give me the facts without window dressing," "I want to see your results, not listen to excuses," and "Why don't you get to the point?"

In each of these cases the speaker wants specific data without quali-fications and shows distinct signs of single-principle imperialism since all texts lie within contexts that give them meaning. In con-trast, a manager from East Asia may feel that his relationship with a customer is far more crucial than the latest profit statement. Profit derives from the relationship.

## 4. Neutral versus Affective

This concerns the legitimacy of showing or controlling emotions while at work.

| | | |
|---|---|---|
| Detached | versus | Enthusiastic |
| Serious | versus | Humorous |
| Professional | versus | Engaged |
| "Don't get personal" | versus | "Do get personal" |
| Poker-faced | versus | Transparent |
| Praise is taboo, | versus | Praise is lavish, |
| e.g., "I am not a child" | | e.g., "brilliant, terrific" |
| Long pauses | versus | Frequent interruptions |

We are especially prone to express emotion in indirect ways. For example, jokes are used to discharge feelings and some people talk about feeling anger without showing it. The issue of how much pas-sion should be revealed is typically discussed in the seven contrasts listed above. The issue is, in fact, a lot more complex than whether emotions should be hidden or revealed. Many cultures, especially in East Asia, are very respectful of human feelings – yet soft-pedal these to suggest "feelings too deep for words."

## 5. Inner-directed versus Outer-directed

This concerns the "locus of control." Is it inside each of us, or outside in our environments to which we must adapt? The conflicts are as follows:

| | | |
|---|---|---|
| Authorities are "authors" | versus | Authorities mediate |
| Dauntless entrepreneur | versus | Public benefactor |
| Driven by conscience and conviction | versus | Responsive to outside influence |
| Originate products | versus | Refine products |
| Consensus difficult | versus | Consensus easier |
| Top-down communication sold | versus | Bottom-up communication heeded |
| Bureaucratic hierarchy | versus | Organic hierarchy |
| Quick to invent | versus | Quick to adopt |
| Pioneer industrialist | versus | Fast follower |
| Strategic orientation | versus | Consensus orientation |

In inner-directed cultures like the USA the word "authority" derives from authorship. Those in charge are expected to have originated ideas. In outer-directed cultures, like China and Japan, authorities may be there to receive the ideas of others, so that bottom-up communication can exist in quite hierarchical cultures because it is high status to listen.

The inner-directed leaders want to pioneer and originate strategy. The outer-directed leaders may be content to fast follow and develop consensual relationships with customers. All ten descriptions are equally legitimate.

## 6. Achieved status versus Ascribed status

This is about why status is conferred on people. Is this because they have achieved, or because of what they are? The conflicts here include the following:

| | | |
|---|---|---|
| Pay for performance | versus | Vindication of worth |
| Share options | versus | Basic pay |
| Fast promotion with low attention | versus | Slow promotion with close attention |
| Meritocracy | versus | Human development |
| Status follows success | versus | Status precedes success |

| | | |
|---|---|---|
| "Up or out" | versus | Long-term employment |
| Headhunting | versus | Nurturing people in-house |
| Learning at school | versus | Learning at work |
| Employee of the month | versus | Crown princes of high scholarship |

Why is pay for performance about achieved status, not ascribed status? It rewards what you do, not who you are, and cannot perceive your potential as a person. Headhunters go out to look for achievers. Other cultures treat employees as valuable before they have achieved and hope to develop them. The nine vexed issues listed above are much more likely to turn up in interviews than Achieved versus Ascribed status per se.

## 7. Sequential time versus Synchronous time

This has to do with whether one sees time as passing in a sequence, or coming around again and again. Cultures think of time as a sequence or as a synchronization and coordination. Thus...

| | | |
|---|---|---|
| Taylorism/Fordism | versus | Just in time |
| Do one thing at a time | versus | Do several things |
| Keep strictly to schedule | versus | Be easily distracted |
| Sequential processing | versus | Parallel processing |
| Keep machine running | versus | Reduce inventory |
| Make haste | versus | Make connections |
| Win the race | versus | Shorten the course |

Informants almost never discuss time in high-sounding terms like "sequential." But doing operations fast and doing them just in time, doing them one after the other or at the same time is a lively topic, especially in manufacturing. Modern automobile plants have integrated fast sequences learned from the USA with just in time coordination learned from Japan.

To summarize, if interviewers keep in mind the multiple variations on the seven dimensions, with no fewer than seventy-four dilemmas listed above, then it is possible to think in both the abstractions of the Researcher's models and in the more concrete resemblances of the Informant's models. The Informant's models are, in effect, subsets of the Researcher's models, although they are every bit as important. In time an interviewer learns to spot the contrasts in the minds of the people who are being interviewed. If they want this particular value, what is the contrasting value that they are overlooking? The good interviewer teases out this contrast in the informant's minds by persistent questioning.

## EXPLAINING SUCCESSES IN RETROSPECT

It has never been our position that dilemmas have only been reconciled after we began to identify and write about them. Creative and successful people have reconciled dilemmas since time began. What is new is the modeling of this process, not the process itself. Ask any innovative person how they do it and you are likely to be disappointed. Dilemma reconciliation has been called "flair," "genius," "good judgment," "brilliance," "superlative performance," and so on. When we see it in business we throw money at it and hope it stays around. Very rarely do we understand it or model it so that others can build on these accomplishments or manage the knowledge that emerges.

It follows that most successful accomplishments can be regarded as reconciled dilemmas. Where such achievements have been wrought spontaneously, it can be of value to explain these in retrospect via dilemma theory.

Take, for example, a piece of creative intuition two thousand years old. Archimedes was the chief scientist to the King of Syracuse, who had been given a silver crown. He suspected that it was not pure silver but adulterated by base metals and gave Archimedes the job of finding out if this were true. Archimedes knew the cubic weight of silver and could weigh the crown, but did not know the crown's volume. He would destroy its fine filigree were he to melt it down. Frustrated by his problem, he finally decided to take a bath. As the water rose up the inside of his bathtub he saw the answer. The crown would also displace water equal to its own volume. "Eureka!" he shouted. His breakthrough is depicted in Figure 7.2.

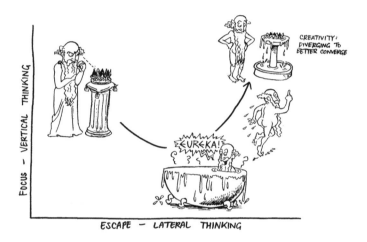

**Figure 7.2** Vertical versus Lateral thinking

We could argue that several dilemmas are involved here; for example, vertical thinking, where you focus hard on the issue, and lateral thinking. You could argue that the conscious mind had interacted with the unconscious, and that Archimedes' thoughts were convergent then divergent. While all these contrasts help us to understand innovative behavior, they are not by themselves enough. The creative connection was unique, never fully explicable by the styles of thinking used. And so it must remain: Dilemma thinking has insights into the process of creativity but cannot guarantee its occurrence.

At THT we have recently accounted for business unit successes at ABN AMRO, the Dutch international bank, by arguing that in each case dilemmas were resolved – albeit quite different ones. We interviewed those responsible for the success and they generally appreciated the system of explanation: "I never knew that I was so smart." This also provides a comparative framework to record successes, manage knowledge, and communicate this to other units.

## FEEDING THE CLIENT'S DILEMMAS BACK TO THE CLIENT

The researcher or interviewer does not have the right to define the client's dilemmas unilaterally, much less impose that definition upon the client and there is no need to do so. Yet in some cases they might have to add the missing half of the dilemma.

Let us take an example. This time we are talking to a single-principle imperialist, although a worried one. Our imperialist thinks sales push is good; you cannot push hard enough. Nevertheless, customers are complaining and that is not good. In this event half the map, or one axis, is your informant's and the second, qualifying part of the map has been supplied to you, as in Figure 7.3.

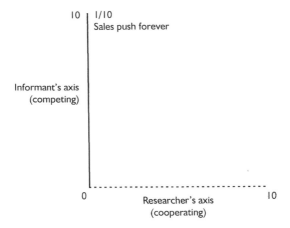

**Figure 7.3** Informant's versus Researcher's axes

Hence, even in the worst case, faced by a linear enthusiast, the map is co-created between the Informant and the Researcher. You do not have to deny the validity of the Informant's values, only qualify these with your own and argue that both are valid. How can the company sell like hell while still pleasing customers?

Accounting for a corporation's successes via dilemma theory is an important step in getting that logic used throughout the corporation so that it becomes a way of managing knowledge in general.

## Web-based assessments

At THT we have had increasing success in recent years in administering assessments electronically over the web. In this event, we ask publicly for dilemmas and paradoxes occurring in the work setting.

As an illustration, our instrument has been designed to draw out some of the basic issues or perceptions that exist in a company before a particular event where they are to be discussed. Using a short, anonymous, web-based questionnaire (WebCue), we compile and analyze the collective information from a specific company. Participants from this company are asked to describe their issues in "on the one hand versus on the other hand" terms; see below for an example.

| On the one hand . . . | On the other hand . . . |
|---|---|
| The company is aiming for global knowledge sharing in order to get consistent forecasts, plans, and expectations on likely outcomes of comparable performance | The company has decentralized sales organizations with the autonomy to fine-tune knowledge to local conditions |

An advantage for using WebCue is, firstly, that all answers remain confidential and are treated anonymously. Participants are allowed to use nicknames when completing the questionnaire. Secondly, filling in the WebCue is not time-consuming; it takes approximately ten minutes to answer the questions. Thirdly, in a very short time a very detailed view is created on the client's problems, and, fourthly, it is relatively easy to capture and process a lot of company data.

## Analyzing dilemmas

When analyzing the WebCue results for a specific company THT first investigates the input. This input is the so-called "raw dilemmas." After that we categorize these dilemmas, using the seven dimensions of culture model as a frame of reference, and as a result we get "principal dilemmas," mostly between 4–8 in number. Finally we try to apply each principal dilemma to a business function, like Human Resources, Strategy, Organizational Structure, etc. We then present both the WebCue output as principal dilemmas and as functional issues to the client.

## The results so far

In the first book in this series, *Business Across Cultures*, we looked at the use of WebCue in eliciting dilemmas; what follows here is therefore a brief illustration. At THT we have been using WebCue since the beginning of 2001, and it is proving a great success. At the moment more than 40 international companies have used it, resulting in around 2000 dilemmas, with more accumulating fast.

For this book we have looked at all the output from WebCue so far; below you will find a summary of our findings, including the six "principal business dilemmas" and how they relate to business functions.

| | % |
|---|---|
| **Dilemma** | |
| Global organization interest versus Local subsidiary interest | 25 |
| Cost versus Investment | 11 |
| Individual department/person versus Total organization/unit | 10 |
| Short-term versus Long-term focus | 8 |
| Internal organization versus External focus on environment | 7 |
| Focus on specific issues versus Breadth of options | 3 |
| Other | 13 |
| **Non-dilemmas** | |
| Lack of integrity/management (complaints about the management) | 10 |
| Lack of integrity/respect (complaints about stakeholders) | 8 |
| Others | 5 |

Here are the dilemmas organized by business function:

| Dilemma/business function | Strategy (%) | Leadership (%) | Knowledge Management (%) | Human Resources (%) | Operations (%) | Organization (%) |
|---|---|---|---|---|---|---|
| Global organization interest versus Local subsidiary interest | 36 | 20 | 16 | 8 | 4 | 24 |
| Cost versus Investment | 63 | 18 | 9 | 9 | – | – |
| Individual department/person versus Total organization/unit | 10 | – | 10 | 30 | 30 | 20 |
| Short-term versus Long-term focus | 75 | 25 | – | – | – | – |
| Internal organization versus External focus on environment | 28 | 29 | 14 | – | – | 29 |
| Focus on specific issues versus Breadth of options | 67 | – | – | – | – | 33 |

These business dilemmas affect the HR function in organizations and it is useful to anticipate these. But there are also some dilemmas that are specific to HR in our database:

1.  Objective observation/evaluation versus Subjective observation/evaluation

2.  Evaluate behavioral differences versus Evaluate intuitive differences

3.  Priority for HR development versus Productivity

4.  BSC as development tool versus BSC as evaluation tool

5.  Development as professional versus Development as generalist

6.  Technical logic versus Business logic

7.  Taking risks versus Avoiding failures

8.  Individual accountability versus Team responsibility

9.  Task orientation versus People orientation

10. Entrepreneurship versus Control/accountability

11. Flexibility versus Efficiency

12. Exploitation versus Exploration

13. Mentoring versus Managing

Finally, we need to ask what the WebCue approach misses and does not accomplish, as personal diagnosis and interviewing are still necessary:

- It does not surface anything that respondents are unwilling to discuss among themselves or electronically.

- It tends to mirror internal discourse and is limited to the insights present in that discourse.

- It tends to become a cerebral "game," in which the respondent enumerates conflicts without considering their pain or their implications for the company.

- The responses are shaped by the perceived reasons for the consultant's forthcoming visit with little that is new or unexpected. It rarely touches on deeper levels of meaning, nor does it explore the "far side" of linear thinking.

- It is very influenced by the latest management fashions and buzzwords, i.e., "Global versus Local," which is by now a cliché.

- It cannot turn linear thinking into dilemmas but classifies these as nondilemmas, although complaints about lack of leadership are quite easy to formulate as dilemmas.

But the WebCue approach can still give us some unique insight. It is perhaps most powerful when it plots the dilemmas discovered by personal interviewing and opens these up for general discussions online. To go properly through the sequence of awareness, respect, and reconciliation, you have to talk intimately to people to become aware of and respect their opinions; only then are effective reconciliations possible. Since this pattern of dilemmas tends to repeat and repeat across an organization, you need talk intimately to only a few to grasp the problems of many.

Whilst groups of managers or leaders can work together during a facilitated workshop session to elicit and structure dilemmas in order to seek their reconciliation, the momentum to maintain this new way of thinking and working needs to be embedded in the organisation. If not, there is a danger that the impetus developed during the consultant-led workshop might not to be sustained and thereby the benefits never fully realized.

For this reason we have developed our blended learning approach. The online WebCue provides an initial capture of the main dilemmas before such a workshop, as explained above. The workshop provides a forum for managers and leaders to develop their understanding of the methodology for reconciling dilemmas. They can also practice with some relevant case examples from their own agenda, gleaned from the WebCue.

However, the real benefit and sustained adaptation comes after the workshop when managers are available to participate in our DCOL (Dilemma Community OnLine). Here participants can return to the web and join their own community in which participants work through a structured step-by-step procedure to elicit, structure, and reconcile their own or organizational dilemmas. These dilemmas are archived in a database and can then be shared across their community. At the same time the consultant can maintain support to the various dilemma communities by providing a role of editor and commentator on both specific dilemmas as well as providing a holistic and guiding hand.

This blended learning solution provides the vehicle for embedding this philosophy across the organization.

In this chapter we have tried to illumine how dilemmas are identified in the first place. You can find these dilemmas within the Informant's model, either consciously owned or betrayed by hesitations, ambivalences, inner conflicts, doubts, forebodings, etc. The Informant's model contrasts with the Researcher's model featured in much of this book. On occasion dilemmas become social conflicts, which makes them easy to spot but difficult to heal, since managers have taken sides. Such conflicts are often characterized by single-principle imperialism. Here a polarized value is extolled and its opposite condemned. You can seek to rescue these submerged values by posing killer questions.

Another way of moving from the Researcher's model to the Informant's one is to see the latter as subsets of our seven dimensions. Academics and consultants like us think abstractly, while managers are responsible for more concrete operations. Their dilemmas, while every bit as important and vital, are expressed at lower levels of abstraction while being very similar structurally.

Yet a third way of moving from Researchers' to Informants' models is to study unexpected corporate successes, explaining these in retrospect as reconciled dilemmas. This works because people have been reconciling intuitively since time began. The Researcher's only contribution is to model this.

# CHAPTER 8

# Steps towards resolving dilemmas

W e are often asked about a methodology for resolving dilemmas. It is a good and simple question. We wish that the answer was equally simple and that the results of our instruction equally good but, in truth, the more dilemmas you reconcile the more the process becomes intuitive rather than rational. The logic by which we reconcile becomes inaccessible, even to us. This is a very old problem. Try asking creative people how they create. You will be very disappointed with their answers. They are not being coy. They really do not know and cannot explain how their feats were achieved.

The best we can do is to reconstruct the logic by which we approach dilemmas. If you follow the steps we propose, at least the barriers to seeing the solution will be removed one by one. The "steps" are all interconnected and are merely a means to an end. So leap to your conclusion as soon as it occurs to you. The steps are just promptings to help you see. If one step helps you more than others then go with that one.

This chapter looks in detail at two specific situations. We will first deal with a famous international dispute between Australia and Japan and then turn to a conflict between international HR directors in a beverage company.

## THE AUSTRALIAN–JAPANESE SUGAR NEGOTIATIONS

In the late 70s a famous misunderstanding between Australian sugar cane growers and Japanese sugar refiners occurred. It rumbled on for years. Both parties were indignant and perplexed at the other's "bad behavior," as they saw it.

The Japanese refiners had signed a ten-year, long-term contract to buy Australian sugar at the then market price, less $5. The Australians would get the security of a ten-year sales agreement. The Japanese would get guaranteed supplies at a competitive price vis-à-vis other refiners. Everyone seemed happy and the deal was signed.

Hardly was the ink dry on the paper than the price of sugar on world markets crashed by $10 a ton. The Japanese refiners faced the prospect of paying more for their raw sugar than anyone else, a cost that would fatally impact on the price of refined sugar and everything made from it.

Up to this point, both cultures probably saw eye to eye. It had been a good deal but now circumstances had changed and the Japanese refiners faced genuine difficulties. The cultural split occurred over what to do about this. The Japanese suggested to the Australians that the contract be renegotiated. After all the Australians could not possibly wish their partners to lose money; mutual satisfaction and lasting relationships were surely the ideal.

The Australians pointed out that a contract was a contract. The Japanese had given their word. Fluctuations in the world price of sugar were not unusual. All business involved risks. Had the price risen, not fallen, the Australian growers would have been the losers. You cannot go crying to your partner every time markets shift.

If we want to reconcile this conflict we first have to examine the value differences at stake. If these are not formulated correctly the conflict cannot be solved, the cultures cannot cooperate. What is dividing these cultures is:

| | | |
|---|---|---|
| Contract | versus | Relationship |
| Letter of the law | versus | Spirit of the law |
| Rule | versus | Exception |

It will help us to see possible solutions if we compare these dilemmas (or bifurcations) to at least four of the seven dimensions, outlined in Chapter 3. A theme running through this dispute is whether a universal rule applies or particular circumstances make this rule unjust and inappropriate. This was dimension 1, Universalism versus Particularism.

A second dimension touching on this conflict is Individualism versus Communitarianism. Is each individual partner responsible for his own profitability and fortune or do they share one fate as a community? A third dimension was Specificity versus Diffusion, and this too is involved in this particular conflict. The letter of the law, the small print in the contract, is specific, while the spirit of the law and the goodwill associated with mutual relationships are both diffuse.

Finally, there is even a touch of Achieved versus Ascribed status, a fourth of the seven dimensions. The Australians say that you "achieve what you bargain for, no more and no less." The Japanese say that the ascription of being a business partner should override what each achieves from their bargain.

It should come as no surprise that Australians are overwhelmingly Universalist, Individualist, Specific, and Achievement-oriented, while the Japanese are much more Particularist, Communitarian, Diffuse, and Ascriptive of status. This was a conflict waiting to happen.

If there is a universal obligation for individuals to honor the specific letter of the law, then the Australians are right. If there is a particular reason to form a better community and respond to the diffuse spirit of the law, in exceptional circumstances, then the Japanese are right.

## Mapping

Our first step is to map this dilemma. Instead of putting the conflict at opposite ends of a rope, and just pulling back and forth, we can create a dual axis "map," see Figure 8.1.

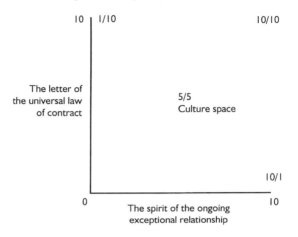

**Figure 8.1** Dual axis map

Three things need to be noted about this map. First, by creating a dual axis, we have made for ourselves a "culture space" where various outcomes can be compared. Second, the labels on both axes are "good." We have expressed what the Australians sincerely believe on the vertical axis and what the Japanese sincerely believe on the horizontal axis. Thirdly, we have shown that each value can be maximized at the other's expense at 10/1 and 1/10, compromised at 5/5, or synergized at 10/10. Reconciliation involves synergy.

## Strategy and making epithets

Step two is to stretch each principle as far as it will go, noting the good and bad points of doing this. If we take sanctity of contract to its logical conclusion, then this has clarity, legal sanction, freedom of contract – but also rigidity, inflexibility, and closure. If we take a special and exceptional relationship to its logical conclusion, we get subtlety, flexibility, harmony, but also ambiguity, relativism, and broken promises.

It helps to create epithets, rude words about extreme positions, typically used in rhetorical exchanges between Australians and Japanese when they are arguing. Hence the Australians might call the Japanese "slippery customers" and the Japanese might call the Australians "tablets of stone inscribed." An epithet can also be used for the middle 5/5 position to remind ourselves that cutting our principles in half is not what we want. Let us call this "half way to meet the bastards." Our map now looks like Figure 8.2.

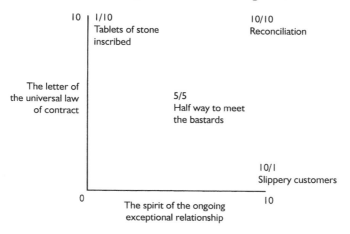

**Figure 8.2** Dual axis map, step 2

Note that 1/10, 5/5, and 10/1 are on a straight line. We have not yet escaped from our tug of war. However, we have made fun of our own extreme positions and we have admitted to some downsides of taking our values to extremes. If you can laugh together over absurd extremes there is less chance of crying later on. If you can admit that your own position can be satirized, not just that of your opponent, then this is a step forward.

## Five steps to reconciliation

These are as follows:

- Processing
- Framing and contextualizing
- Sequencing
- Waving/Cycling
- Synergizing

Let's go through these one by one and see if they throw up any ideas about reconciliation. If such ideas occur to you, then forget the remaining steps. As we've noted, they are just stepping stones enabling you to cross from one reality to another.

### Processing

One assumption we have continually challenged is that values are things. "The sanctity of contract" conjures up the image of a legal document, which specifies exactly what we must do. The special relationship is another potential idol, inviting worship. Aristotle told us that two opposite things could not occupy the same space and ever since then we have been running away from the specter of contradiction.

But if values are processes not things, then we have left the world of solid objects and entered the "frequency realm," the world of waves, vibrations, frequencies, spectra, and fields. Instead of "rock logic," we have "water logic," to use Edward de Bono's terms. The easiest way to convert values from things to processes is to add "ing" at the end. Hence, not contract but contracting, not law but legislating or drafting, not exceptions but making exceptions, not relationship but relating.

Does this make any difference? Yes, quite a lot. Relating and contracting do not sound very polarized at all. Nor do ruling and finding exceptions. If logic is like ripples of water why should not these form elegant and aesthetic patterns?

## Framing and contextualizing

All values and communications are a text within a context or, if you prefer, a picture within a frame. Values remain integral so long as the text is not separated from the context, or the picture from its frame, nor the figure from its ground.

The simplest context is two levels of abstraction:

To create a contract

We are relating

So as to clarify our relationship

We are contracting

The higher level is the context. The concrete process is the text.

The utility of a picture and a frame is to show that one value surrounds or embraces the other.

 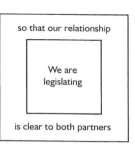

What the crash in the world price of sugar has done is to tear the text from the context and the picture from the frame. Any reconciliation is going to have to put these together again.

## Sequencing

Dilemmas look worse than they are when they confront us simultaneously in traumatic situations: "To be or not to be, that is the question." We cannot honor a contract and break a contract at the same time, but we could do both in a sequence. We could honor the existing contract, but negotiate an additional one, compensating the Japanese in some degree for their likely losses on the first contract. We are contracting, before making exceptions, before recontracting.

Alternatively, we could take Japanese "exceptionalzing" seriously and redraft the contract to give them a $5 reduction per ton on raw sugar below the existing market price, whatever that price might be. This would bring the volatility of markets into the contract terms. You could specify that a 5 percent reduction or rise in world prices would trigger an automatic renegotiation but that a lesser volatility would not.

Indeed, here the crisis looks more and more like an opportunity to improve both contracting and relating – and at the end of this process there will be a much better agreement.

## Waving/cycling

A waveform is, of course, a rolling cycle. It is a short step from creating a sequence to turning this into a learning loop.

272

The Japanese are right; improving relationships between partners is the name of the game. Between you, you can generate more and more value. But the Australians are also right that these relationships, however subtle, need to be codified into legally binding reciprocal obligations. The rule of law is indispensable. What these laws have to do is cover more and more particulars. Exceptions are there to test good laws and who does not want to be in some way exceptional? Good legislation leaves room for this. It puts freedom within the law (as picture and frame).

## Synergizing

Synergy, we may recall, means to "work together". We must improve our relating so that we can improve our contracting. We must continue finding exceptions so that our later agreements cover more eventualities. We know that synergy is present as we move towards 10/10 on our original map, so that both contract law and exceptional relationships optimize each other.

Now it is not easy to draft a contract that anticipates many contingencies and leaves both parties with discretion to meet unforeseeable problems, but it is possible and laws that enshrine our freedoms are on the statute books. It was Brandeis, the great American jurist, who said that the US Constitution was a charter for learning. On a much more modest scale, that is what a new contract between Australian growers and Japanese refiners has to be. The reconciled dilemma looks like Figure 8.3.

Note that our cycle has turned into a helix that winds its way upwards achieving better relations through better contracting and better contracting through better relating. At top left the evolving relationships have been brilliantly codified.

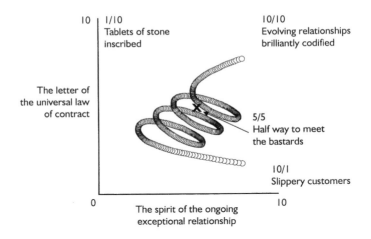

**Figure 8.3** Helical reconciliation

If all this sounds grandiose let us consider in detail the reconciliations of the quarrel between Japanese refiners and Australian growers. Among our suggestions would be these:

*For the Australian growers:* Ask that the existing contract be honored and in exchange draft a new contract that secures further business but helps to ameliorate the refiners' current losses. This contract should offer a $5 concession on the world price of sugar, whether it rises or it falls.

*For the Japanese refiners:* Ask to renegotiate the contract but pledge to honor it without alteration for a specified time period, unless the fluctuating price falls outside a $10 band, in which case negotiating starts again. Make sure the new contract incorporates all aspects of the ongoing relationship that can be codified, while protecting areas of discretion for both parties. Make the new contract a celebration of the rapport, which you have already achieved and the even better mutuality to which you aspire.

Now let's look at our second situation.

## STAFF APPRAISAL AT QUENCHY INTERNATIONAL

Our second illustration of how values can be reconciled using the mapping process and the five steps comes from "Quenchy International," a multinational beverage corporation based in the US. Despite fast growth during the 80s, their progress dipped significantly in the 90s and it was decided to revitalize the company via a cross-cultural staff appraisal system for the entire company. Against this background J. A. Daniels, the Human Resources Director, has sent out the memo set out in Box 1. Attached to this memo are some "Guidance Notes" or "10 Wise Lessons" for staff appraisal. These are set out in Box 2.

---

### BOX I
### Quenchy International Memo

Date:     August 10

Subject:  Meeting – Introduction of ASAS (Advanced Staff
          Appraisal System) October 2, 9.00 a.m.,
          US Headquarters

From:   Human Resource Director – Quenchy International
        USA

To:     National Human Resource Directors:
        Mr(s) Yakomoto    Quenchy International Japan
        Mr(s) Mantovini   Quenchy International Italy
        Mr(s) Klaus       Quenchy International Germany
        Mr(s) Khasmi      Quenchy International Iran
        Mr(s) Jones       Quenchy International USA

I am happy to invite you for a "brainstorming meeting" on the

---

introduction of our new Advanced Staff Appraisal System (ASAS). Until recently, Staff Appraisal has been a relatively underappreciated element within the realities of our organization. But times have changed. Motivated employees are essential to meeting increased competition. More and more we realize that Staff Appraisal should be the cornerstone of our company's Human Resource policy. Indeed, employee involvement is vital to their sustained motivation. One of the strongest motivational forces one can think of is the linkage between individual performance and income. Therefore, one of the main points of our new ASAS should be the pay-for-performance principle. It is my belief that this is crucial to guarantee the continuity of our company.

Your group will be responsible for producing:

1.    A statement of the Purpose and Objectives of the Appraisal/Pay-for-Performance Process.

2.    A list of what should be appraised.

3.    A description of the ideal process.

The objective of having this group discuss the process is that it is important that the process is the same in all the countries we operate in.

I enclose a list of "10 Wise Lessons for Staff Appraisal" that I have always found personally useful.

I look forward to your conclusions.

J. A. Daniels

Human Resources Director, Quenchy International USA

## BOX 2
## GUIDANCE NOTES
### 10 wise lessons for an effective staff appraisal meeting

J. A. Daniels

Please find a number of tips we could use as part of the Guidance Notes – an appendix that will be sent to all appraisers of Quenchy's local operating companies for the next staff appraisal round.

Please read them very carefully, I have always felt them to be most useful. I would be very happy to hear your comments.

1.  ASAS should focus on appraising *specific results* as output, and *function-specific behavior* as input.

2.  Base your judgments on *performance and business results:* do not be misled by any kind of personal preference; do not be biased by prejudices and leave "the person," as opposed to actual performance, out of consideration.

3.  Evaluate each appraisal criterion *in isolation.* Do not let strong or weak points of the appraisee influence your evaluation of other criteria.

4.  Don't be influenced by previous experiences you have had with the appraisee (a recent success or blunder should not bias the actual appraisal).

5.  Evaluate on the basis of *this year only.* Past performances should not be taken into account.

6.  Base judgments on *concrete facts:* not on notions or

assumptions. The appraisal must be as *objective* as possible.

7. Don't be afraid of giving low ratings if necessary. A boss who always tries to stay in the safe middle is doing injustice to other well-performing employees.

8. Evaluate on the basis of *fair company norms*, even if the requirements of the job are not well defined and performance is difficult to measure.

9. *Be honest, open, frank, and direct.* Don't be wary of confrontations.

10. Make sure that ranking procedures for rewards are *consistent* with the actual appraisal. The staff appraisal should justify the salary increases.

To make cultural analysis of this document easier we have italicized all those suggestions made by Daniel that emphasize American cultural values. We must, however, ask "if these values are being emphasized, what is being relatively de-emphasized?" We should recall that values are differences, so you cannot extol one end of a values' continuum without inferring that the contrasting value is less important.

Daniels emphasizes:

Specific results not general goodwill
Function-specific behavior not cross-functional connections
Actual performance not personal aspiration
Isolated criteria not overall configurations

Current achievement not work history

Concrete facts not broader contexts

Objectivity not inter-subjectivity

Unambiguous success/failure not face-saving tact

Frank, outspoken, direct communication not subtle,
suggestive communication.

The individual not social circumstances

Rewards consistent with ranking not rewards for
trying/improving

Short-term (this year only) not long-term career

Of course, Daniels does not say he is against the list of values on the right and since he does not state his opposition, we have been forced to infer what he means. But given what he extols, it is at least probable that the values on the right will suffer in comparison with those on the left, whether he intends this to happen or not.

Like most people, Daniels regards concrete facts about current achievements as good things. It does not occur to him that he may be subordinating the broader contexts and work history of employees as a result of his enthusiasm.

As readers will have guessed, his "wise lessons" caused widespread dismay to Messrs. Yakomoto of Japan, Mantovini of Italy, Klaus of Germany, and Khasmi of Iran. Only Jones of the USA was in favor and, even there, there were some doubts. For the reasons we must turn back to the seven dimensions of cultural difference set out in Chapter 3. In fact, the values praised by Daniels and those (accidentally) damned are close family resemblances (see Chapter 7) to several of our dimensions. For example:

| Specificity | _____ | Diffusion |
|---|---|---|
| Results | _____ | General goodwill |
| Concrete facts | _____ | Broader contexts |
| Function specific behaviors | _____ | Cross-functional ties |
| Frank, outspoken | _____ | Subtle, suggestive |
| Isolated criteria | _____ | Overall configurations |
| | | |
| **Individualism** | _____ | **Communitarianism** |
| The person | _____ | Social circumstances |
| | | |
| **Achieved status** | _____ | **Ascribed status** |
| Current score | _____ | Work history |
| Unambiguous success/failure | _____ | Face-saving tact |
| Rewards equal ranking | _____ | Rewards for improvement |
| | | |
| **Sequential time** | _____ | **Synchronous time** |
| Short-term (this year) | _____ | Career development |

Note that the values on the right are also "good," even if J. A. Daniels is not aware of their importance. The graphs on Specificity versus Diffusion, Achievement versus Ascription etc., in Chapter 3 show that Japan, Italy, and Iran for example are all less specific, less individualistic, and less achievement-oriented than is the USA.

Why is general goodwill important, in addition to specific results? Because believing that someone means well, has good intentions, and is generally positive in their orientation towards you is crucial to building trust and keeping clients. Indeed specific instances of poor results may be overlooked or regarded as honest mistakes where general goodwill is manifest. Similarly, concrete facts are interpreted by way of broad contexts.

Unless you want an organization subdivided into silos, you must regard cross-functional connections as at least as important as function-specific behaviors. Some cultures regard frank, outspoken, and direct communication as praiseworthy and authentic. But Iranians,

Japanese, and Italians find this unsubtle, obvious, rude, and aggressive. Subtle suggestions and hints that an employee might improve will be understood, only if that employee is ready to change. The subtlety and nuance is intended as a tribute to the employee's sensibility and perceptiveness.

If you isolate appraisal criteria, you lose sight of the significance of their co-occurrence. An idealistic person should also be realistic or the ideals will come to nothing. The overall configuration of sensing and intuiting, thinking and feeling, judging and perceiving on the MBTI is very important, as we discussed in Chapter 2. To look at the "person" and ignore social circumstances penalizes team solidarity and conduct that helps and supports others. Is this what Daniels wants?

To consider current achievements alone means "you are only as good as your last film." Your work history or track record give a sounder indication of your worth. Innovative people, especially, are prone to occasional errors. If you rank all your people and tell the bottom 50 percent where they stand on this linear yardstick, you are likely to lose a lot of employees. This is especially likely to happen in Germany, Japan, Iran, and Italy, whose cultures perceive in multiple dimensions, with each person proud of what they do well.

The Germans invented *gestalt* psychology along with continental philosophies with their dialectical values. The way they think is *ganzheitlich* (holistic). Italy is a culture of grand artistic visions and aesthetic elaboration. Japanese *kanji* form delicate syntheses of contrasting ideas. All this is a long way from "good/bad," "pass/fail," and "49th percentile: below average, I'm afraid." Culturally diverse values cannot be prioritized on single yardsticks without denying their diversity. An apple is neither better nor worse than an orange. The aesthetics of a Roman Catholic chapel in Florence, with its rich elaborations, are no better and no worse than the white-painted simplicity and parsimony of a New England Protestant church. Rather they are different and together make for a more varied and fascinating world. Claiming that either one has greater "merit" or "achievement" and rank-ordering them is not objectivity but cultural imperialism. What Daniels sees as universally "wise" and "objective" are American cultural preferences.

None of this denies that Daniels and Jones have a legitimate point of view. We do need individual employees to take responsibility. We must take note of results, but the views of Daniels and Jones can, as we shall see, be reconciled with those of the other HR directors. The values of various cultures are complementary. To understand both ends of the continuum is better than to understand just one.

## A simulation exercise

In order to bring these differences home to readers in corporate environments we recommend simulation exercises. Let different trainees play the roles of Jones, Yakamoto, Montovini, Klaus, and Khasmi. Brief them in advance on their underlying assumptions and how these anchor the positions they take. Then have them argue with each other in front of an audience. You will witness quite a fierce debate with each cultural persuasion becoming more and more firmly entrenched in opposition to the other. Such a simulation is set out in Appendix A. It will help to bring to life some very real issues between cultures.

In Appendix B is a reconciliation template for this exercise. You now have the participants read the contents of this chapter and set them the task of reconciling their earlier quarrels. The fiercer their disputes the clearer the issues will become. Can these be reconciled? Let us go through the process of mapping, stretching, making (or

remembering) epithets before going through the five steps to reconciliation. The objective is to come out of this conflict with a better
appraisal system satisfying to all.

## Mapping, stretching, and epithets

This should not be too difficult. Cultural disputes tend to clarify
positions and the maps should be easier to draw after a really heated
argument full of epithets. Figures 8.4–8.6 are the kinds of maps you
are likely to get.

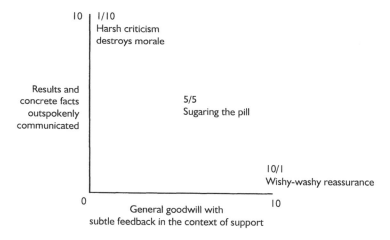

**Figure 8.4** Report versus Rapport

Daniels and Jones are both gunning for wishy-washy reassurance,
10/1. If you pull your punches, the truth about how well an
employee is doing will not be communicated and will not register
with that person. But Yakamoto is likely to see this as an unaccept-
able loss of face for the employee and a source of shame, shattering
to morale. Mantovini is likely to see it as a mortal insult that will
make the subordinate furious with his supervisor. For many Italians
a person's performance *is* that person. Criticize what they do and
you are rejecting that person entirely. For Khasmi, the lack of sup-

port and goodwill towards Iranian operations is the reason for their modest sales. Khasmi will resist the instruction that they start to blame each other for this neglect. They need more help, not more criticism.

We have characterized this dispute as Report versus Rapport. Daniels and Jones are urging that honest reports about how well employees are doing is all that is required for better assessments. Khasmi, Mantovini, Yakamoto, and Klaus believe that unless there is better rapport between supervisors and supervisees, critical feedback will devastate morale and trigger resignations. You have to be subtle and supportive or your people will be fatally discouraged. Klaus questions whether supervisors understand well enough the expertise of their subordinates to make rankings. They should perceive not judge.

A second map, Figure 8.5, has to do with Function-specific behaviors and isolated criteria versus Cross-functional ties and overall configurations.

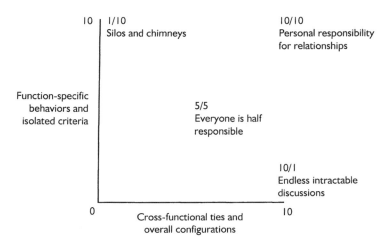

**Figure 8.5** Differentiation versus Integration

The problem with itemizing function-specific behaviors and using isolated criteria is that you reinforce the tendency of the organization to form silos and chimneys. Everyone maximizes the operations of their single function and what suffers is the organization as a whole, which becomes a prisoner of its own mental categories. Klaus is especially eloquent on this criticism, seeing Quenchy as far too segmented. But Daniels and Jones think there is far too much talking across divisions and functions that gets the organization nowhere; the recent heated argument being a good example. They would have done better to be at work in their units producing results. The problem with allowing interfunctional, interunit relationships into the equation is that everyone is half responsible and no one wholly responsible. People can simply pass the buck to the unit that did not do as they requested.

A third map, Figure 8.6, has to do with Single rankings of merit versus Plural forms of excellence.

The objection to taking rank orders to their logical conclusions is that most people lose. This is not simply those in the bottom 50 per-

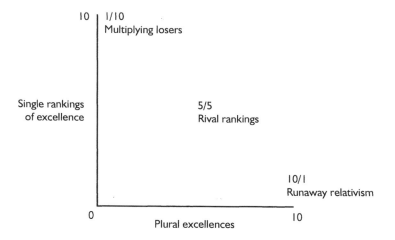

**Figure 8.6**  Single yardsticks versus Plural excellences

cent but those whose own definition of excellence puts them in the top 5 percent, while the company's definition relegates them to 25th percentile or lower. They are naturally aggrieved. Is there anything more important than marketing the Quenchy brand? Yet a marketer is put beneath the head of the bottling factory ... single yardsticks make for invidious comparisons.

The case for plural excellences might seem very strong. In Khasmi's view making high sales in Iran is so much harder than making these elsewhere, that the whole team deserves a medal; instead their sales are compared to those in New York. Could anything be more ridiculous? Klaus believes that the new fastener designed in the Frankfurt research laboratories is in a league of its own technologically. Complaining that it has yet to produce results is obtuse. Use it more widely. Give it time.

But Daniels and Jones believe that if everyone claims to be a special case no concept of best practice can emerge. Is not the whole point to identify winners and get other people to learn from these? You cannot do this if everyone is running a private race. Runaway Relativism – 10/1 – makes all performances incomparable and fatally obscures the type of conduct necessary to business survival.

Another undesirable outcome of plural definitions of excellence is Rival Rankings, 5/5. Employees who have done well on a ranking system exclusive to them will attack the ranking systems used by other units and functions. Disagreements on what constitutes excellence become entrenched and the corporation argues "matters of principle" when it should be performing.

We are now in a position to go through the five steps of reconciliation here, that is Processing, Framing/Contextualizing, Sequencing, Waving/Cycling, and Synergizing.

## Step 1: Processing

*Dilemma 1: Concretizing and communicating results very plainly versus Supporting and placing results in a context of goodwill.*

Once again we have retained the essence of both value polarities but they are far less combative. There is no inherent reason why the concretizing of results should not be seen as supporting the individual and should not be communicated to that person in an atmosphere of goodwill.

*Dilemma 2: Isolating and specifying certain behaviors versus Tying together functions in new configurations.*

Here the opposition has virtually vanished. Why not specify behaviors that tie together functions in addition to those who serve single functions?

*Dilemma 3: Ranking persons by merit to find the best versus Pluralizing the dimensions along which you rank.*

We do not necessarily lose the merit principle by having several dimensions of merit, especially if these are complementary.

## Step 2: Contextualizing/framing

This treats one side of the dilemma as "text" or "picture" and the other side as "context" or "frame", so, for our first dilemma:

Or:

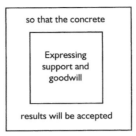

so that the concrete

Expressing
support and
goodwill

results will be accepted

And for the second dilemma:

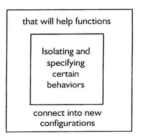

that will help functions

Isolating and
specifying
certain
behaviors

connect into new
configurations

For the third dilemma:

on several dimensions

Ranking
persons by
merit to find
the best

important to different
cultures

By putting these one-time conflicts into frames and pictures, contexts and texts, ground and figure, we have rendered them complementary rather than adversarial.

## Step 3: Sequencing

This step places one side of each dilemma before the other in time, for example.

| | |
|---|---|
| *First*, create a context of goodwill and support for the person assessed. | *Then* start communicating results that might otherwise damage morale |
| *First* isolate and specify certain behaviors | *Then* use these in tying together functions in new configurations |
| *First* start ranking people on one yardstick of excellence to see who is best | *Then* generate additional measures and celebrate pluralities of merit. |

In many cases these sequences could be reversed. For example, you could look at your more dire results and then build the contexts of rapport that would make these communicable. You could define plural excellences and then start ranking people on all of these.

## Step 4: Waving/cycling

A sequence can easily give way to a loop, so that the second value feeds around to influence the first. These can be turned into learning loops, so for the first dilemma:

This can be used on our second dilemma:

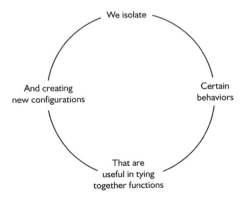

Finally, a learning loop encompasses our third dilemma as well:

## Step 5: Synergizing

To establish synergy we must not only encompass both sides of the dilemma or bifurcation at higher levels of salience, i.e., more merit on more dimensions, we must create a system or innovation that transcends the previous dichotomies. Thereby we are following Albert Einstein's dictum that a problem may be insoluble in its initial formulation and may need to be redefined.

Let's go back to our three original maps and see if we cannot generate innovative outcomes by resolving the original dilemmas. The first is shown in Figure 8.7.

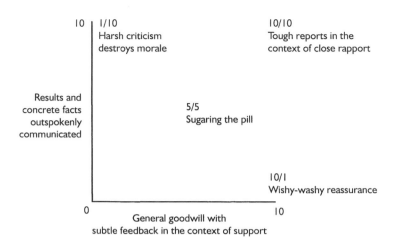

**Figure 8.7**  Report versus Rapport

At 10/10 something new has emerged. The assessed person is firmly held in a context of goodwill and strong rapport. Their boss is dedicated to the employee's future. Reassured by this strong bond the assessed person is confronted with what they must do to improve, however tough this is. Believing the supervisor to be genuinely on their side, the person internalizes the communication and is motivated to change.

Now let's look for the synergy of our second dilemma (see Figure 8.8).

If we wish to reward specific behaviors and relationships why not pinpoint profitable relationships between functions that contribute to customer satisfaction? People who take responsibility only for themselves are only moderately responsible. The really responsible person accepts more than their fair share in making business relationships effective.

In fact it is relationships, not individuals, who create wealth. You cannot do it without the customer responding. Similarly, if two busi-

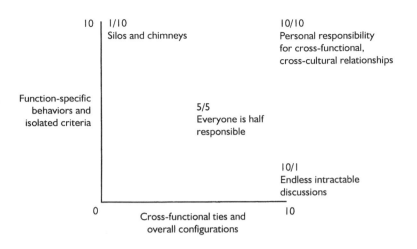

**Figure 8.8**  Differentiation versus Integration

ness units combine to cross-sell to a customer why not credit their cross-unit or cross-functional relationship? That would demonstrate the value of the synergy between functions or units. You can get the units themselves or the relationship manager to apportion credit for a sale. Soon those working together would outperform those working apart.

Another way of apportioning credit is to hold people responsible according to their relative salary levels for the relationships they form. A boss earning three times as much as his secretary is 75 percent responsible for their relationship, because that is what he is being paid for. If his secretaries quit, he is not doing his job; you do not have to prove that he has behaved improperly. Good or bad relationships are much easier to identify than good or bad behaviors. He is not earning his keep if his relationships fail.

If you wish your company to be more diverse then give greater credit for relationships that span different cultures.

Our third difference between HR directors from the USA, Japan,

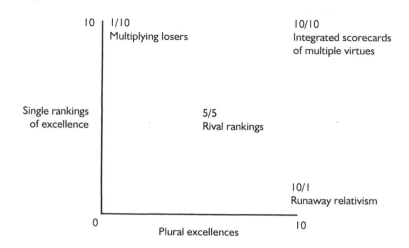

**Figure 8.9** Integrating plural values

Iran, Germany, and Italy was about Single ranking of excellence versus Plural definitions of excellence, as in Figure 8.9.

The synergy of Integrated Scorecards comes about because one dimension of virtue helps promote a second and a third. If an employee is very competitive this is a virtue, provided they are also cooperative. Persons of very high intelligence may or may not be creative. If they are also creative this greatly increases the likely effectiveness of their business unit. We saw in Chapter 3 that balanced scorecards were likely to become unstable unless they were integrated. Few companies give as much importance to learning goals in the future as they do to (past) financial results. If balance is to be maintained you have to show that learning goals sustain financial results, that higher scores on internal benchmarks satisfy external customers: Without this, "balance" is pious hope. You need to make the connection.

The future of global companies is to let each culture specialize in what it values and does best. Graduates from southern India are highly numerate and make excellent data processors. Malaysia is one of the most multilingual cultures in the world; what better place to locate an Asian call center? The automobile of the future may be styled in Italy, engineered in Germany, its safety systems made in Sweden, and its car computer supplied from Japan while the skilled assembly is done in Singapore.

To summarize, we began with a quarrel between HR directors summoned to a meeting on assessment, where values were over-whelmingly American and would have upset employees in Japan, Italy, Germany, and Iran had the assessment rules been simply rolled out and implemented as Daniels originally envisaged them.

Yet the closer we looked at these objections, the more we saw that assessments would actually be improved if these contrary views were recognized and respected. Out of conflict could grow a very much better assessment system suitable to an international com-pany. To go further into this vital issue we recommend the role-plays outlined in Appendices A and B; you can play out for yourselves the roles of Daniels and the HR directors.

CHAPTER 9

# Creating an assessment center

**W** e examined the topic of assessment and selection in Chapter 2. Here we will go deeper and look at the likely future of Assessment Centers now being set up in various corporations and aimed at winning the war for talent. We will examine:

- The culture of assessment centers.
- Assessing candidates in all four cultural quadrants.
- International leadership assessment.
- Cultures of career development.
- Career development in different national cultures.

We will see that assessment centers themselves presuppose a certain type of culture. Can these be remotely fair to those of other cultures? They can if we deliberately pull those other cultures into our assessment centers. Can we assess how people might operate in a culture other than their own? It is possible to do this, as we shall see. We will examine what "career development" means in various cultures. Is the whole notion of "career" becoming obsolete? We shall examine the validity of different meanings.

## THE CULTURE OF ASSESSMENT CENTERS

Centers are a product of a Guided Missile culture, the top right hand quadrant of our four cultures. These expect their members to be flexible, goal-seeking, team-oriented, and literally "rise to the occasion" by hitting a moving target. Candidates are typically confronted by unanticipated challenges and they perform for the benefit of those making the assessment. The premium is on spontaneity, finesse, interpersonal competence, and problem solving in situ. Candidates must be prepared to put their "best foot forward" and show off their dynamic personalities and problem-solving skills.

These are precisely the kind of behaviors the Guided Missile culture demands, the ability to influence a number of "stranger groups," made up of people's diverse experiences and of temporary duration, which solve problems and then divide in favor of another challenge and another team. Such people should be able to engage with a variety of new issues and unfamiliar companions. It is not difficult for assessment staff to simulate such situations.

They may form a team of people being assessed and throw a succession of hot topics at them, a charge of sexual harassment here, a complaint there from an important customer about lack of service in an area in which the company is hesitating to move. Another topic could be that a boss has left a critical appraisal of a young employee on the staff member's voicemail. This employee is refusing to come into work. What would the candidates for assessment do about these and other situations? This is designed to evoke from candidates their problem-solving skills and their abilities to communicate with the team and it with them. They can take it in turns to be the team leader and suggest solutions to team members.

All this makes for good assessment, but is it fair on those who come from other cultures and who may be slow to realize that they are supposed to display their prowess for public consumption? The whole concept of simulating virtuous conduct is alien to some cultures. Let's look more closely at this.

## ASSESSING CANDIDATES IN ALL FOUR CULTURAL QUADRANTS

Let us return for a moment to our four culture quadrants: the Incubator, the Guided Missile, the Eiffel Tower, and the Family. All four can have their virtues measured, but it takes different kinds of metrics to do this. Figure 9.1 is a suggested typology.

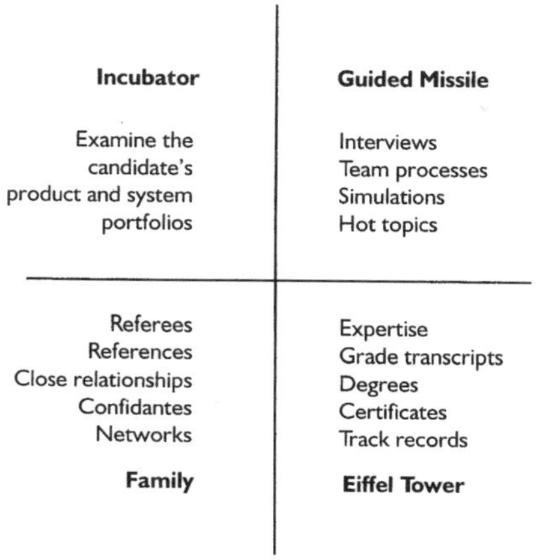

| Incubator | Guided Missile |
|---|---|
| Examine the candidate's product and system portfolios | Interviews<br>Team processes<br>Simulations<br>Hot topics |
| Referees<br>References<br>Close relationships<br>Confidantes<br>Networks | Expertise<br>Grade transcripts<br>Degrees<br>Certificates<br>Track records |
| **Family** | **Eiffel Tower** |

**Figure 9.1**   Assessing candidates in the four quadrants

We have already described the Guided Missile culture. Here assessors want to discover how candidates conduct themselves under challenging conditions. Among such are interviews with probing questions, teams voicing various opinions, simulated crises and difficulties, and hot topics likely to constitute dilemmas requiring resolution. All this is very good and necessary, but is not enough. At least three other cultures must be dealt with and their values included in any assessment.

Where you are dealing with an Incubator culture and people used to this culture, what matters to them are their actual creations, which you will find in their product and system portfolios, provided, of course, that you have asked to see these. . . . It could be an error to assume that their personalities would sparkle or that they would be socially pleasing and adept. In many cases they have poured their personalities into their products and creations and expect these to speak for them.

Quite a large number of highly inventive people are shy. It has been said that a major motivation for their innovative conduct is to earn the love and admiration they might not otherwise attain. If you assess them and not their creations, you will miss much of their genuine value. What drove them to create this product or that system? What are they excited about now? Highly creative people are easy to underestimate, but you pay a stiff price. They may develop products at your expense and then resign on the eve of a breakthrough success, going into business with co-inventors or even with a competitor.

Members of an Incubator culture are not very loyal to their companies. They are loyal, tenaciously so, to their own ideas, and if your company takes these seriously they will stick with you, but not otherwise. It was said of Silicon Valley in its boom days that most creative products were hatched in coffee shops, often with the help of people actually employed elsewhere. Co-inventors change their employers more readily than their car pools or coffee-shop companions. Does your assessment system capture the fleeting allegiance of such individuals? Do not judge people by their surface plausibility alone, but by what they have created and seek to create in the future.

Assessors may seriously underestimate candidates coming from Family cultures. This is because the assessors take their own Guided Missile values for granted. Candidates are expected to perform, but those from Family cultures may not be willing to exhibit themselves and are so unused to doing so that – even if they try – they often fail to impress.

In the Family everyone knows everyone in some depth. You have no need to show off because people know the secrets of your soul. Indeed, younger people in such cultures are excessively modest, behaving like children in the presence of their parents and only speaking up when invited to do so. Such modesty is seen as a sign of their worth. They have nothing to prove, so high do they stand in the appreciation of close "relatives" and close customers.

Senior members of a Family culture may seem presumptuous in the eyes of assessors, so used are family elders to the respect of their subordinates. They may even see the assessor as a subordinate, who should have done his homework on the deference due to the candidate. If the assessor does not see the inner worth of the Family leader then too bad. The fathers of a Family have nothing to prove to outsiders; their loyal and affectionate cultures speak for themselves.

Family cultures can be very successful and it is a serious mistake to assess them by your own values alone. You need to look very carefully at the candidate's referees and references, at their close relationships and circles of loyalty and the number of close and valued confidantes in the network. If a Family elder brings twenty or more customers with life-long loyalties along, then the value to your company could be inestimable. But you must discover if the admiration claimed is genuine and if the relationships are indeed enduring and trustful. More time spent in talking to intimate acquaintances may be of higher relevance to the candidate's excellence than performance in a simulation, where the pretence and play-acting may seem wearying and artificial.

For those coming from an Eiffel Tower culture the process of "selling your own virtues" to Guided Missile assessors is both shallow and insincere. Several times in their lives these people have confronted examinations and other tests of proficiency and professionalism and come through with credit; it is on their transcripts for the assessor to read. A brilliant record of past performance needs no embroidery; there is nothing more to be said. They were tested. They succeeded. If an assessor wants to discuss qualifications further, then well and good, but if the assessor wants their instant reaction to some social

## CASE CAPSULE
### American and Chinese Candidates at XYZ

An American and a Chinese candidate had been shortlisted for a top divisional job at XYZ Electronics. Both visited the Assessment Center. As was usual, each candidate was rated "blind," that is, their records were scrutinized and a judgment was made about relative qualifications. Each was then called in for lengthy interviews and was asked to discuss simulated crises in which a product had failed and the company faced scandal and legal claims.

The Chinese candidate was rated slightly superior on the blind test of professional expertise. But all three assessors (from France, the US, and UK) scored him lower than the American on the interview and much lower on the simulated scandal. The Chinese candidate had begun the interview by saying how unworthy he felt to work for this famous company. "I asked him," laughed one assessor, "why, in that case, did you apply for the job in the first place? He said nothing." During the discussion of the failing product he was far too polite to the complainant's lawyer. He did not stand his ground or try to defend the company. "He should have shown more guts," said the same assessor.

The assessors planned to recommend awarding the job to the American on the morning after, but in the meantime took both candidates out for an evening meal. To everyone's surprise the Chinese candidate charmed everyone with his wit and conversation. Over dinner with a couple of drinks his reserve and compliance completely vanished and the assessors began to wonder whether the job was worthy of *him*; he was so confidant, erudite, poised, and convivial. What a change!

embarrassment, then they have better ways to spend their time. The point of life is not to look good or sound impressive; it is to complete complex assignments to the highest professional standards and that has been done consistently. They therefore refuse to posture or to bluster. Assessors should just look at the record in front of them and be quiet. All these silly trick questions, psychological profiles, and invasions of private space are attempts to undermine professional excellence, which stares assessors in the face if they will only pay attention. Conflicts are solvable by going out and gaining the necessary knowledge. Unfortunately, the assessor knows virtually nothing about – say – automobile engineering and is thus forced to judge people by their gestures and their babble.

If assessment centers wish to engage Eiffel Tower cultures they must take proficiency in the company's leading technologies very, very seriously indeed. They must question those with excellent track records about the quality of that excellence and not minimize a quality simply because they do not share it.

We have dwelt at some length on the many ways that Guided Missile assessors can misunderstand the three other quadrants, yet there is no inherent reason why Incubator values, Family values, and Eiffel Tower values cannot be prominently featured in an assessment center. It especially helps to know where candidates come from. If you acknowledge early on that in which their cultures take pride, then you will be off to a good start.

## INTERNATIONAL LEADERSHIP ASSESSMENT

For many years we and other cross-cultural researchers at THT compared different cultures on our seven dimensions and predicted that if the culture profile of the individual differed substantially from the profile of the destination culture, then the foreign assignments

**Your personal Profile compared to China**

This is your cross-cultural profile *compared to* the average profile from **China** from the Trompenaars' cross-cultural database.

**Relative scores**

**Figure 9.2** Individual Culture Profile and Profile of Destination Culture

would prove difficult. We created charts like the those in Figure 9.2 and sent them out to clients.

While these profiles provided insight, they did not succeed in anticipating how much difficulty expatriate managers would face and whether they would fit well into the destination culture. One problem is that having the "same" profile can cause as much difficulty as having different ones. If both cultures are high in universalism, they may clash over who makes the rules. If both are inner directed they may fight over whose direction will prevail.

Our clients at THT were asking for a tool that could measure values integration and cultural reconciliation. Suppose leaders and managers differed in their capacities to grasp the values of another culture and make these consistent with their own, how could we discover this and measure it? We came up with a measure of trans-cultural competence which changed the finite games played – e.g., Rules versus Exceptions, Competing versus Cooperating – into infinite games, rules being ever modified and improved by exceptions, competitors being ever strengthened by the cooperation from customers they had won over.

Finite games are zero-sum philosophies, rival antitheses, win–lose conflicts in which one value always subtracts or is subtracted from its opposite. Infinite games are mutual, transformational, synergistic, and involve learning. You learn how far a theory can be extended before exceptions multiply, how modifying that theory can increase its range and validity. You learn what is truly exceptional in going beyond theoretical bounds. You learn how competition can reveal the very best ideas around so that former rivals can then cooperate. These "games" never end, competing the better to cooperate, finding exceptions the better to reform the rules. In preparation for an infinite game you need:

1.     Awareness (of cultural difference)

2.     Respect (for both)

3.     Reconciliation (between these).

We touched on the story of the car and the pedestrian in Chapter 2, yet the simple choice between Universal rules and Particular exceptions is a finite game. To make it an infinite learning experience, we need five possible answers, not two. So now let's look at a version of this dilemma in the light of finite/infinite games. Firstly, let's revisit the dilemma itself:

## The car and the pedestrian

You are riding in a car driven by a close friend who hits a pedestrian. You know your friend was driving at least 45 miles per hour (70 km/hr) in an area of the city where the maximum is 30 miles per hour (50 km/hr) . Your friend's lawyer says that if you testify under oath that your friend's speed was only 30 miles per hour (50km/hr), it may save your friend from serious consequences. There are no other witnesses.

How would you (and others in your organization) act in this case?

(a)     There is a general obligation to tell the truth as a witness. I will not give false testimony in court. Nor should any real friend expect this from me.

(b)     There is a general obligation to tell the truth in court, and I will do so, but I owe my friend an explanation and all the social and financial support I can organize.

(c)     My friend in trouble always comes first. I am not going to desert my friend before a court of strangers based on some abstract principle.

(d)     My friend in trouble gets my support, whatever my friend's testimony. Yet I would urge my friend to find in our friendship the strength that allows us both to tell the truth.

(e)     I will testify that my friend was going a little faster than the allowed speed and say that it was difficult to read the speed-ometer.

It is clear that "a" and "c" are polarized answers, part of a finite game: "a" puts down friendship, "c" puts down abstract principles (or truth). The infinite game players or the trans-culturally compe-tent would choose "b" or "d." The first tells the truth, then tries to repair friendship. The second persuades friends to tell the truth. "e" is a fudge or compromise. In our research we found that the 21 lead-ers in our book *21 Leaders for the 21st Century* were substantially more reconciled than our average for top managers. If you can reconcile one dilemma there is a strong likelihood that you can reconcile many more. Reconciliation is a pattern of thinking.

The way in which people reconcile and their reasons for doing so are clearly articulated in the interviews that should accompany all metrics. That a person scores in a particular way is only half the issue, we need to know why and in interviews many of the secrets of good leadership emerge.

There is a final form of assessment already touched upon. We refer to simulations. One of these will be taken up in detail at the end of the book.

## CULTURES OF CAREER DEVELOPMENT

Are careers dying? Is there any future in the concept of career development?

Over the last decades the notion of a "career" has taken several hard knocks, especially the idea of a career with one company. Is it still reasonable to expect that young, well-educated recruits can chart their progress up a company's hierarchy for a decade or more? Should such expectations be encouraged? Is it not wiser to stress "employability"? The company promises to increase the qualifications of its recruits to be employed within its industry, allowing them to seek out the best opportunities for themselves. The company cannot promise them a future career path extending over a lifetime. Trading conditions are simply too turbulent. What we all face is permanent white water in which each one of us must shift as best we can.

In our view the concept of a career is vital, although we need to define this term in several ways, depending upon the culture of the corporation. People's lives take the form of narratives or learning journeys. These may have planned destinations or consist of open-ended explorations. What is common to them all is a sense of continuity amid change. Each one of us steers a personal course and accumulates a unique combination of experiences in which we discover meanings. This gives to our lives a sense of direction so that, even where we are deflected from our course, we seek to persevere in a chosen direction.

Corporations would be wise to collect, to chart, and to study these "subjective careers" because among their richness and their variety can be discovered future directions for the company itself. Not only may several managers share the same aspirations, these may have the power to transform the company's current policies and alter its destiny. Most senior executives seek to leave a legacy behind them, as Motorola discovered in the 90s. To tap into these legacies is to grasp the significance of ongoing lives, to discover what your highest contributors have been living for, and what they wish their successors to learn. Ideally a score of learning journeys can potentially culminate in a new reality for a company as a whole. When you are about to let go, you are concerned to pass the torch to the next generation and help them fare better than you did.

The disappearance of visible ladders up which people plan to ascend does not foreclose new meanings within the concept of a career. The four quadrants of culture, the Incubator, the Guided Missile, the Eiffel Tower, and the Family, also help to illumine the changing nature of careers (see Figure 9.3). The most familiar and most traditional notion of a career is that of a career ladder (bottom right). This remains strong in cultures with long-term professional qualifications in a chosen discipline. This cumulative learning makes individuals supreme in their functions and a lifetime can still be spent perfecting such functions. All the way from the bottom to

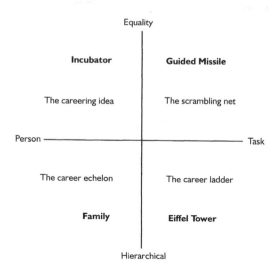

**Figure 9.3**    Career Development in the four cultures

the top are calibrated levels of qualification and expertise. It takes a lifetime to master a discipline or function and even if people change companies they will not quit their professional ladders. Such individuals will still be – say – automobile systems engineers, no matter which auto manufacturer employs them.

The career echelon consists of several people within age cohorts or with filial-type relationships between masters and apprentices. In either case the metaphor of the family and of the highly qualified community of persons, at a level above other, less distinguished groups, remains strong. These are not separate ladders but an elite group of intimately related persons, whose fates and futures are shared. They are quintessential insiders with information held between them, confidentially or *entre nous*. They are the *crème de la crème*. It is no coincidence, as we shall see, that the French have many phrases descriptive of such cultures.

The career ladder becomes a scrambling net as we move top-right into the matrix organization or Guided Missile culture. Now there are two criteria of excellence. How well one's function is discharged is one strand of the net and the success of the whole project of which one's function is a part is the other strand. You have scrambled from project to project as the teams in which you have temporary memberships fulfill their purposes and then dissolve. Your career consists of serial encounters with new teams and their members, in each one of which you represent your function.

Finally, at top left on Figure 9.3, we have the careering idea. In an Incubator culture you hatch innovations upon which your future then depends. Your career shares its fate with the new technology, product, system, or service you have created. Fellow members of the company are similarly tied to the fortunes of the new enterprise. If they are all successful, they will occupy the top rungs of their own "ladder" and can ask newer recruits to climb up it. For the time being, however, they potentially "own" the ladder itself and have helped design it. The highest rung is that of invention.

## CAREER DEVELOPMENT IN DIFFERENT NATIONAL CULTURES

Culture has a great influence on the way an organization understands and practices career development. It also frames the career goals and expectations of individuals and groups in different cultures. Evans, Doz, and Laurent of INSEAD have described the different career developments typical of organizations in particular cultures. These are also examined in *The Global Challenge* by Evans, Pucik, and Barsoux.

All successful business cultures are based on achievement and meritocracy at school. Where they differ markedly is in their concept of career development after school. So French, Japanese, American, British, German, and Dutch cultures all use their educational systems to select those who will go on to higher attainments in the corporation.

Those cultures high in communitarianism have a tendency to believe that, childhood being over, elite scholars should now stop competing and start cooperating. To achieve this they ascribe very high status and almost guaranteed preferment to those who have distinguished themselves academically and they ask and expect that these people will now model a life of public service.

Let's look at career development in a variety of national cultures.

## Career development – Japan

In this tradition we will briefly discuss the Japanese and the "Latin" or French approaches. Both cultures subject students to variations of "examination hell." Education is teacher-centered, hierarchical and highly structured with the most disciplined, not the most creative, emerging at the top. Evans, Doz and Laurent's research indicates what happens in the Japanese model, seen in Figure 9.4.

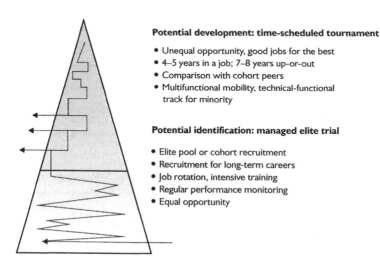

**Potential development: time-scheduled tournament**

- Unequal opportunity, good jobs for the best
- 4–5 years in a job; 7–8 years up-or-out
- Comparison with cohort peers
- Multifunctional mobility, technical-functional track for minority

**Potential identification: managed elite trial**

- Elite pool or cohort recruitment
- Recruitment for long-term careers
- Job rotation, intensive training
- Regular performance monitoring
- Equal opportunity

**Figure 9.4**  Elite cohort approach – the Japanese model

Students go from college as an elite age cohort, anticipating long-term careers (although without an improvement in the Japanese economy this may not prove possible). The zigzags at the lower end of the hierarchy show job rotation, which includes work on the factory floor, trade union membership, and often representation of the union's position. The Japanese have strong cultural emphases on different perspectives. Rather than attempting an objective view they believe that a view from multiple perspectives leads to a larger, more inclusive vision of reality. Future leaders should therefore assume multiple viewpoints as part of their training. Promotion is slow and typically age cohorts are promoted together at this stage of their careers, getting equal opportunities to show their mettle but not put ahead of each other.

Cohorts are encouraged to look after the cohorts directly beneath them in an elder brother–younger brother, family-type relationship. Relative performance is carefully monitored and assessed but is a private and not a public matter.

In the second stage managers are kept on average four to five years in a job, before being switched from one function to another, still in search of all-round experience. After seven to eight years they must move up or out. Enough information on relative performance has now accumulated to give the best jobs, with the greatest opportunities, to the best managers who have the self-fulfilling status of high flyers. They must compete with their peers by being more cooperative and helpful towards them, an art resembling a political tournament, in which alliances are formed, sponsors are won, and coalitions formed. Competing while cooperating takes on the character of a game, in which the more you do for others, the greater your personal advantage.

## Career development – France

The French model (Figure 9.5) has no rotations at the lower level and the elite are segregated from the working class. While their peers in Japan would have started work the French elite are still at a Grande Ecole getting science Ph.Ds, or MBAs from INSEAD. So great is the prestige of such schools that their star pupils are expected to achieve once they join a corporation. The corporation may blame itself if a distinguished pupil fails to flower. A graduate of one of the best known Grandes Ecoles has a 90 percent chance of becoming a company president.

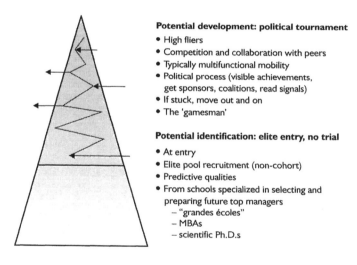

**Potential development: political tournament**
- High fliers
- Competition and collaboration with peers
- Typically multifunctional mobility
- Political process (visible achievements, get sponsors, coalitions, read signals)
- If stuck, move out and on
- The 'gamesman'

**Potential identification: elite entry, no trial**
- At entry
- Elite pool recruitment (non-cohort)
- Predictive qualities
- From schools specialized in selecting and preparing future top managers
  - "grandes écoles"
  - MBAs
  - scientific Ph.D.s

**Figure 9.5**   Elite political approach – the "Latin" model

At this point elite managers are rotated, but often do not remain in their jobs long enough to prove themselves. Indeed, they are held to have proved themselves educationally and it now remains for the corporation to find the best ways of bringing their proven talents to bear. As in the Japanese system they are higher flyers in multifunctional roles and shifting coalitions in what is essentially a political process of demonstrating talent.

In both cases the system is familial, meritocratic, and hierarchical, drawing heavily on Eiffel Tower and Family cultures. Who you know tends to be as important as what you know. Michel Crozier has referred to *camaraderies d'association* with a *mafia de collègues*.

One problem with both these systems is that you lose competitive advantage by leaving Japan or France. This tends to make their elites quite parochial. Those Japanese going abroad deprive themselves of their high context culture in which tacit communications of great subtlety and intimacy occur – but, unfortunately, not with foreigners. Culturally specific forms of achieving rapport prove to be non-exportable.

The French suffer similarly when deprived of their native language, the carrier of much of their civilization. Nor do the magic circles of elite understand travel well outside national boundaries; see the Ha Je Sey capsule case opposite.

While consultancy companies themselves typically operate as Guided Missile cultures sending in trained teams to deal with clients, the clients themselves are often Family or Eiffel Tower cultures and may welcome a "comrade" from their old school. In both the Japanese and French models we witness the strong particularism which, as we saw in Chapter 3, characterizes these cultures. A mixture of expertise and political power orientation is the name of the game.

## Career development – Germany

In view of the importance of technical expertise for managers' authority, careers in the German model deviate significantly from the Latin approach. We can vividly remember the first encounter we had with the "Nachwuchs Gruppe" (the high-potential, young grad-

## CAPSULE CASE
### Ha Je Sey

During a training session in one of the big five consulting firms, an English senior partner asked our advice about the selection process for an elite multicultural group of consultants. He was worried that the criteria he and his colleagues used were inappropriate because too many Northwestern Europeans seemed to dominate the game. He told us the following story: "We use test interviews in our assessment centers. A Frenchman was the best of all, but he failed in the interviews. We all agreed he was the best candidate but he avoided anything about his achievements. We couldn't assess his ambitions. We asked him about his achievements directly and he kept on saying something about his grades at Ha Je Say.* No clue what that was. But we have a rule: if in doubt, don't hire."

*Ha Je Say is the French phonetic pronunciation of HEC (Hautes Études Commerciales), one of France's elite management schools.

uates) of Daimler Benz in Stuttgart. In the first break we went to the organizers to ask whether we were dealing with a middle management group since this quite intelligent crowd seemed, on average, to be in their late twenties. Daimler's HR Staff looked puzzled and explained to us that the average age was 28 since everyone in this group of high potentials, with just a few exceptions, had a doctorate. This is no big deal in Germany. After a six-year graduate study, ranging from law and engineering to economics and sociology, doing a Ph.D. is a very common step.

In the larger German, Swiss, and Austrian Eiffel Tower cultures of

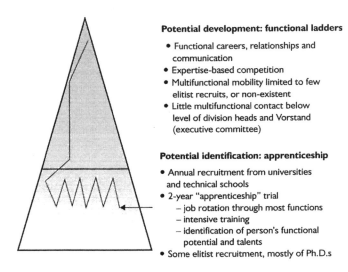

**Potential development: functional ladders**

- Functional careers, relationships and communication
- Expertise-based competition
- Multifunctional mobility limited to few elitist recruits, or non-existent
- Little multifunctional contact below level of division heads and Vorstand (executive committee)

**Potential identification: apprenticeship**

- Annual recruitment from universities and technical schools
- 2-year "apprenticeship" trial
  - job rotation through most functions
  - intensive training
  - identification of person's functional potential and talents
- Some elitist recruitment, mostly of Ph.D.s

**Figure 9.6**   Functional approach – the "Germanic" model

corporations (with some Dutch and Scandinavian exceptions) it is quite common that well-educated graduates add an extra academic specialization to their curriculum through the Herr or Frau Doctor title. Everything is focused on preparation for functional careers. After an extremely selective one-year recruitment process (where the depth of their expertise is tested in rigorous ways), candidates typically go through a two- or three-year apprenticeship period that combines a company job and special assignments with intensive training. This development program does not only serve to broaden candidates' knowledge, but also serves to identify their functional potential and talent.

The big decision, made early in a young recruit's career, is in which function to specialize. Several may be tried out – see the vertical zig-zags in Figure 9.6 – but once the die is cast, it is on an up with great expertise in a single function. Mentors may guide this fateful choice, each one potentially willing to take on the recruit as an apprentice. Once a function is chosen, the recruit must build a network within it.

There is little inter-functional mobility below the level of *vorstande* (the executive committee). At the end of this highly "within-functional" challenge, we see many Herr or Frau Doktors and even Herr or Frau Professors become heads of functional divisions. At times it seems almost obligatory for managers to take a part-time professorship in order to deepen the knowledge they require even further. This is in great contrast with the Anglo-Dutch system of career development, where even the start of one's career can appear to be hindered by having a Ph.D.

## Career development – North America and Northwestern Europe

Beginning with the founding of business schools in the USA in the late 20s and early 30s, America has always believed in the general manager, the "master of business administration," capable of operating not just across functions, but in a great variety of different businesses. As the great entrepreneurs died off, business emancipated itself from Family cultures to become an administrative "science." Its earlier formulations were in the Taylorist, Eiffel Tower mode but, thanks in part to HRM, business scholarship and American consulting practices, the Guided Missile culture emerged as the dominant cultural model and the matrix became the preferred way of operating.

This form of career development confronts the manager with a series of ever-changing encounters with groups of strangers who learn to work with one another before breaking up and tackling new issues and problems with a new set of colleagues. The work is problem-centered with far less respect for the highly educated specialist. The Dutch author was once advised by an Englishman to remove the "Dr" from his business card as "English CEOs might find out that you have thought about a subject, which diminishes your status as a consultant." Fons assumed he was joking until he heard an American friend confirming the low status of a Ph.D in business.

While Eiffel Tower cultures tend to be tightly structured, as in the German automobile industry, the Guided Missile structure is loosely structured, as in the British and American financial services industry. You develop in such cultures by finding solutions in case after case, with detailed feedback on success or failure. Getting on with other team members and synthesizing their suggestions is at least half the battle. Social skills are as important as technical skills. Much use is made of assessment centers because of the complexity of judgments. During assessment, subjects are expected to model dynamic leadership behavior and team leadership skills. Their performance is typically rank ordered by assessment staff.

The Case Method used in MBA teaching, with class discussions, is good practice for this kind of culture. In fact, employees may be studying for part-time MBAs or taking eighteen months out for a full-time MBA. The case comes first. The principles necessary to solving the case are derived inductively. All those present are encouraged to participate. The instructor is a facilitator of the group's discussion. This approach has neither the deep social knowledge of colleagues present in the Family culture, nor the expert knowledge of technological systems and scientific principles present in the Eiffel Tower culture. It operates best in situations of high uncertainty and insufficient knowledge, where swift action is imperative and mistakes can be used for learning.

In this model you begin as a specialist. Harvard Business School recruits as MBA students those who have excelled as graduates in the sciences and humanities, avoiding undergraduate business studies students.

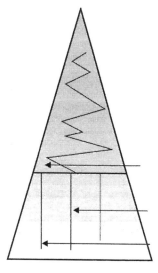

**Potential development:**
**managed potential development**

• Careful monitoring of high potentials by management review committees
• Review to match up performance and potential with short- and long-term job and development requirements
• Importance of management development staff (often reporting to GM/CEO)

**Potential identification:**
**locally managed functional trial**

• Little elite recruitment
• Decentralized recruitment for technical or functional jobs
• 5–7 years trial
• No corporate monitoring
• Problem of internal potential identification via assessments, assessment centers, indicators
• Possible complementary recruitment of high potentials

**Figure 9.7** Managed development approach – the North American and North-western European model

When candidates have reached "Master's level," whether still in school or in the corporation, they start zigzagging across functions or across disciplines. While bright students are preferred, academic attainment is by no means the only criterion. The capacity to make practical use of ideas and information is carefully monitored by assessment staff in situ, in role plays, and in simulations. Because multiple skills are necessary for success, assessment is quite complex and seen as important and "psychological" in its orientation. Methods may be controversial and testing procedures are sometimes challenged. Assessors make claims about the objectivity of their methods, but in practice you need to be part of the Guided Missile Culture in order to come well out of tests. Candidates strive to appear "dynamic" and "motivated," qualities that the Eiffel Tower culture would regard as bluffing and the Family Culture would regard as shallow posturing.

## Career development in innovative settings

The concept of a career has its hardest time in highly creative contexts like Silicon Valley, Silicon Glen, the Cambridge Phenomenon, etc. Entrepreneurs routinely develop ideas at the expense of their employers and then resign to exploit it. In part they do this for personal advantage and in part because their ideas are not being treated seriously. Hence "the Fair Children" grew out of Fairchild, Apple grew out of Xerox Parc, Applied Materials grew out of Bell Labs, etc. In none of these cases did the parent company see the same potential in products under development which the principals themselves recognized. Even so, the parent companies did see themselves as sponsoring creativity. They still missed the actual creations emerging from their sponsorship.

In this event the "career" jumps from company to company. Protagonists are still embarked upon an adventure and a learning journey. They resign from one company, then start their own which is often purchased by a third company. The connectivity is very clear and very important to that individual even if others do not perceive the unfolding story.

The ability to identify these careers remains extremely important to any company valuing innovation. The British author worked recently for Scottish Enterprise, a government agency charged with facilitating innovation in Scotland. Despite some very successful start-ups 80 percent of all innovative companies had been acquired by American corporations within ten years of their founding. Why? This was not because US companies outbid their rivals, but because the Scottish entrepreneurs themselves felt that their innovations were in the most appreciative hands. US acquirers had done their homework. They knew the real value of what they were buying.

So career development is vitally important in Incubator cultures as well, even if that career jumps from company to company and appears to have no stable anchorage. It may be wise for HR departments to have an inventory of employees' aspirations, what they dream of doing if ever anyone gave them to freedom to do it.

## Career development in trans-national companies

A good way of developing careers across cultures is to encourage every participating nation to play from their own strength. Send German Eiffel Tower experts out to befriend fellow experts in a client's organization so that they become united in the appreciation of precision engineering. Send the cream of your French scholar-aristocrats out to meet colleagues who appreciate their sophistication and want to bond with them intellectually.

In the Cassini-Huygens mission to Saturn and Titan, the Italian engineers came up with most of the creative ideas in an Incubator-style culture, while the Germans took charge of the integration of scientific instruments aboard the Titan IV rocket, a task needing incredible precision and discipline, requiring Eiffel Tower virtues. In the meantime, the Americans had set up a "trading system" (which was mentioned briefly earlier, in the Capsule Case in Chapter 7) in which Principle Scientists could barter with others on the amount of mass, power, and cost that their own instruments would consume. Mass points could be exchanged for power points and cost points, all expressed as a single currency, so that the scientific teams self-organized into optimal patterns of mutuality. This was a creative adaptation of Guided Missile team dynamics.

As corporations spread around the globe there is increasing evidence of decentralized centers of excellence, in which functions are performed wherever the local culture is most suited to this. Hence

ABN AMRO, the Dutch multinational bank, has located its information processing in Southern India where numeracy is excellent and accuracy highly valued, while placing its call center for East Asia in Malaysia, where multilingual teams field calls in twelve languages or more. Some major innovations have emerged from Taiwan.

In conclusion, it is important to judge the development of executives' careers against their own values. Some people do not show off verbally because they do not value that kind of Guided Missile articulation. They do not enthuse over the brilliance of their colleagues in 360° Feedback, because all colleagues are brilliant in elite Family cultures and because the performance of those colleagues is already registered in an Eiffel Tower's records and there is nothing more to say. If you show wonderment and surprise it suggests you are not accustomed to high performance; encouragement is for children, not professionals and experts.

If you ask those whose careers you seek to develop what their aspirations are, what in the best of all possible worlds they would seek to accomplish, they will tell you in what kind of culture they would thrive, what sort of response from others they are seeking and what legacy they would like to leave behind them.

It is wise to remember that not all forms of talent exhibit themselves or believe in exhibition. An extremely talented Chinese woman recently applied to do a Ph.D. with the British author. Her record was second to none, but her application began with the words "I am sure you have many candidates more deserving than I." In fact, there were no such candidates. Potential in people does not always advertise itself. It remains to be discovered.

# CHAPTER 10

# Varieties of culture shock

There has been one glaring omission from this book thus far. We have given scant attention to emotion. This comes about in part because this topic is consciously or unconsciously taboo in most "rational" explanations of culture and management. Even so, it is crucially important and we do not begin to grasp the extent to which our subject matter is haunted until a point of sheer dread until we have looked squarely at this problem.

There have been various estimates of the number of people who were murdered in the twentieth century because they happened to be of the wrong color, race, ethnicity, or national culture. From the British concentration camps for Boers at the beginning of the century, through the Turkish massacre of Armenians, to the Nankin massacre of the Chinese by Japanese occupiers, to the Holocaust in Nazi Germany, to Soviet Gulags, to Kosovo, Rwanda – some 60–70 million people have died because they have been identified with the wrong group.

Differences of race, color, culture, religion, creed, etc., can arouse human beings to the fury of genocide. It has happened again and again, and those who speak blithely of globalism would be wise to heed history's warnings. The worm in the apple, eating out the core of human integrity, is anxiety. In this chapter we will discuss two topics at the center of visceral anxiety, culture shock and women and men encountering each other in the workplace. There is also a simulation we have designed about a visit to an imaginary culture called "Derdia."

## CULTURE SHOCK

Anxiety may be a vague and pervasive feeling, but its physical manifestations are clear and measurable. When we are anxious our hearts beat faster, pumping blood which can be used for emergency action, the electricity on the surface of our skin increases, the rate of our breathing increases markedly so that we have the oxygen to resist attack, and we begin to sweat as the body lubricates itself. All this is accompanied by some frustration because we may lack any avenue through which to discharge our tensions. There is no visible threat to focus upon. We are with strange people in a strange land, yet what can we actually do about this? The sheer relish and delight with which majorities have persecuted minorities for imagined crimes testifies to this huge surfeit of energy with nowhere to go.

In one sense a book like this is a defense against anxiety. People believe that if they are forewarned about the misunderstandings involved in encountering people who are different from themselves, then such encounters will be managed more smoothly and with less embarrassment all round. You first study such situations through the pages of a book, or attend seminars, then go out and conduct cordial negotiations with foreigners.

In fact, you probably learn more and faster from immersing yourself in foreign cultures than you will from reading or discussing possibilities in advance. There are only two problems. It hurts and it costs. We are not talking of agony, but something akin to persistent, low-level toothache. People fear any source of direct threat, be that a rogue driver, a gunman on the loose, a leaking gas pipe, or a terrorist attack. You fear specific objects or persons, and because you have identified the threat you can often remove it.

But we are not talking of fear but of anxiety. Anxiety is our response to an ill-defined threat in which we feel dread but do not know why or what to do about it. The threat cannot be located precisely. It is everywhere, yet nowhere. It is all pervading. It is anxiety we feel when we enter an unfamiliar culture. We feel awkward. We cannot read social cues correctly. We feel that something will go wrong at any moment, potentially costing us millions if a contract is at stake. Yet we do not know how to prevent this. The dilemma is shown in Figure 10.1.

**Figure 10.1**   "Like us, yet not like us" breeds anxiety

These people are in some ways like us, recognizably human with resources we want and needs we should be able to understand. They have rights. We are supposed to respect these and respect them, and yet they are in other ways very unlike us, with strange clothes, different complexions, and some bizarre ways of behaving. This tension of like–unlike causes a continuing anxiety within us that constitutes culture shock, or more accurately culture shocks, which slowly wear us down and exhaust us long before the end of the working day.

In situations like this you find yourself doing all manner of things designed to control your anxiety. You smile a lot. Thank your foreign hosts effusively. Make largely empty, ritual speeches of salutation. Chatter away because you find silence awkward, even though you are boring yourself…and your hosts may be every bit as anxious as you, may do the same, with elaborate diplomacy and formality. You both go through the motions of professing a friendship you do not actually feel.

One reason people do this is because other ways of controlling anxiety are a lot nastier. Colonial masters would insist on their own social and ethnic superiority. They would force indigenous peoples to defer to them. If you can control people and make them crawl, then you thereby control the anxiety within yourself. If there is a misunderstanding you start to shout orders. The local inhabitant is wrong, by definition, and must obey your dictates.

While imperialist behavior is now much more rare than it once was, its root cause, culture shock or anxiety, does not go away. You simply have to use different methods to combat it. Being very formal, very polite, deferring to your hosts, affecting a gaiety you do not feel, apologizing or becoming convinced that the foreign culture is somehow better than your own are simply different ways of assuaging the mild "toothache" of day-to-day mis-involvements. Instead of making the unfamiliar people crawl, you crawl to them.

When husbands and wives are sent abroad it is often the one who stays in their new home who feels the greater shock. The partner who goes to the office is well protected by indigenous staff, while the spouse left in the house, possibly with children and usually the woman, must face contractors, repairmen, school officials, and "helpful" neighbors. Why are her children shouting and playing in the garden? Does she not know that the town council has designated this as a quiet time? It is often partners who find culture shock too much and cry "enough!"

Culture shock may not strike immediately. There is often what Clyde Sergeant calls the "honeymoon" period in which people feel obliged to welcome you or are naturally curious to meet you. You are also excited and expectant. Culture shock typically strikes after this introductory period is over, in what Sergeant calls the "Sauerkraut" stage, when you must take the initiative to meet new friends or go without them. When local inhabitants no longer feel they owe you hospitality, you may conclude that they do not like you. If you are shy in such situations, the sensation of having two left feet and stamping accidentally on people's toes may never leave you. Suddenly you are irritated by everything. The symptoms of culture shock are those of mild neuroses: skin rashes, appetite loss, depression, sleeplessness, swellings, palpitations, etc.

You can, of course, hang out with other "shocked" persons from the expatriate community and discuss endlessly how dreadful the locals are, but this is unlikely to improve your trans-cultural competence or your sense of curiosity about the host culture. You might legitimately question why you went abroad in the first place if you only bitch about it.

The truth is that culture shock persists unless you set out to confront it and hopefully break through it. You can shorten the period of pain by being as extrovert as possible and going out and about. Mistakes are inevitable and embarrassment will abound but the sooner you experience these barriers the better. It is like learning a language. It is quicker if you are unafraid to make a fool of yourself and are inured to puzzled pauses in conversation when you get things wrong. Serious mistakes are unforgettable and a good laugh – in hindsight. The female executive who excused herself for not finishing her meal by explaining that she was "trés pleine" took a long time to forget the look on the headwaiter's face. She had just inadvertently told him she was very pregnant – not a mistake she would make again.

The fact is that mild shocks are excellent teachers and their memory traces are vivid. You will find that your native hosts will readily forgive errors provided they are convinced of your goodwill and sincerity. After all, a well-intentioned person is only rude by mistake and once your intention to learn their ways is clear, much will be forgiven and they will be flattered that you are trying so hard to get to know them.

## Two routes for severe culture shock

Around 20 percent of expatriate managers suffer severe culture shock. There are two routes, the D route and the C route. Both journeys begin after the *Sauerkraut* Stage. Five percent suffer the D route in which locals are actively despised. It usually sets in after six months. These expatriates are dying psychologically and cannot cope. Alcohol, isolation, and very poor work performance are among the symptoms. They should be returned home as soon as possible.

Three quarters of those of the "severe" category are in the C route. Poor work is continually blamed on living conditions and locals, who will "never learn" how to behave properly. C route people search out other malcontents and make group complaints. They are not personally isolated, as in the D group, but form complaining factions, citing their spouses and families as perpetual victims of an unjust local culture. These individuals should also be considered for return or placed with those adapting best.

## Two routes of relative adjustment

The B group is distinguished by adequate job performance, but complaints of homesickness, especially around festivals and anniversaries, make them count the days before the end of their assignments. These people constitute about 40 percent of the whole. People in the A group – the final 40 percent – have been strengthened and expanded by the time spent abroad. Their performance has actually improved and their enjoyment of variety has been enhanced. They have grown in their jobs and become more innovative. They often regret that they must go home. And it is on their return that HR lets many of these people down.

## Problems with reentry

The perils of culture shock do not end with acclimatizing to new cultures abroad. Problems often arise when you return home. Because you have been out of sight of HQ staff, you may also have been out of mind and they will assume that you have accomplished nothing of significance in the interval of your absence.

In truth, you probably have got more of importance to tell them than if you had stayed at home, but no one seems interested in listening to you. In thinly staffed offices abroad, people must often take on responsibilities they would never shoulder at home, as well as playing multiple roles and discovering abilities they never knew they had. Foreign operations are typically more innovative, more risky, and more surprising. Yet when you try to tell people about the extraordinary opportunities and of your adventures in – say – Thailand, they will dismiss these as peripheral, as in one sense they are.

Our company has been paid to inform companies about foreign cultures when those companies have not even bothered to debrief their own returnees from those self-same cultures. The best way for HR to educate employees who are about to spend time in a particular culture is to have them talk to your own well-adapting returnees. This will give everyone a chance to learn from the culture concerned. For example, you could arrange for returnees to feature on panel discussions entitled "Missed and Seized Opportunities in Malaysia: Can we double our revenue there?" Try to get officers with responsibility for that part of the world to attend.

Western companies often attract an unusual caliber of native recruits. These people seek entry to global operations and are willing to let go of the safe and familiar business opportunities preferred by indigenous elites. Such well-educated "outsiders" are rare and potentially very precious to an international company. Another reason for carefully debriefing expatriate managers is to learn about locally hired staff. Which of these show enough promise to qualify as global leaders? What do they think and believe? How can they be developed?

## WOMEN AND MEN ENCOUNTERING EACH OTHER IN THE WORKPLACE

Among the victims of the underlying anxiety of the male majority are women in the workplace. This has all the usual hallmarks of irrational prejudice. Women's academic records on emerging from school are at least as good and often better than those of men. There are many, many examples of their exemplary work. Almost no one publicly defends gender inequality any more, especially at work. Yet discrimination persists. We resort to such expressions as "the glass ceiling" to indicate that the barriers are very real yet, curiously enough, invisible. Women do not progress, despite their victories in most rhetorical battles. Why?

Again the reasons are deep down. In order for men to engage women successfully in their private lives, they need confidence and to know in advance that their attentions to the opposite sex are welcome. Although men actively desire a few women in the workplace, criticism, self-assertion, negativity, and nay-saying by any woman may stir inner anxiety about rejection, impotence, unmanliness, etc. A woman exhibiting completely justifiable doubt, skepticism, critical acumen, exacting standards, and strong preferences of any kind can awaken gnawing anxieties about the nonresponsiveness of more intimate partners. Some men may actually dislike women for doing what any job in business demands because it reminds them of past difficulties in their private lives. These anxieties are alleviated if working women behave affably and girlishly, but this ill fits them for promotion. They are damned for behaving like men and damned if they do not, a classic double bind.

And yet there are some interesting examples of breakthrough. Some women employees may do better abroad than at home and the reasons why are interesting. Nancy Adler looked at six hundred North American women sent to Latin America and Southeast Asia. Their satisfaction rating was appreciably higher than the satisfaction reported by men from the same companies. There were some obvious reasons, such as it being cheap and easy to get help with children and housekeeping. Successful women vouched for by a multinational corporation seem both interesting and attractive to the local population. Their abilities are not questioned and their success evokes admiration.

Adler also found that her female expatriates, having played complementary roles vis-à-vis North American males for much of their lives, were better listeners and better at establishing rapport with local business leaders than were their male counterparts. They were able to elicit more information from local sources and their styles of interaction were more "Latin" and "Eastern" than those of American males. They found these cultures easier to engage.

The reason women may do better abroad is complex but potentially important because it is a great potential career avenue for them. Many countries discriminate against women in business. This discrimination takes roughly the following form.

"As a rule women do not do as well at business as men, but there are exceptions." In Britain, for example, two of the most successful monarchs in history – Elizabeth I and Victoria – have been women. Yet women did not even get the vote until 1919. A culture can acknowledge a fact, but still believe that this fact is exceptional, a belief lasting many years. Rules versus Exceptions are very close to the first of our seven dimensions introduced in Chapter 3, Universalism versus Particularism.

Yet being the exception to a "universal" rule has many advantages. We nearly all want to be "exceptional" as people. We tend to attract admiration, curiosity, and respect if our achievements are unexpected. Indeed, disadvantage is often seen as a springboard for greatness, as in the case of Nelson Mandela. We marvel at the prisoner-statesman or the blind pianist because these people are exceptional and have transformed their own circumstances.

Hence the position of a high-flying North American female expatriate in Malaysia, Singapore, San Paulo, Santiago, etc., is that she is a certified exception. A big corporation is vouching for her talent and has awarded her high status. She is both exceptional and demonstrably competent. If she is also relatively young and personable she has everything going for her. She is more interesting, more visible, more reliable, and more distinguished than a male colleague with a similar position. A corporation would be very smart to build up such women, as in the following capsule case.

---

**CAPSULE CASE**
**An exceptional Dutch woman in Shell**

Senior Shell executives heard through the grapevine that an important Japanese client was angry that a delegation of Shell negotiators was to be headed by a woman. They believed that this signaled to them that the forthcoming negotiations had been downgraded in importance. Shell was extremely reluctant to ask the woman to step aside. She was extremely well qualified for her leadership position and it would have been palpably unjust to leave her out.

She had friends at the University of Tokyo where she had studied. They extended her an invitation to deliver a lecture on one of the evenings she would be in town. The Japanese client was told that this exceptional female scholar, invited to speak at the University, had graciously agreed to extend her stay in order to lead the team of Shell negotiators, and that Shell was extremely fortunate to secure her services. When she entered the boardroom the entire Shell negotiating team applauded her and spoke of her and to her with reverence.

The negotiations went very well and the Japanese hosts joined in their gratitude and admiration for her.

---

You do not directly attack a culture's prejudices where you deem a woman's talents to be exceptional. In time, as exception piles on exception, that culture will be forced to change its rules on the subject of women. In the meantime, exceptionality includes a measure of status that expatriate women can enjoy.

There is another hidden advantage in sending western women abroad. We probably only pay for being different once. Hence, if you are already a foreigner, and therefore different, you might as well be a female foreigner as well. This will not double your difference but help explain it, even excuse it. North Americans are "strange people" and giving high positions to women is among the strange things they do, so come along and talk to her. She must be highly competent; they would not risk their money otherwise – American business is successful.

The anxiety we feel upon encountering strangers has a lot to do with fears that the encounter will be embarrassing, awkward, and unsuccessful. If we are told in advance that the person we are about to meet is a woman of exceptional talent then we are more likely to be excited than anxious, more confident than doubting.

Although the differences between people can be characterized as exciting, instructive, novel, and enlightening, and this certainly helps, not all differences can be glamorized or framed advantageously. Culture shock is a fact of life and we need the emotional muscles to deal with being surprised and confounded in our expectations. If we can prove that global business is successful and enlightening, the horrors of the last century may finally be behind us.

Now let's look at our simulation.

## SIMULATING CULTURE SHOCK: MEET THE DERDIANS

We have helped develop a simulation entitled "Towers for the

Derdians." It "educates the viscera" and teaches us about our own emotions.

Derdia is an imaginary village inhabited by people very different to the visiting team of technicians from the corporation. The job of the technicians is to help the villagers build paper towers. The Derdians like and admire paper towers, which confer great prestige upon them. They are anxious to learn from the visiting technicians, who are similarly keen to serve their corporation in this new and difficult assignment.

Although towers must be built in the approved fashion with only right-angled folds the technology itself is not the problem. The technicians could probably impart the necessary skills in short order were it not for the cultural differences between them and the Derdians. The details of how the simulation is played are set out in Appendix C. Here we will deal with the elements of that simulation that produce culture shock.

Derdians continuously *touch* each other for mutual reassurance; not touching shows disapproval.

They greet by *kissing the shoulder,* but always the shoulder opposite to the one on which the person was first kissed. Irregular forms of kissing are insults. Holding out your hand means "please go away."

Derdians *never say "no."* Instead an exaggerated nodding means "no."

Although Derdian men and women can use tower-building instruments – paper, pencils, scissors, and rulers – women *may not use paper and scissors in the presence of men. Men may not use pencils or rulers in the presence of women.*

Derdian males will *refuse to greet a male stranger unless introduced by a woman*, of whatever group.

When these social norms are acted out they naturally impinge upon the technicians' attempts to instruct their clients on constructing towers. Indeed technical work is persistently obstructed by social and cultural systems.

The technicians will typically misread the Derdians, calling them "childlike," "retarded," "uninterested in towers," or "touchy-feely." The Derdians find the technicians "rude," "direct," "insulting," "arrogant," and "obsessed."

The value of the simulation lies in the mild culture shock imparted by the two groups. It is mild because both groups know it is an exercise but both feel the discomforts and awkwardness of mis-involvements and unsuccessful social encounters. Participants also learn about themselves, about how difficult it is to impart simple technical instructions when you cannot understand or predict the behavior of the locals, about how irritating and frustrating they find incoherent conduct to be and how it renders sensible communication almost impossible.

It helps to give participants a taste of culture shock without the associated trauma, which is real enough when the company sends people out to a cultural environment with which they cannot cope. Some participants are adept at learning quickly about Derdian taboos, but others learn nothing and offend repeatedly while blaming their hosts. Because Derdia is imaginary, prejudices are seen for what they are, anxieties within us, not as something necessarily associated with a defective out-group. We also learn that Derdian norms are consistent and derive logically from their assumptions.

All becomes clear when the assumptions are spelled out. For precise instructions on visiting Derdia, see Appendix C.

In conclusion, we learn about culture not simply through books and seminars that anticipate the difficulties we may face and provide intellectual understanding of these, but through making errors and suffering cultural shocks. Culture shock is a form of inner anxiety that gnaws away at us, so that we try to control our anxiety by myriad devices, most of which impede accurate communication. It may be better to confront our own errors and learn from these, instead of exhausting ourselves by evasions. The degree of shock can be classified from severe to mild.

Even those who learn valuable lessons from global experiences may not be properly debriefed when they go home and locally grown talent may be underestimated.

Women who play complementary roles to men during early socialization may be more adept at establishing rapport with foreigners, since they are used to engaging Western men in styles similar to those used by foreigners. Women can use their disadvantage as a springboard to become notable exceptions to local rules. They can make themselves interesting rather than threatening.

However, the shock of engaging foreign cultures never goes away completely and cannot be wholly pleasant. Those destined for foreign engagements need to build up emotional muscles and learn how anxiety can sap their energies. For these purposes the Derdian simulation is recommended.

# Endnote

The human race suffers from a curious malady. We have a brilliantly advanced understanding of the world of things and individuals, and yet an abysmal grasp of values and relationships. The world of things/individuals is a world that lends itself readily to analysis, reduction, and objectification. This is a real world, which makes very good sense. Most of us marry one partner or another, live in one house or another, drive one car or another, spend our money or save it. Everywhere we face either/or choices between hard realities. We stand at proverbial crossroads using "swords of decision" to cut off all directions save one. We would not dream of negating this logic and this paradigm.

Yet there is another world and the road to it is one rather less traveled or understood. Values and human relationships do not yield their secrets to means–ends rationality or technical reason. This is because values are not things at all but differences, which presuppose continua with diverse extremities. The logic by which values and the persons holding those values relate is wholly different from our manipulative habits of mind. Worse still, it appears "contradictory" and irrational to the keepers of our conventional wisdom. In this book we hope to have said enough to bring you with us on this neglected path to an understanding vital to our future. Human Resources are not like physical and material resources. They cannot be grasped by the same paradigm. They need and deserve a circular logic of their own, what Paul Tillich called "Encompassing Reason" in his book *The Courage to Be*. This has been an attempt to introduce such logic. If you read this you must have persevered to the very end. Thank you for your patience. We hope it was rewarded.

# Appendices

## APPENDIX A: ROLE-PLAY IN THE QUENCHY INTERNATIONAL CASE

Quenchy International is a large multinational beverage company with its headquarters in the USA. While it grew rapidly in the 70s and 80s, its results from 1990 to date show a flattening followed by a slight decline. International HR seeks to halt this decline with a world wide Advanced Staff Appraisal System (ASAS), which will locate merit wherever this occurs, learn from it and reward it.

The case is initially described in Chapter 8. Especially important are Boxes 1 and 2, including a memo from J. A. Daniels and his Guidance Notes. All participants should read these before the role-play commences.

When doing role-play, it is better not to give those playing the part of various HR directors any scripts. Instead, brief them on the underlying assumptions and attitudes of the persons they are playing. This is done in the pages that follow. The individual actors can then come up with their own interpretations of their roles and characters. This will sound more convincing and may convert the actor to the role being played, so that they clearly understand the Japanese/Iranian/German/Italian points of view. All points of view are logically coherent and derive rationally from underlying assumptions. This exercise should dramatize the high plausibility and consistency of different cultural viewpoints, which when spelled out make good sense. We judge others as "irrational" when we have not grasped their basic assumptions.

### Exercise

Re-enact the meeting in J. A. Daniel's office between Mantovini, Klaus, Yakamoto, Khasmi, and Jones. Each party has half an hour to work out arguments and half an hour for the ensuing discussion. None of the characters should be rude or misbehave. Each is trying very had to explain the probable fate of Daniels' "Wise Lessons" in the culture they know only too well. You may show frustration and exasperation but try to keep the discussion civil. Daniels also defends the wisdom of his own position and explains why everyone should understand it. Jones understands Daniels or may, if wished, play a mediating and reconciliatory role. Jones, as opposed to Daniels, is widely traveled and respects diversity.

We will now go through the cultural role-briefs.

## Cultural role-brief for Mr(s) Jones – USA

Cultural dimensions for you to integrate into your attitude:

| | |
|---|---|
| Universalism | Individualism |
| Specific | Neutral |
| Achievement | Internal control |
| Sequential | Strong task/result orientation |

The Guided Missile culture is most natural for you.

- Obviously, you are very satisfied with your own boss's proposal. You want the group to reach agreement but are quite sure that your boss has outlined an ideal ASAS.

- You feel especially strongly about the individualized system of pay for performance (Individualism). According to you, those who work hardest deserve the best and introducing financial incentives will certainly lead to better business results.

- You also like the idea of limiting the system by rewarding only the highest salary groups. Those are, by definition, the people who work hardest. You feel you need to praise and reward them for that. (Achievement.)

- Also, you would be quite disappointed if your colleagues were to reject the idea of a universal and standardized ASAS. You believe it would be wise to stick to the proposal. In the US it works so well; why shouldn't it work in other countries? Only if your colleagues come up with reasonable arguments will you be willing to compromise (Universalism).

- You like the idea of separating the person from the task. According to you, this is the only way to ensure objectivity and fair play. (Specificity.) Staff appraisal should definitely focus on achieving results.

- Ideally everyone should be in charge of their own track record, controlling their destiny, shaping their own future, making their mark. The appraisal system develops autonomy (Inner Direction). Results follow logically and sequentially from greater efforts.

However, you have traveled extensively in Italy and visited Japan four times and are very concerned that employees in other regions should not be offended. You are keen to discover if what they prefer can somehow be reconciled with what Daniels wants. You intend to listen to all objections very respectfully and make constructive suggestions.

## Cultural role-brief for Mr(s) Khasmi – Iran

Cultural dimensions for you to integrate into your attitude:

| | |
|---|---|
| Particularism | Communitarianism |
| Diffuse | Affective |
| Ascription | External control |
| Synchronic | |

The Family culture is most natural for you.

- You are relatively happy with the way performance measurement is presented. However, you have one footnote to add: the achievement of results can never be objective. Indeed, there are several aspects playing an important role:
  – The difficulty of the fixed target (how big is the effort that is to be made)?
  – The influence of the unstable Iranian business environment on the possibility of reaching targets; i.e., under which circumstances do targets have to be reached? (External Control.) HQ has no conception of how relatively poor Iranians are and how well your people have actually done in difficult circumstances.

- You do not believe in the principles of individual pay for performance as favored by Daniels. You believe it is unfair to reward individuals at the cost of the team. You think it is more motivating to reward a group (department/division) than individuals. If the group is motivated to work hard and receives a salary increase, every single individual will benefit from that. But it does not work the other way around. On the contrary, if an individual is given extra rewards for outstanding results, this might even demotivate the group (why are we all working so hard if we are not allowed to share in the profit?). Hence the competitive aspect detracts from the functioning of a team. People who think too much about their own rewards also tend to neglect customers and proper service. (Communitarianism.)

- Although you are not against having a standardized, worldwide ASAS, you think it is wise to attune some aspect of it to the traditions and values of local operating companies (Particularism). People know almost nothing about Iran and the particular difficulties under which it labors.

- For the same reasons you fear that many of the "Wise Lessons" are not applicable in your country due to cultural constraints, such as the issue of separating the task from the person (Diffuse), and the advice of being frank, open, and confrontational, which risks the loss of face and insults the sense of honor. The great advantage of indirection is that employees will understand if ready to understand. Otherwise, oblique critiques will pass them by.

- You have some good ideas about Appraisal Criteria and you will put them forward in the meeting; "respectful, modest, dutiful, and pious" should be on the list. After all, we are one Family.

## Cultural role-brief for Mr(s) Mantovini – Italy

Cultural dimensions for you to integrate into your attitude:

| | |
|---|---|
| Particularism | Communitarianism |
| Diffuse | Affective |
| Ascription | Internal control |
| Synchronic | |

The natural culture for you is the Family Incubator.

Overall, you are not very happy with the outline proposed by Daniels. The "Wise Lessons" run counter to too many of the countries' and national organizations' cultural values. You believe the outline for the ASAS is an ethnocentric one. Actually, Daniels' memo has quite upset you. You are absolutely sure that it would never be accepted in the Italian subsidiary. This opinion is based, among others, on the following considerations:

*Jokes around the Italian company*
- On several partitions in the open plan office are cartoons of faces with business results plastered across them so as to expunge their features.

- In another cartoon a woman wears a baseball cap labeled "top performer." Her friend is asking "but how were your results achieved?" In the background is a heap of the bodies of the dead and injured.

- In a third cartoon a masseur is working on several prone statistics. "You'll feel a lot better when I've massaged these," he says.

*Pay for performance*
- Although you believe that it can, under some circumstances, be a motivational tool, you don't like the idea that it should be individualized. In

your opinion the proposed system of individual pay for performance can negatively impact group morale. (Communitarianism.)

- Imagine person A gets a salary increase because they have reached all the fixed targets and assume that this person could only reach targets thanks to the continuous help and input of person B (who, because of help given, could not reach their own targets). It would be utterly unfair and unwise to reward person A and not person B, because next time person B will think twice before supporting A. In your situation individual pay for performance works against teamwork (Communitarianism).

As an alternative, you would like to propose that rewards are based on departmental/divisional performance. A bonus for high performance (i.e., reaching the divisional targets) will then be equally distributed amongst all employees in that department/division.

In your view creativity is its own reward and you fear that if performance is defined in advance creativity could suffer. You also worry that dialogue between appraiser and appraisee, with its subtle blend of supporting the person while improving performance, could be weakened by the either/or decision of giving or withholding rewards. This, in your view, is too specific and insufficiently affective, diffuse, and ascriptive. What counts in being creative is the particular person.

## Cultural role-brief for Mr(s) Klaus – Germany

Cultural dimensions for you to integrate into your attitude:

| | |
|---|---|
| Universalism | Individualism |
| Diffuse | Neutral |
| Achievement | Internal control |
| Sequential | |

Your natural culture is the Eiffel Tower.

- On the whole you feel there is some merit in the memo written by J. A. Daniels. You are particularly keen on registering expertise using the ASAS. You believe it is great to have, finally, a universal measure that you can use as a yardstick to work on career and staff planning at Quenchy. With the new Staff Appraisal reports, you will finally have a universal and standardized document at hand (Universalism).
- You are inclined to support any proposal with an orientation to developing higher levels of expertise.
- You are particularly serious about one issue; appraisees should also be

evaluated on their compliance with rules, procedures, and company regulations (Universalism).

- You support individualized systems of pay but believe these should be oriented to accumulating knowledge (Individualism/Achievement).
- You support the idea of a standardized staff appraisal system worldwide. Adapting ASAS to the different requirements of the various operating companies would inevitably lead to confusion!

Your major problem is with the fragmentary nature of the appraisal system and its neglect of knowledge of the whole corporation, which must diffusely flow through the organization. With the help of an English dictionary you locate the word "suboptimal" and point out individual achievements can be sub-optimal to the enhancement of the whole organization. "Anglo-American empiricism is reductive," you announce although most people in the room look puzzled. "My view is holistic," you add, but puzzlement continues. "It is fine to record successes, but we must also ask why. This system is a good start but lacks insight." Klaus feels quite isolated.

## Cultural role-brief for Mr(s) Yakomoto – Japan

Cultural dimensions for you to integrate into your attitude:

| | |
|---|---|
| Particularism | Communitarianism |
| Diffuse | Ascription |
| External control | Neutral |

Harmony between people as way of improving tasks

Your natural culture is the Guided Family.

- According to you, too much emphasis is usually placed on the task aspects of the job. It seems that the human dimension is often underappreciated. You would like to appraise people not only on the basis of what and how much they achieved, but also on the basis of how they achieved it (with creativity, by successfully working in teams, etc.). Quality and integrity are just as important as output.
- As far as competencies are concerned you believe that far more emphasis should be placed on leadership skills and the ability to coach and develop others. If a person is excellent at achieving business results, but hopeless in developing teamwork, coaching, and leadership skills, that employee has done only part of their job. You find it important that staff appraisal is not seen as an isolated thing, a boring form that has to be filled in once a year, but as an integrated part of total management.

Therefore the ASAS should stress both task management and people management. Just as you have to deal with an employee as a total person, you must appraise them on the basis of relationships formed. (Diffuse).

- Furthermore, you believe it is a shared responsibility of both superior and manager to improve performance. Evaluating performance is not sufficient. The appraiser should not act only as judge but as coach. It is their responsibility to support and lead the appraisee to even better performance by practicing mentorship, making document/training plans, etc. Therefore you find it necessary that the ASAS gives due credit to mentors and does not pretend that the employee is solely responsible for good performance. It is rather the relationship that "performs" (Communitarianism).

- You do not think it is wise to standardize ASAS worldwide. Each culture is different and has different ways of solving problems. For example, the "Ten Wise Lessons for an Effective Staff Appraisal" would be totally counterproductive when applied to your country: how can you isolate a person from a job? How can you evaluate on the basis of this year only? Should you not take efforts and progress into account? So-called facts have been torn from their contexts (too specific). If you use these to be confrontational, you will wreck the very system you are trying to improve.

After the one-hour exercise, throw open the discussion to all participants and to any audience. What did they notice? Get those who played the various roles to discuss their underlying beliefs. Did they feel others were listening? If Daniels imposes this system what do they think will happen?

If there is an audience for this role-play get them to form teams and "map" the positions of the six principals on the dilemmas or dimensions they see operating. You will find the Dilemma Template in Appendix B. Copy and redistribute three or four of these to each team and ask them to locate the arguments of each of the HR directors in the role-play. They may ask this director additional questions if they wish, so as to discover where they stand.

Now ask the teams to reconcile these dilemmas and design a truly cross-cultural appraisal system, referring back to Chapter 8, if they need to.

# APPENDIX B: THE DILEMMA TEMPLATE

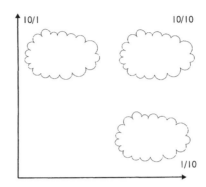

Fill in the template above whenever you are trying to "map" someone's position. Do not forget to map your own position. All we ever discover is other people's reaction to our own inputs, so the difference between you and the other is crucial to any understanding.

Please guard against the following common errors: The two dimensions must both have positive or at least neutral descriptions along the vertical and horizontal dimensions. Try to make these equally attractive. In contrast, the epithet words inside each box at top left and bottom right are rude and satirical. Here you are mocking a value taken too far or over the top. Again, the two epithets should be equally insulting. The idea is to place boundaries around any conflict that will not be crossed. All parties agree that their ideas, if pushed to excess, become absurd.

This is not designed to exercise your imagination, but to enable you to map what is really going on. Be as truthful as you can about your culture, as you know it.

# APPENDIX C: SIMULATION EXERCISE FOR TECHNICIANS VISITING DERDIA

## Situation

You are all inhabitants of the village of Derdia. A team of international experts is coming to visit you and will stay with you in your village for a limited period of time (30 minutes). They are coming to teach you how to build paper towers, according to skills only they are familiar with. You are all very interested in this skill since your prime interest is in mastering the skills of building paper towers.

Tower-shaped constructions have always been a source of status in your country and by mastering the skills that the international experts have, you can increase the prestige and income level of your village. In addition, an agreement made in your capital calls for you to receive money and food from experts in exchange for your work on building the tower, an agreement which is less important to you and which, anyway, you took for granted to be the case. You are expected to learn from the experts by building the tower in cooperation with them and are highly motivated to build this tower.

## Rules for social behavior

*Touching:* Derdians have the habit of touching each other all the time. While working, and even in passing, they touch each other. Not touching means the same as "I'd rather you'd go away."

*Greetings:* The way of greeting is a kiss on the shoulder. If you give a kiss on the right shoulder, you are kissed on your left shoulder. If you gave it on the left shoulder, you are kissed on the right one. Simultaneous kissing is therefore not possible. Any other form of kissing is seen as an act of humiliation. The Derdian will react to that with abuse, explaining to offenders that they have no reason to be so insulting. Holding out a hand to someone means "Please be so kind as to leave me alone. Go away please."

*Yes/No:* A Derdian never uses the word "no." Instead, "no" is expressed by saying "yes" with an exaggerated nodding at the same time.

*Taboos:* All the men and women in Derdia know how to use paper, pencils, scissors, and rulers. They are very well acquainted with these materials. But there is a gender-related taboo concerning the use of them. Women will never use paper and scissors in the presence of men and men will never use a pencil or ruler in the presence of women.

*Strangers:* Derdians are always friendly to strangers. Naturally, they expect the stranger to behave according to their rules. A Derdian male will never make contact with a male stranger unless a female first introduces that stranger to him, no matter if she is a Derdian or an outsider. A Derdian never speaks about (explains) his own behavior code and always sticks to it in the presence of strangers. Derdians have a strong sense of social control among themselves.

## Assignments

You have 30 minutes to learn how to build the tower, since the experts will have to return to their own country after that time. Try to build the tower within the given time. You will have 30 minutes to practice the Derdian behavior and prepare yourself on how to cooperate with the experts. About 15 minutes after you start your preparation one or two experts will visit you for no longer than 5 minutes in order to exchange information.

Points for discussion after the exercise.

- What is your opinion about the experts' skills in their transfer of knowledge?
- What did the experts do particularly well?
- What could they have improved?
- Give a short summary of yourselves as a team.
- Give a short description about the success of the project.
- What would you change to be more effective next time?
- Does this exercise/simulation relate to your own work/job?

### The Derdian case used as an assessment simulation

In order to help the selection process to be able to assess whether a person has talent to become an international manager, it is important to know the competencies you need to look for. As we described in the first three chapters of *21 leaders for the 21st Century*, the successful international leader needs to be aware of, respect, and reconcile cultural differences. During the Derdian simulation both the experts and the Derdians can be assessed on those competencies.

## Awareness of cultural differences

The first test for the awareness of cultural differences is during the preparation for the brief advance visit of the experts to Derdia. Some experts are so focused on the technical aspects that no mention is made of possible cultural differences. This occurs despite the fact that the exercise is introduced as a cross-cultural simulation. But the Derdians are also very focused on preparing themselves for the right behavior as described in their brief. It is only seldom that an individual Derdian raises the issue of the technicians' possible cultural differences.

The second time to assess these qualities is the advance visit of the technical experts to Derdia. In most of the cases we see that the technically-prepared experts visit Derdian society with a highly task-oriented focus. We therefore see initially that this technical focus becomes a hindrance to being sensitive towards Derdian culture and vice versa. Here the first assessment can be made. The assessors attribute extra points to both technicians and Derdians who show they are aware of the differences. More than 85 percent of them don't even raise the issue of cultural differences and are therefore quite surprised and, in the case of the technicians even shocked, by the odd behaviors of their counterparts.

## Respect for cultural differences

Even in cases where either technicians or Derdians are quite prepared for cultural differences, there is rarely much respect for these differences. The feedback for those who score a low number of points is typically along these lines: "These Derdians are a bunch of retarded people from the local asylum. They tap each other on the shoulder continuously. They always say yes, as infants do, and on top of that they kiss each other on the shoulder," or "They are not interested in our towers at all. When we try to explain to them they walk away, and raising a ruler or pair of scissors make them kiss. I don't think they understand English. It's an underdeveloped culture. Let's give up and go back home."

From the Derdian side, we often hear after the advance visit that the technicians are not interested in Derdian culture and don't respect their principles of introduction and greeting. All in all there are only a few individuals who try to respect their counterparts' culture and who are eager to understand it without judging at first glance. From the technicians' side, the lack of respect shows most clearly in the complete underestimation of the Derdians' level of knowledge. Both in the advance visit and the actual exercise you can see the technicians being patronizing. They may ask whether the Derdians know what a ruler is and it is not exceptional to see technicians walking around with scissors clicking, asking "Do you know what these are for?" The best answer we recorded was a Derdian saying "Yes; for cutty, cutty." When you treat people from another culture as children they are either insulted or play the child.

The Derdians' lack of respect is clearly shown by the frequent lack of interest in the modus operandi of the technicians. Moreover, the responsibility for the success of the transfer of technology is often put into the hands of the technicians. In our experience we have found that the key to success is often in the hands of the Derdians, because they are not only in the majority but have the knowledge about the cultural differences. This (prior) knowledge is so much more powerful than the knowledge of building towers. A child of six would know how to build this simple type of tower.

### Reconciliation of (cultural) differences

Once our international candidates on the technical or Derdian side have shown some awareness and respect for the obvious cultural differences the main challenge starts. Successful candidates will reconcile the major dilemmas that these differences raise. In most cases the Derdians reconcile from different starting points than the technicians. Let's start with the major dilemma.

## 1. The technical and social side of the transfer of technology

Every process of technology transfer has a social and a technical side. The type of interaction between the two will make or break the exercise. An interesting aspect of the Derdian exercise is that both parties have the same or complementary objectives: building towers and the exchange of technology. The dilemma is best represented as follows: If the technicians keep to their technical brief the risk is that they will just ask the Derdians to shut up and listen. Similarly, the Derdians might only exaggerate their role-play and continuously keep on introducing Derdians to the newcomers and kissing them on the shoulder. This is very realistic, since many Derdians and technicians tend to stereotype their own roles, particularly in cases where pressure builds up.

Successful technicians will soon take the (fairly simple) technical materials for granted and focus on showing respect for Derdian culture. Open questions are frequently asked and more relate to how Derdian cultural idiosyncrasies can help them in building towers.

On the Derdian side we see that the most talented people will find ways to implicitly demonstrate Derdian culture to the technicians without giving their culture away. Successful Derdians and technicians will try to bridge the gap between the cultures without giving up their own roles.

## 2. Be prepared for the other culture or be yourself

The second dilemma relates to the individual participant's level and how much they are prepared to give up on their own values for the sake of the others. The dilemma is perhaps best phrased as "on the one hand you need to build on your own strength while on the other you want to adapt to the values of others." We know very well what happens when both parties stick to their own values. It is against them. The more the experts focus on the technical side, the more the Derdians start to focus on their social brief.

There is an interesting dynamic unfolding where both parties adapt to each other. We have seen HR practitioners playing the roles of experts so shocked by their unexpected experiences during the advance visit that they turned into people demonstrating socially sensitive behavior. So sensitive did they become that the Derdians at a certain stage started shouting "We want towers. We want towers!"

Participants who score highest on the assessment sheets are the ones who know exactly what their uncompromising values are so that they can easily adjust other values and behaviors. This is true for both Derdians and technicians. A good example of effective behavior on the Derdian side is when they introduce and greet themselves amongst Derdians to show the visiting technicians how it is done. An corresponding example for the technicians is for them to take some Derdians aside – after being introduced properly – to explain to them the beginnings of tower building.

In neither of the cases is too much given away from the cultural assumptions, though enough flexibility is shown to bend toward the other side.

A final footnote on the reconciliation of this dilemma is that the exercise doesn't invite the experts to be culturally well prepared for the venture. The degree to which one is culturally prepared is often seen as one of the most crucial areas for being successful across cultures. In real life technical preparations, like those so often summarized in the "Dos and Taboos" kind of books, are useful but not really sufficient. Preparation through multiple sources seems most effective. The accumulation of viewpoints of a culture through movies, local novels, cross-cultural books, and historical accounts is much more effective than the "dos and don'ts" approach so often referred to. For the Derdians this is much less necessary. They might expect what is coming from the visitors. Once people are better prepared culture shock is much reduced.

## 3. Overestimating versus underestimating the knowledge level of the Derdians

A third dilemma concerns the correct estimation of the Derdians' knowledge level about tower building.

On the one hand – in the (likely) event that you underestimate the knowledge of the Derdians – you might insult them (remember "Do you know what these are for?") or invite them to play stupid. The best example we ever encountered was an American engineer who had his first job abroad in Moscow. When he first met his Russian colleagues he took an electrical wire and clearly articulated the word "electricity" while showing it to them. One of the Russians replied by asking whether it was the same electricity they used on their MIR spaceships.

On the other hand, by assuming too much knowledge, you might well ask the Derdians if they have understood the ideas, and get a collective nodding as the result. Very often across cultures this is even more important.

Effective international managers continuously show that they respect the level of intelligence of the people they face. Zooming in a little below the actual knowledge level is shown to be most effective. But how can one get there without aiming too high or too low? The answer lies in asking open questions, questions without too much cynicism. The place where questions are asked is crucial. We have seen that, during the simulation, the most effective experts took Derdians aside and asked them about what they knew. there was no group pressure nor possibilities of loss of face.

## 4. Individual survival versus Group sharing

It is amazing how embarrassed the technicians can get when confronted with the Derdians' "odd" behaviors. Furthermore, the introductions and greetings are very individual. Therefore you see very quickly that the individual experts have to rely on themselves in order to survive. In survival mode it is not easy to share experiences with other expert team members. This often means that one tries to find individual breakthroughs in order to find a way out of this odd situation. However, we have often seen that one of the experts might find the key to the greeting by kissing the right shoulder, while simultaneously a colleague was still struggling with it.

This is a real dilemma because once you act as an expert group there is often too little learning, and when operating as an individual there is not enough sharing. Once the pieces of the individual puzzles are put together the team can get the whole picture and the Derdian culture is "cracked" much more quickly. On the other hand, we have seen experts who stuck together but didn't learn anything as a group because they were inaccessible.

The best way to get the Derdian culture cracked is to learn individually but plan for time-outs where best practices and learning can be shared. Because of the chaotic environment, one needs to plan for these time-outs. Too often people are carried away by their individual excitement.

# Bibliography

Adler, N. J. (1994) *Competitive Frontiers*, Oxford: Blackwell Business.

Allinson, R. E. *et al.* (1989) *Understanding the Chinese Mind*, Hong Kong: Oxford University Press.

Argyris, C. (1980) *The Concept of Rigorous Research*, New York: Academic Press.

Argyris, C. (1986) "Skilled Incompetence," *Harvard Business Review*, September/October.

Argyris, C. (1985) *Strategy, Change, and Defensive Routines*, Boston: Pitman.

Argyris, C. with Putnam, R. and Smith, D. M. (1985) *Action Science*, San Francisco: Jossey-Bass.

Argyris, C. and Schön, D. (1978) *Organizational Learning*, Reading, MA: Addison-Wesley.

Baden-Fuller, C. and Stopford, J. (1992) *Rejuvenating the Mature Business*, London: Routledge.

Barber, B. R. (1995) *Jihad vs. McWorld*, New York: Times Books.

Bartlett, C. A. & Ghoshal, S. (1991) *Managing Across Borders*, Boston, MA: Harvard Business School Press.

Bateson, G. (1978) *Steps to an Ecology of Mind*, New York: Jason Aronson.

Bateson, M. C. (1991) *Our Own Metaphor*, Washington, DC: Smithsonian Institution Press.

Belbin, R.M. (1996) *Management Teams: Why They Succeed or Fail*, London: Butterworth-Heinemann

Bell, D. (1976) *The Coming of Post-Industrial Society*, New York: Basic Books.

Bell, D. (1976) *The Cultural Contradictions of Capitalism*, New York: Basic Books.

Benedict, R. (1934) *Patterns of Culture*, Boston: Houghton-Mifflin.

Bennis, W. (1989) *On Becoming a Leader*, Reading, MA: Addison-Wesley.

Bennis, W. and Nanus, B. (1985) *Leaders: The Strategies for Taking Charge*, New York: Harper and Row.

Bennis, W. and Townsend, R. (1995) *Reinventing Leadership*, New York: William Morrow.

Berle, A. and Means, G. (1932) *The Modern Corporation and Private Property*, Portland, OR: Transaction Publishers

Berlin, I. (1953) *The Hedgehog and the Fox*, New York: Simon & Schuster

Berlin, I. (1958) *Two Concepts of Liberty*, Oxford: Clarendon.

Bion, W. R. (1961) *Experiences in Groups*, London: Tavistock.

Blake, R. R. and Mouton, J. S. (1964) *The Managerial Grid*, Houston: Gulf Publishing.

Bohm, D. (1996) *On Dialogue*, New York: Routledge.

de Bono, E. (1982) *Lateral Thinking*, London: Penguin.

de Bono, E. (1994) *Water Logic*, London: Penguin.

Brandenburger, A. and Nalebuff, B. J. (1996) *Coopetition*, New York: Doubleday

Burns, J. M. (1978) *Leadership*, New York: Harper and Row.

Burns, T. and Stalker, G. M. (1961) *The Management of Innovation*, London: Tavistock.

Cameron, S. K. and Quinn, R. E. (1999) *Diagnosing and Changing Organizational Culture*, Reading, MA.: Addison-Wesley

Campbell, J. (1971) *The Portable Jung*, New York: Viking.

Capra, F. (1975) *The Tao of Physics*, San Francisco, CA: Shambhala.

Carlzon, J. (1986) *Moments of Truth*, New York: Harper and Row.

Carrol, R. (1988) *Cultural Misunderstandings*, Chicago: University of Chicago Press.

Chakravarthy, B. and Lorange, P. (1991) *Managing the Strategy Process*, Englewood Cliffs, NJ: Prentice Hall.

Chesbrough, H. W. (2003) "The Era of Open Innovation," *MIT Sloan Management Review*, Spring.

Christensen, R., Andrews, K., Bower, J. *et al.* (1987) *Business Policy: Text and Cases*, Homewood, IL: Irwin.

Collins, J. C. and Porras, J. I. (1994) *Built to Last*, London: Century.

Csikszentmihalyi, M. (1990) *Flow: The Psychology of Optimal Experience*, New York: Harper.

Davis, S. and Meyer, C. (1998) *Blur: The Speed of Change in the Connected Economy*, Reading, MA: Addison-Wesley

de Geus, A. P. (1997) *The Living Company*, London: Nicholas Brealey.

de Geus, A. P. (1998) "Planning as Learning," *Harvard Business Review*, March/April.

de Wit, B. and Meyer, R. (1999) *Strategy Synthesis: Resolving Strategy Paradoxes*, London: International Thomson.

Deming, W. E. (1982) *Quality, Productivity, and Competitive Position*, Cambridge, MA: MIT Press.

Deming, W. E. (1986) *Out of the Crises*, Technology Center for Advanced Engineering Study.

Douglas, S. and Wind, Y. (1987) "The Myth of Globalization," *Columbia Journal of World Business*, Winter.

Drucker, P. (1954) [reissued 1993] *The Practice of Management*, New York: HarperBusiness.

Drucker, P. (1999) "Knowledge Worker Productivity: The Biggest Challenge," *California Management Review*, vol. 41, no. 2, pp. 79–94

Drucker, P. (1999) "Managing Oneself," *Harvard Business Review*, March

Evans, P., Doz, Y. and Laurent, A. (eds) (1989) *Human Resource Management in International Firms*, New York: Macmillan Press, pp. 113–143.

Evans, P., Pucik, V. and Barsoux, J.-L. (2002) *The Global Challenge: International Human Resource Management*, New York: McGraw Hill, pp. 372–375.

Festinger, L. (1957) *A Theory of Cognitive Dissonance*, Evanston, IL: Row Peterson.

Florida R. (2002) *The Rise of the Creative Class and How It's Transforming Work, Life, Community, and Everyday Life*, New York: Perseus Books

Follette, M. P. (1987) *Freedom and Coordination: Lectures in Business Organization*, New York: Garland.

Frank, R. H. and Cook, P. J. (1995) *The Winner-Take-All Society*, New York: Free Press.

Freeman, E. and Reed, D. (1993) "Stockholders and Stakeholders: A New Perspective on Corporate Governance," *California Management Review*, vol. 25, no. 3, Spring.

Friedman, T. (1999) *The Lexus and the Olive Tree*, New York: HarperCollins.

Getzels, J.W. and Jackson, P.W. (1962) *Creativity and Intelligence Explorations with Gifted Students*, New York: Wiley.

Goulder, A. W. (1964) *Patterns of Industrial Bureaucracy*, New York: Free Press

Hall, E. T. (1959) *The Silent Language*, New York: Doubleday.

Hall, E. T. (1983) *Dance of Life: The Other Dimension of Time*, New York: Doubleday.

Hall, E. T. (1989) *The Cultures of France and Germany*, Yarmouth, MA: Intercultural Press.

Hall, E. T. and Hall, M. R. (1987) *Hidden Differences: Doing Business with the Japanese*, New York: Doubleday.

Hamel, G. (1996) "Strategy as Revolution," *Harvard Business Review*, July/August.

Hamel, G. and Prahalad, C. K. (1989) "Strategic Intent," *Harvard Business Review*, May/June.

Hamel, G. and Prahalad, C. K. (1994) *Something for the Future*, Boston, MA: Harvard Business School Press.

Hamel, G., Doz, Y. and Prahalad, C. K. (1989) "Collaborate with your Competitors and Win," *Harvard Business Review*, January/February.

Hammer, M. and Champy, J. (1993) *Reengineering the Corporation: A Manifesto for Business Revolution*, New York: Harper Business

Hampden-Turner, C. M. (1973) *Radical Man: Towards a Theory of Psycho-social Development*, London: Duckworth.

Hampden-Turner, C. M. (1974) *Sane Asylum: Inside the Delancey Street Foundation*, New York: William Morrow.

Hampden-Turner, C. M. (1981) *Maps of the Mind*, New York: Macmillan.

Hampden-Turner, C. M. (1984) *Gentlemen and Tradesmen*, London: Routledge and Kegan Paul.

Hampden-Turner, C. M. (1985) "Approaching Dilemmas," *Shell Guides to Planning*, No. 3.

Hampden-Turner, C. M. (1992) *Creating Corporate Culture*, Reading, MA: Addison-Wesley.

Hampden-Turner, C. M. (1994) *Charting the Corporate Mind: From Dilemma to Strategy*, Oxford: Basil Blackwell.

Hampden-Turner, C. M. and Teng-Ki, T. (2002), "Six Dilemmas of Entrepreneurship: Can Singapore Transform itself to Become an Innovative Economy?," *Nanyang Business Review*, vol. 1, no. 2 July–December.

Handy, C. (1978) *The Gods of Management*, London: Souvenir Press.

Handy, C. (1989) *The Age of Unreason*, London: Business Books.

Handy, C. (1994) *The Age of Paradox*, Boston, MA: Harvard Business School Press.

Harrison, R. (1981) "Start-up: The Care and Feeding of Infant Systems," *Organizational Dynamics*, September.

Hedley, B. (1997) "Strategy and the "Business Portfolio," *Long Range Planning*, vol. 10, February, pp. 9–15.

Hofstede, G. (1980) *Cultures' Consequences*, Beverly Hills: Sage.

Hofstede, G. (1991) *Cultures and Organizations: Software of the Mind*, New York: McGraw-Hill.

Huizinga, J. (1970) *Homo Ludens: A Study of the Play Element in Culture*, New York: Harper.

Hurst, D. K. (1984) "Of Boxes, Bubbles and Effective Management," *Harvard Busienss Review*, May/June.

Hurst, D. K. (1995) *Crisis and Renewal*, Boston, MA: Harvard Business School Press.

Imai, M. (1986) *Kaizen: The Key to Japan's Competitive Success*, Chicago: McGraw-Hill

Inzerilli, G. and Laurent, A. (1983) "Managerial Views of Organization Structure in France and the USA," *International Studies of Management and Organization*, XIII(1–2).

Jacobi, J. (1973) *The Psychology of C. G. Jung*, New Haven: Yale University Press

Jacques, E. (1976) *A General Theory of Bureaucracy*, London: Heinemann.

Jacques, E. (1982) *The Form of Time*, New York: Crane Rusak.

Jacques, E. (1982) *Free Enterprise, Fair Employment*, New York: Crane Rusak.

Johnson, B. (1992) *Polarity Management: Identifying and Managing Unsolvable Problems*, Amherst: HRD Press.

Joynt, P. and Warner, M. (2001) *Managing Across Cultures*, Florence, KY: Thomson Learning

Jung C. G. (1971), *Psychological Types*, London: Routledge & Kegan Paul

Kaplan, R. S. and Norton, D. P. (1992) "The Balanced Scorecard: Measures that Drive Performance," *Harvard Business Review*, January.

Kelly, K. (1998) *New Rules for the New Economy*, New York: Viking.

Kelly, M. (1999) *The Divine Right of Capital*, San Francisco: Berrett-Kohler.

Kohn, A. (1992) *Published by Rewards*, Boston: Beacon Press.

Kwak, M. (2003) "The Paradoxical Effects of Diversity," *MIT Sloan Management Review*, Spring.

Laing, R. D. (1965) *The Divided Self*, New York: Penguin.

Laurent, A. (1983) "The Cultural Diversity of Western Conceptions of Management," *International Studies of Management and Organization*, XIII (1–2).

Laurent, A. (1986) "The Cross Cultural Puzzle of International Human Resource Management," *Human Resource Management*, 25(1).

Laurent, A. (1991) "Cross Cultural Management for Pan European Companies," in Spyrous Makridiakis (ed.) *Europe 1992 and Beyond*, San Francisco, CA: Jossey-Bass.

Lawler, E. (1986) *High Involvement Management*, San Francisco, CA: Jossey-Bass.

Lawrence, P.R. and Lorsch, J. W. (1967) *Organization and Environment*, Boston, MA: Harvard Division of Research.

Lecky, P. (1945) *Self-consistency – A Theory of Personality*, New York: Island Press.

Levitt, T. (1983) "The Globalization of Markets," *Harvard Business Review*, May/June.

Lewin, K. (1951) *Field Theory in Social Science*, New York: Harper.

Lipman-Blumen, J. and Leavitt, H. J. (2001) *Hot Groups: Seeding Them, Feeding Them, and Using Them to Ignite Your Organization*, New York: Oxford University Press Inc

Lorange, P. and Vancil, R. F. (1997) *Strategic Planning Systems*, Englewood Cliffs, NJ: Prentice Hall.

Lorenzoni, G. and Baden-Fuller, C. (1995) "Creating a Strategy Center to Manage a Web of Partners," *California Management Review*, vol. 37, no. 3.

McGregor, D. (1960) *The Human Side of Enterprise*, New York: McGraw-Hill

McKenzie, J. (1996) *Paradox: The Next Strategic Dimension*, New York: McGraw-Hill.

Maruyama, M. (1963) "The Second Cybernetics," *American Scientist*, 51.

Maruyama, M. (1982) "New Mindscapes for Future Business Policy and Management," *Technological Forecasting and Social Change*, 21.

Maruyama, M. (1989) "Epistemological Sources of New Business Problems in the International Environment," *Human Systems Management*.

Maslow, A. (1954) *Motivation and Personality*, New York: Harper and Row.

Miller, D. (1990) *The Icarus Paradox: How Excellent Companies Bring About their Own Downfall*, New York: Harper Business

Mintzberg, H. (1976) "The Manager's Job: Folklore or Fact?" *Harvard Business Review*, July/August.

Mintzberg, H. (1988) "Opening Up the Definitions of Strategy," in J. B. Quinn, H. Mintzberg and R. M. James (eds), *The Strategy Process*, Englewood Cliffs, NJ: Prentice-Hall.

Mintzberg, H. (1989) "Crafting Strategy," *Harvard Business Review*, March/April, pp. 66–75.

Mintzberg, H. (1994) *The Rise and Fall of Strategic Planning*, New York: Free Press

Mintzberg, H., Simons, R. and Basu, K. (2002), "Beyond Selfishness," *MIT Sloan Management Review*, Fall, no. 44(1), pp. 67–74.

Mintzberg, H. and Waters, J. A. (1985) "Of Strategies: Deliberate and Emergent," *Strategic Management Journal*, July/Sept.

Monks, R. A. G. (1998) *The Emperor's Nightingale*, Oxford: Capstone.

Morgan, G. (1986) *Images of Organization*, Beverly Hills: Sage.

Morita, A. (1986) *Made in Japan*, New York: Dutton.

Natanson, M. (ed.) (1963) *Philosophy of the Social Sciences*, New York: Random House.

Nock, S. L. and Rossi, P. H., "Achievement vs. Ascription in the Attribution of Family Social Status," *American Journal of Sociology*, 84(3).

Nonaka, I. and Takeuchi, H. (1995) *The Knowledge-Creating Company*, New York: Oxford University Press.

Ohmae, K. (1982) *The Mind of the Strategist: The Art of Japanese Business*, McGraw-Hill: New York.

Ozbekhan, H. (1971) "Planning and Human Action," in P. A. Weiss (ed.), *Systems in Theory and Practice*, New York: Hafner.

Parsons, T. and Shils, E. A. (1951) *Towards a General Theory of Action*, Cambridge, MA: Harvard University Press.

Pascale, R. T. (1984) "Perspectives in Strategy: The Real Story behind Honda's Success," *California Management Review*, 26(3).

Pascale, R.T. and Athos, A. G. (1981) *The Art of Japanese Management*, New York: Simon & Schuster.

Pfeffer, J. (1994) *Competitive Advantage Through People*, Boston, MA: Harvard Business School Press.

Pine, B. J. (1993) *Mass Customization*, Boston, MA: Harvard Business School Press.

Porras, J. I. (1987) *Stream Analysis*, Boston, MA: Addison-Wesley.

Porter, M. E. (1980) *Competitive Strategy: Techniques for Analyzing Industries and Competitors*, New York: Free Press.

Porter, M. E. (1990) *The Competitive Advantage of Nations*, New York: Free Press.

Prahalad, C.K. and Hamel, G. (1990) "The Core Competence of the Corporation," *Harvard Business Review*, May/June.

Quinn, J. B. (1982) *Intelligent Enterprise*, New York: Free Press (1982).

Quinn, J. B., Mintzberg, H. and James, R. M. (1988) *The Strategy Process*, Englewood Cliffs, NJ: Prentice-Hall.

Quinn, R. E. (1988) *Beyond Rational Management*, San Francisco: Jossey-Bass.

Rappaport, A. (1981) *Creating Shareholder Value: The New Standard for Business Performance*, New York: The Free Press.

Robbins, H. and Finley, M. (1998) *Transcompetition*, New York: McGraw-Hill.

Roethlisberger, F. and Dickson, W. (1939) *Management and the Worker*, Cambridge, MA: Harvard University Press.

Rogers, C. R. (1951) *Client-centered Counseling*, Boston, MA: Houghton-Mifflin.

Rohwer, J. (1996) *Asia Rising*, London: Nicholas Brealey.

Romig, D. (1996) *Breakthrough Teamwork*, Chicaco: Irwin Professional.

Rotter, J. B. (1996) "Generalized Experiences of Internal versus External Control of Reinforcement," *Psychological Monographs*, 609.

Savage, C. (1996) *Fifth Generation Management*, Boston: Butterworth-Heinemann.

Saxenian, A. L. (1999) *Silicon Valley's New Immigrant Entrepreneurs*, San Francisco: Public Policy Institute of California.

Schein, E. H. (1985) *Organization, Culture, and Leadership*, San Francisco: Jossey-Bass.

Schein, E. H. (1996) *Strategic Pragmatism*, Cambridge, MA: MIT Press.

Schön, D. A. (1971) *Beyond the Stable State*, New York: Random House.

Schön, D. A. (1979) "Creative Metaphor: A Perspective on Problem Setting in Social Policy," in A. Ortony (ed.), *Metaphor and Thought*, Cambridge, Cambridge University Press.

Schön, D. A. (1983) *The Reflective Practitioner*, New York: Basic Books.

Schutz, W. (1961) *The Interpersonal Underworld*, Palo Alto, CA: Science and Behavior Books.

Schumpeter, J. A. (1975 [1942]) "Creative Destruction," *Capitalism, Socialism and Democracy*, New York: Harper, pp. 82–85.

Sculley, J. and Byrne, J. A. (1987) *Odyssey: Pepsi to Apple: A Journey of Adventure, Ideas, and the Future*, New York, HarperCollins

Senge, P. M. (1999) *The Fifth Discipline: The Art and Practice of the Learning Organization*, London: Century.

Slywosky, A. J. and Morrison, D. J. (1999) *Profit Patterns*, New York: John Wiley.

Stacey, R. (2000) "Strategy as Order Emerging from Chaos," *Long Range Planning*, vol. 26, no. 1, pp. 10–17.

Stalk, G., Evans, P. and Shulman, L. (1992) "Competing on Capabilities," *Harvard Business Review*, March/April

Tannen, D. (1990) *You Just Don't Understand*, New York: Ballantine Books.

Tannen, D. (1998) *The Argument Culture*, New York: Random House.

Tatsuno, S. M. (1990) *Created in Japan*, New York, Morrow.

Taylor, F. W. (1947) *The Principles of Scientific Management*, New York: Norton.

Trist, E. and Emery, F. (1960) "Socio-technical Systems," in *Management Sciences; Models and Techniques*, Oxford: Pergamon Press.

Trompenaars, F. (1981) "The Organization of Meaning and the Meaning of Organization," unpublished dissertation, Wharton School, University of Pennsylvania.

Trompenaars, F. (2003) *Did the Pedestrian Die?* Chichester: Wiley Capstone.

Trompenaars, F. and Hampden-Turner, C. M. (1998) *Riding the Waves of Culture*, New York: McGraw-Hill.

Trompenaars, F. and Hampden-Turner, C. M. (2000) *21 Leaders for the 21st Century*, Oxford: Capstone.

Tuckman, B. and Jensen, M. (1977) "Stages of Small Group Development Revisted," *Group and Organizational Studies*, vol. 2, pp. 419–427.

Tung, R. L. (1988) *The New Expatriates*, Cambridge, MA: Ballinger.

Tung, R. L. (1997) "Managing in Asia: Cross-cultural Dimensions," in Joynt, P. and Warner, P. (eds), *Managing Across Cultures*, Singapore: International Thompson.

Waldrop, M. M. (1992) *Complexity: The Emerging Science at the Edge of Order and Chaos*, New York: Simon and Schuster.

Warner, M. (1996) *Comparative Management: A Reader*, London: Routledge.

Watson, W. E., Kumar, K. and Michaelson, L. K. (1993) "Cultural Diversity's Impact on Interaction Process," *Academy of Management Journal*, vol. 36, no. 3, pp. 590–602.

Watzlawick, P. (1977) *How Real is Real?* New York: Vintage.

Watzlawick, P., Beavin, J. H. and Jackson, D. D. (1967) *Pragmatics of Human Communication*, New York: Norton.

Weber, M. (2001) *The Protestant Ethic and the Spirit of Capitalism*, London: Routledge Classics

# Index

# Trompenaars Hampden-Turner
## Culture for Business

Trompenaars Hampden-Turner provides consulting, training, coaching and (un) learning services to help leaders and professionals manage and solve their business and culture dilemmas. Our clients are primarily Global Fortune 500 companies. We are based in Amsterdam, The Netherlands and Boston, USA. In addition, we have a network of associates throughout the world.

We particularly focus on cross-cultural consulting services around:

- mergers and acquisitions integration
- globalization
- corporate vision and values.

We take pride in using the client's own language and discourse, although we make subtle changes to its underlying structure to render it more coherent. Topics may include diversity, communication, learning, training, teamwork, culture, coaching, knowledge management, leadership development, integrity and balanced scorecards. For us these are all parts of a system. We also aim to introduce you to a paradoxical logic of human and organizational development. We aim for minimalist interventions yielding maximum results.

## Introduction to our offerings

We work with all business implications of culture. These may be part of an organization's globalization process, external growth and integration strategies, corporate identity and corporate communications, international change management, or the worldwide 'roll-out' of building cross-cultural competencies.

We work with organizations through a highly customized and integrated approach including:

## Global human resources management

- Create top-of-mind recognition of and respect for cross-cultural HRM issues
- Develop culture-for-business competencies into competitive advantage
- Help HR managers solve critical culture-for-business dilemmas
- Ascertain awareness of and respect for cross-cultural diversity among staff
- Develop the ability to leverage global diversity

## Consulting on culture-for-business management

- Conduct cross-cultural due diligence
- Facilitate your vision and value to strengthen your corporate identity
- Surface cultural challenges and dilemmas which may be creating obstacles
- Systematically reconcile cultural differences in order to maximize the business value of cultural diversity
- Assist in creating a business climate of mutual respect and trust in order to link people from different cultures in productive and positive ways

## Executive coaching

- Cross-cultural executive coaching helps leaders and managers with wider perspectives, cultural sensitivity and the ability to

- work with diversity in a productive and innovative way to achieve organizational goals.
- Cross-cultural coaching helps the individual or team assess its own strengths and challenges. It assists with positive changes in behavior and perception. It also helps individual integration without sacrificing diversity and integrity, within the organization.

## Employee training and (un) learning

- Raise awareness of how culture-for-business competencies can help improve bottom line
- Build awareness and respect for cross-culture and diversity issues
- Provide support in "unlearning" negative cultural attitudes and stereotypes
- Develop the ability to value and work with diversity

Amsterdam Office:
A.J. Ernststraat 595D
1082 LD Amsterdam,
The Netherlands,
Tel: +31 20 301 6666   fax: +31 20 301 6555
email: info@thtconsulting.com

USA Office:
14 Arrow Street, Suite 10
Cambridge, MA 02138-5106,
USA
Tel: +1 617 876 5025   fax: +1 617 876 5026

Made in the USA
Lexington, KY
15 February 2013